Assessing Grammar

THE CAMBRIDGE LANGUAGE ASSESSMENT SERIES

Series editors: J. Charles Alderson and Lyle F. Bachman

In this series:

Assessing Vocabulary by John Read
Assessing Reading by J. Charles Alderson
Assessing Language for Specific Purposes by Dan Douglas
Assessing Writing by Sara Cushing Weigle
Assessing Listening by Gary Buck
Assessing Speaking by Sari Luoma
Statistical Analyses for Language Assessment by Lyle F. Bachman

Assessing Grammar

James E. Purpura

CAMBRIDGE
UNIVERSITY PRESS

PUBLISHED BY THE PRESS SYNDICATE OF THE UNIVERSITY OF CAMBRIDGE
The Pitt Building, Trumpington Street, Cambridge, United Kingdom

CAMBRIDGE UNIVERSITY PRESS
The Edinburgh Building, Cambridge CB2 2RU, UK
40 West 20th Street, New York, NY 10011-4211, USA
477 Williamstown Road, Port Melbourne, VIC 3207, Australia
Ruiz de Alarcón 13, 28014 Madrid, Spain
Dock House, The Waterfront, Cape Town 8001, South Africa

http://www.cambridge.org

© Cambridge University Press 2004

First published 2004

Printed in the United Kingdom at the University Press, Cambridge

Typeface 9.5/13pt Utopia   *System* QuarkXPress™   [SE]

A catalogue record for this book is available from the British Library

Library of Congress Cataloguing in Publication data

ISBN 0 521 80281 4 hardback
ISBN 0 521 00344 X paperback

I dedicate this book to Steve Albanese (M-L)

Contents

Series editors' preface to *Assessing Grammar*

Grammar, the structural glue, the "code" of language, is arguably at the heart of language use, whether this involves speaking, listening, reading or writing. Grammar has also been central to language teaching and assessment historically, from the Middle Ages, when "rhetoric" was a key component of a university education, to the "skills-and-components" models of the 1960s that informed both language pedagogy and language testing.

However, although the way grammar is currently viewed, both in theoretical and applied linguistics, and in language learning and language teaching, is vastly different from the perspective that informed grammar tests in the 1960s, very little has changed since then in the way language testers conceive of grammar and in the way it is assessed in practice. Thus, many of the grammar tests that are currently in use, both in large-scale and in classroom assessment, reflect the perspectives of structural linguistics and discrete-point measurement. This book takes a completely new look at the assessment of grammar, placing it in the context of current views of linguistic pragmatics and functional grammar. It thus brings the assessment of grammar into sync with current thinking and practice in applied linguistics and language pedagogy.

The author of this book, Jim Purpura, has extensive experience not only in teaching and assessing grammar, but in training language teachers in grammar and assessment. In this book, he presents a new theoretical approach to defining grammatical ability that provides a basis for designing, developing and using assessments of grammar for a wide range of uses. This approach reflects the belief that grammar cannot be treated as an isolated component of knowledge, but must be assessed in the larger context of language in communication.

This book provides a coverage of L2 grammar assessment that is both theoretically grounded and practical, discussing the relevant research and theory, and clearly discussing the practical implications for test development of his approach to defining grammatical ability. The author leads the reader through the process of designing and developing tests to measure L2 grammatical ability. He discusses how L2 grammatical ability can be defined for different types of assessments, and describes the characteristics of assessment tasks that can be used for assessing grammatical ability in a variety of settings, illustrating this with examples of a wide range of grammar assessment tasks. He provides critical reviews of several grammar tests that have been developed professionally, using his framework of L2 grammar ability as a basis for analyzing these.

But this book is not just for language testing professionals. It is also for classroom teachers, as the author devotes an entire chapter to assessments of grammatical ability aimed at supporting learning and instruction. In the closing chapter, the author provides a retrospective overview of how grammar assessment has evolved over the past fifty years. He also discusses some persistent challenges in how we define grammatical ability, how we assess meanings, in the kinds of assessment tasks that are needed to both assess grammatical ability and provide authentic and engaging measures of grammatical performance, and in assessing the development of grammatical ability over time.

In summary, this book is timely, in that it provides a fresh perspective on the assessment of grammar, a perspective that is long overdue, and that brings grammar assessment into line with current theory and practice in language teaching and other areas of applied linguistics. This book provides a principled approach to the design, development and use of grammar assessments, and thus epitomizes what we as series editors hope to achieve in this series: the integration of theory and research in applied linguistics into language assessment in a way that is useful for both the test developer and the classroom teacher.

J. Charles Alderson
Lyle F. Bachman

Acknowledgments

In the late 1990s when Lyle Bachman and Charles Alderson invited me to write a book on assessing grammar, the resurging interest in grammar in the field of applied linguistics had already been well underway, and I was delighted. I knew there was no other book on assessing grammatical ability, and I knew this would be a challenge. In the next five years, I worked continuously on this book and am deeply grateful that Lyle, Charles and Mickey Bonin, then of Cambridge University Press, never lost faith that I would finish the manuscript. Having now completed it, I have many people to thank. First, I would like to thank Lyle, Charles and Mickey for their endless patience and steadfast support and enthusiasm for this volume. I would also like to thank them for reading the manuscript carefully and for providing constructive and thought-provoking comments. I would especially like to acknowledge Lyle, who selflessly read and reread each chapter, and then provided detailed comments, feedback and guidance. I just don't know that many people who are willing to engage in a three-year discussion and sometimes impassioned debate on the meaning of 'meaning'. I am sincerely grateful to Lyle for contributing to that discussion and for his ongoing mentorship – and, of course, his good humor.

I would also like to thank Teachers College, Columbia University, for its generous support in many stages of this project. I also wish to thank my colleagues in the TESOL and applied linguistics programs for their continued support and encouragement in writing this book. I am especially grateful to Leslie Beebe for engaging in discussions on pragmatics and to ZhaoHong Han for reading carefully selected chapters and for providing valuable comments and feedback. I wish to express my appreciation to Janine Graziano-King from Queens College, CUNY, for her sharp mind and helpful feedback on many aspects of the book. I would like to thank my friends and colleagues at Cambridge ESOL, in particular Nick Saville, Lynda Taylor and Ardeshir Geranpayeh, for reading and commenting on selected chapters.

I wish to thank the many wonderful students who took second language assessment for reading carefully and commenting on the book. I am particularly grateful to those of you who created grammar tests for your final project. I have learned much from you. I would also like to acknowledge the students in my instructed SLA and assessment class for their willingness to debate the issues and for their insightful comments on the multiple drafts. I am particularly grateful to Jaehak Chang, Yunkyoung Cho, Kirby Cook Grabowski, Jee Wha Kim, Hae-Jin Kim, Hyunjoo Kim, Nitza Krohn, Alick Liao, Maria McCormack, E. K. Park, Taejoon Park, Michael Perrone, Mary Regan, Yoko Sato, Joowon Suh, Elvis Wagner and Cynthia Wiseman.

Finally, I would like to thank my friends and colleagues whose ongoing support and belief in me got me through in times when I thought I'd never finish, especially Sara Cushing Weigle, Antony Kunnan, Tim McNamara and Elana Shohamy. I wish to thank my friends, Steve Gudgel, Jimmy Herbolich, Pam Martin, Diane Pinkley, Margie Rosnick and Carmen Velasco for politely letting me blabber on and on about grammar during dinner. Last, but not least, I am deeply grateful to Steve Albanese, who took great care of me during this time, and whose unshakable patience, support and encouragement brought out the best in me. I could never thank you enough.

J.P.

CHAPTER ONE

Differing notions of 'grammar' for assessment

Introduction

The study of grammar has had a long and important role in the history of second language and foreign language teaching. For centuries, to learn another language, or what I will refer to generically as an **L2**, meant to know the grammatical structures of that language and to cite prescriptions for its use. Grammar was used to mean the analysis of a language system, and the study of grammar was not just considered an essential feature of language learning, but was thought to be sufficient for learners to actually acquire another language (Rutherford, 1988). Grammar in and of itself was deemed to be worthy of study – to the extent that in the Middle Ages in Europe, it was thought to be the foundation of all knowledge and the gateway to sacred and secular understanding (Hillocks and Smith, 1991). Thus, the central role of grammar in language teaching remained relatively uncontested until the late twentieth century. Even a few decades ago, it would have been hard to imagine language instruction without immediately thinking of grammar.

While the central role of grammar in the language curriculum has remained unquestioned until recent times, grammar pedagogy has unsurprisingly been the source of much debate. For example, some language educators have argued that foreign languages are best learned deductively, where students are asked to memorize and recite definitions, rules, examples and exceptions. In this approach, the teaching of language obviously involved the transmission of grammar rules from teacher to student, and to know a language meant to know the intricacies of its grammatical system and to recite its rules. Other language educators have maintained that language learning is best achieved inductively. In this approach, students are presented with examples of the target language and led to discover its underlying organizational principles in order to be able to formulate a formal set of rules and prescriptions. To know an L2 here meant to identify and describe the rules of the language system based on an analysis of texts. Still other more traditional language teachers have claimed that the best way to learn an L2 is to study its grammar so that the language could be translated from one language to another. Based upon the assumption that all languages are similar and that Latin could be used as a model for analysis, this practice gave rise to the first grammars for foreign-language learners and to the grammar-translation approach to language learning (Rutherford, 1987), still used in many classrooms around the world today. In this approach, knowledge of a language involves the ability to read and render an accurate translation. In each cited instance of language teaching, grammar has remained the unquestioned focus, and knowledge of the grammar is viewed as a set of rules. Similarly, the assessment of grammatical knowledge is carried out by having students recite rules, by having them analyze texts and state the rules, or by having them translate texts. In short, grammatical assessment was closely aligned with the goals of instruction and, until recent times, was hardly a topic of concern.

It was not until the late twentieth century that the central role of grammar in language teaching was seriously questioned. In reaction to the grammar-translation approach that had become more about learning a set of abstract linguistic rules than about learning to use a language for some communicative purpose, some language teachers began to seek alternative approaches to language teaching based on what students could 'do' with the language. These teachers insisted that the grammar should not only be learned, but also applied to some linguistic or communicative purpose. They recommended that grammatical analysis be accompanied by application, where students are asked to answer questions, write illustrative examples, combine sentences, correct errors, write paragraphs and so forth. To know a language meant to be able to apply the rules – an approach relatively similar to what is done in many classrooms today. In this approach, knowledge of grammar was assessed by having students apply rules to language in some linguistic context.

Other language teachers have been more vehement in their attempt to de-emphasize the role of grammar in language teaching. They believed that foreign languages were best learned in the same way that children learn their native language, through sustained exposure to the language and through interaction. This belief gave rise to the 'natural method', the 'direct method', and, ultimately, to the 'natural approach' to language acquisition (Krashen and Terrell, 1983). Although these language-teaching methods differed in terms of whether first and second language acquisition were assumed to involve identical processes, these methods made little or no provision for the formal instruction of grammar, and students were left to their own devices to identify and learn the rules. In these approaches, grammar was no longer seen exclusively as a set of grammatical abstractions to be recited, but rather as a set of rules to be internalized and used for communication. To know a language meant to be able to use it for some real-life purpose, and the assessment of grammatical knowledge was based on tasks requiring students to demonstrate their ability to communicate in speaking or writing.

Most of the early debates about language teaching have now been resolved; however, others continue to generate discussion. For example, most language teachers nowadays would no longer expect their students to devote too much time to describing and analyzing language systems, to translating texts or to learning a language solely for access to its literature; rather, they would want their students to learn the language for some communicative purpose. In other words, the primary goal of language learning today is to foster communicative competence, or the ability to communicate effectively and spontaneously in real-life settings. Language teachers today would not deny that grammatical competence is an integral part of communicative language ability, but most would maintain that grammar should be viewed as an indispensable resource for effective communication and not, except under special circumstances, an object of study in itself. Current teaching controversies revolve around the role, if any, that grammar instruction should play in the language classroom and the degree to which the grammatical system of a language can be acquired through instruction. These questions have, since the 1980s, produced an explosion of empirical research, which is of critical importance to language teachers. Given the significance of this literature for teachers and the critical role that grammatical assessment plays in this research, I will examine this literature in some detail later on in this chapter.

In summary, language teachers have always acknowledged the inextricable link between teaching and testing, and accordingly have always assessed their students' knowledge of grammar. In other words, the assessment of grammatical ability is nothing new. What has changed over time is what teachers have chosen to assess under the title of 'grammar' and the ways in which these assessments have been carried out. For example, at one point in time, knowledge of grammar was assessed through the ability to recite rules; at another, through the ability to extrapolate a rule from samples of the target language; and at yet another, knowledge of grammar was tested through the ability to provide an accurate translation. Currently, knowledge of grammar might be inferred from the ability to select a grammatically correct answer from several options on a multiple-choice test, to supply a grammatically accurate word or phrase in a paragraph or dialogue, to construct grammatically appropriate sentences, or to provide judgments regarding the grammaticality of an utterance. In many assessment contexts today, knowledge of grammar may be inferred from the ability to use grammar correctly while reading, writing, listening to or speaking the L2 – a practice based on the assumption that all instances of language use invoke the same fundamental working knowledge of grammar and that a lack of grammatical knowledge can severely limit what is understood or produced in communication. In short, language educators have defined and assessed grammatical knowledge in many different ways over the years as the notion of what it means to 'know' the grammar of a language has evolved and instructional practices have changed.

What is striking, however, in the long-standing debate on grammar and its role in language learning is the relative absence of discussion of how 'best' to assess grammatical knowledge or how to determine if grammatical knowledge has been acquired. Even with the sudden increase of research since the mid-1980s on the teaching and learning of grammar, there still remains a surprising lack of consensus on (1) what constitutes grammatical knowledge, (2) what type of assessment tasks might best allow teachers and testers to infer that grammatical knowledge has been acquired and (3) how to design tasks that elicit grammatical knowledge from students for some specific assessment purpose, while at the same time providing reliable and valid measures of performance. In other words, there is a glaring lack of information available on how the assessment of grammatical ability might be carried out, and how the choices we make in the assessment of grammatical ability might influence the inferences we make about our students' knowledge of grammar, the decisions we make on their behalf and their ultimate development.

In this first chapter, I hope to add some clarity to these issues by describing what language educators generally mean when they talk about 'grammar'. I will show the influences of linguistic theory on different conceptualizations of 'grammar' in L2 educational contexts and will demonstrate how these different descriptions of grammar have broadened our understanding of how language is organized. I will argue that it is important for teachers to have a solid understanding of the grammatical resources of language so that instruction and assessment can be tailored to a variety of educational contexts.

What is meant by 'grammar' in theories of language?

Grammar and linguistics

Before attempting to define what it means to 'know' grammar or to be able to 'use' it to communicate in second or foreign language contexts, we first need to discuss what is commonly meant by 'grammar'. This is important given the different definitions and conceptualizations of grammar that have been proposed over the years, and the diverse ways in which these notions of grammars have influenced L2 educators.

When most language teachers, second language acquisition (SLA) researchers and language testers think of 'grammar', they call to mind one of the many paradigms (e.g., 'traditional grammar' or 'universal grammar') available for the study and analysis of language. Such **linguistic grammars** are typically derived from data taken from native speakers and minimally constructed to describe well-formed utterances within an individual framework. These grammars strive for internal consistency and are mainly accessible to those who have been trained in that particular paradigm.

Since the 1950s, there have been many such linguistic theories – too numerous to list here – that have been proposed to explain language phenomena. Many of these theories have helped shape how L2 educators currently define grammar in educational contexts. Although it is beyond the purview of this book to provide a comprehensive review of these theories, it is, nonetheless, helpful to mention a few, considering both the impact they have had on L2 education and the role they play in helping define grammar for assessment purposes.

Generally speaking, most linguists have embraced one of two general perspectives to describe linguistic phenomena. Either they take a **syntactocentric perspective** of language, where **syntax**, or the way in which words are arranged in a sentence, is the central feature to be observed and analyzed; or they adopt a **communication perspective** of language, where the observational and analytic emphasis is on how language is used to convey meaning (VanValin and LaPolla, 1997). I will use these two perspectives to classify some of the more influential grammatical paradigms in our field.

In the syntactocentric view of language, **formal grammar** is defined as a systematic way of accounting for and predicting an 'ideal' speaker's or hearer's knowledge of the language. This is done by a set of rules or 'principles' that can be used to generate all well-formed or grammatical utterances in the language. This approach typically examines sounds that are combined to form words, words that are put together to form phrases, phrases combined to form clauses, and clauses assembled to form sentences. In other words, this approach is predominantly concerned with the structure of clauses and sentences, leaving the literal meaning and contextual use of these forms to other approaches (i.e., to the fields of semantics and pragmatics). To illustrate, consider the following sentence:

(1.1) Reggio and Messina were taken to the vet's this morning.

Some formal grammarians would explain this passive voice sentence by comparing it with its active voice counterpart – *[someone] took Reggio and Messina to the vet's this morning*. They would then derive a number of rules – for changing the past to the past passive (took→were taken), for moving the patient of the action (Reggio and Messina) to the subject position and for deleting the agent (by someone). They would also devise rules for pronunciation and spelling. Some formal grammarians might even explain this sentence by comparing it to a number of ungrammatical passive sentences.

Syntactocentric theories of language have provided L2 educators with a wealth of information about grammatical forms and the rules that govern them. In fact, most classroom language teachers draw extensively on this information as a basis for syllabus design, materials preparation, instruction and classroom assessment. These theories have also informed L2 teachers and testers in their efforts to identify linguistic content for tests so that more general inferences about language ability can be made.

The second general approach to describing language is through an analysis of communication. In this perspective, the structural description of the language is not the primary object of concern; rather, language is viewed as a system of communication, where a speaker or writer uses grammatical forms to convey a number of meanings. In the communication perspective, grammar is treated as one of many resources for accomplishing something with language, and grammarians describe both what the linguistic forms are for and how they are used to create meaning within and beyond the sentence. In other words, while the choice of the right grammatical form and the most appropriate lexical item is important, this perspective focuses more on the overall message being communicated and the interpretations that this message might invoke.

Grammarians with a communicative view of language might explain the passive voice sentence in 1.1 in a very different way. They would first take note of the structural features of the passive voice, just as the formal grammarians did. For example, they would compare the following sentences structurally.

> (1.1) Reggio and Messina were taken to the vet's this morning [by someone].
>
> (1.2) [someone] took Reggio and Messina to the vet's this morning.

However, they would also be interested in the features of the context that required the speaker to choose the passive over the active voice in the first place. In other words, what was the communicative need for the passive? What was the speaker or writer trying to communicate by its use? From a communication perspective, they might determine that the speaker wished to shift the communicative focus from the actors or agent in the sentence (the person who took the cats to the vet) to the recipients of the action (Reggio and Messina). This highlights the fact that Reggio and Messina were taken to the vet's – since as cats they could not go there by themselves. Thus, the patient of the action (Reggio and Messina) becomes the grammatical subject of the sentence rather than the object.

Of equal interest would be the features of the context that allowed the agent to be omitted since we never learn who actually took Reggio and Messina to the vet's. Given more contextual information, we could most likely infer this; however, in a single isolated, 'discrete' utterance, this information is not available. Furthermore, as the agent in this sentence seemed irrelevant, it went unexpressed. This may also be because the agent is unknown, but it is more likely the case that the agent is known from the context and repeating it would have been redundant. The communication perspective of language, therefore, attempts to examine the relationship between the grammatical forms we use and the conceptual meanings we wish to express, given the context in which the utterances were situated. Like the syntactocentric perspective, this perspective has much to offer the L2 educator, especially when it comes to using grammar as a resource for communication.

These two views of linguistic analysis have been instrumental in determining how grammar has been conceptualized in L2 classrooms in recent years. They have also influenced definitions of L2 grammar for assessment purposes. I will now provide a brief overview of some of the more influential linguistic theories that typify the syntactocentric and communicative views of language.

Form-based perspectives of language

Several syntactocentric, or form-based, theories of language have provided grammatical insights to L2 teachers. I will describe three: traditional grammar, structural linguistics and transformational-generative grammar.

One of the oldest theories to describe the structure of language is **traditional grammar**. Originally based on the study of Latin and Greek, traditional grammar drew on data from literary texts to provide rich and lengthy descriptions of linguistic form. Unlike some other syntactocentric theories, traditional grammar also revealed the linguistic meanings of these forms and provided information on their usage in a sentence (Celce-Murcia and Larsen-Freeman, 1999). Traditional grammar supplied an extensive set of prescriptive rules along with the exceptions. A typical rule in a traditional English grammar might be:

> The first-person singular of the present tense verb 'to be' is 'I am'. 'Am' is used with 'I' in all cases, except in first-person singular negative tag and yes/no questions, which are contracted. In this case, the verb 'are' is used instead of 'am'. For example, 'I'm in a real bind, *aren't* I?' or '*Aren't* I trying my best?'

Traditional grammar has been criticized for its inability to provide descriptions of the language that could adequately incorporate the exceptions into the framework and for its lack of generalizability to other languages. In other words, traditional grammar postulated a separate, uniquely language-specific set of rules or 'parameters' for every language. In spite of these shortcomings as a form of linguistic analysis, traditional grammar has had an enormous impact on L2 teachers and testers throughout the centuries, and many L2 educators continue to find it a valuable source of information.

Another influential theory of linguistic analysis grew out of a concerted effort by linguists in the United States both to teach English to Native American Indians and to learn the indigenous American languages so that they could be documented and preserved. However, as these languages in the early twentieth century had no written alphabet and as the native speakers were unable to describe the languages, linguists departed from the long tradition of comparing English to Latin and began to collect samples of the target languages with the goal of providing a description of its **phonology** (i.e., its sound system), its **morphology** (i.e., the study of minimal units of meaning or grammatical function such as in *untrue*→ un + true or *walked*→walk + ed) and its syntax (Chastain, 1976). This work ultimately gave rise to descriptive or **structural linguistics**.

Structural grammars, associated with linguists such as Bloomfield (1933) and Fries (1940), offered a fairly rigorous method for describing the structure of a language in terms of both its morphology and its syntax. In these grammars each word in a given sentence is categorized according to how it is used, and the 'patterns' or 'structures' are said to constitute a unique system for that language. Figure 1.1 shows how a structural grammar might analyze statements and yes/no questions in English.

Statements

	Subject	+	Verb	+	Direct object	+	Prepositional phrase
	Subject	+	*Verb*	+	*Direct object*	+	*Prepositional phrase*
	Steve	+	reads	+	novels	+	during the summer.

Yes/No questions

Auxiliary	+	Subject	+	Verb	+	Direct object	+	Prepositional phrase
Auxiliary	+	*Subject*	+	*Verb*	+	*Direct object*	+	*Prepositional phrase*
Does	+	Steve	+	read	+	novels	+	during the summer?

Figure 1.1 Structural analysis of statements and yes/no questions in English

Unlike traditional grammars, structural grammars are not based on a set of prescriptive rules. Rather, they seek to describe the language as it appears with a strict focus on grammatical form. Although descriptive linguistics has provided numerous insights into the structure of languages, it downplayed the semantic aspects of grammar, and provided little information on how linguistic forms are used in context. Nonetheless, many L2 educators continue to consider this theory a valuable resource for use in syllabus design, grammar teaching and assessment.

Probably the best-known syntactocentric theory is Chomsky's (1965) **transformational-generative grammar** and its later, broader instantiation, universal grammar (UG). Unlike the traditional or structural grammars that aim to describe one particular language, transformational-generative grammar endeavored to provide a 'universal' description of language behavior revealing the internal linguistic system for which all humans are predisposed (Radford, 1988). Transformational-generative grammar claims that the underlying properties of any individual language system can be uncovered by means of a detailed, sentence-level analysis. In this regard, Chomsky proposed a set of phrase-structure rules that describe the underlying structures of all languages. These phrase-structure rules join with lexical items to offer a semantic representation to the rules. Following this, a series of 'transformation' rules are applied to the basic structure to add, delete, move or substitute the underlying constituents in the sentence. Morphological rules are then applied, followed by phonological or orthographic rules (for further information, see Radford, 1988, or Celce-Murcia and Larsen-Freeman, 1999).

According to Chomsky's (1981) theory of UG, knowledge of a language consists of not only knowledge of the universal **principles** shared by all languages, but also knowledge of language-specific rules, or **parameters** of grammatical variation observed between languages or different varieties of the same language. These parameters are triggered by exposure to the target language. More recently, Chomsky (1995) has argued that 'grammars should be described in terms of the minimal set of theoretical and descriptive apparatus necessary' to describe a descriptively adequate depiction of linguistic phenomena (Radford, 1997, p. 265). This minimalist program of linguistic theory stems from a desire to minimize the acquisitional burden for children learning a language in a relatively brief period of time (Radford, 1997). Finally, Chomsky's linguistic program has evolved considerably over the years. The details of this system are complex, and beyond the purview of this book. For our purposes, I will refer to this work simply as UG.

Although UG has deepened our understanding of syntax, it has been criticized for failing to account for meaning or language use in social contexts (Hymes, 1971; Halliday, 1994). In other words, UG's focus on syntax downplayed to some extent the role of **semantics**, or the study of the conventional meanings of words, phrases and sentences, and excluded **pragmatics**, or meanings derived from context-specific use. Nonetheless, both semantics and pragmatics, together with phonology, morphology and syntax, are critical for assessing the communicative success of an utterance within a given context.

To illustrate these shortcomings, consider the following two syntactically identical sentences.

(1.3) **It** is raining.
(1.4) **It** is working.

Both sentences begin with the pronoun subject *it*, followed by the third-person singular form of the auxiliary verb 'be', which carries tense (present). The auxiliary verb is followed by a main verb (*rain* or *work*) in the progressive form. Syntactically, these forms are identical apart from the different main verbs. However, there are obviously many differences in linguistic meaning and contextual use. For example, *it* in 1.3 functions as a 'sentence filler' in the subject position since *it* contains no referent. Sentence fillers are a resource available to those languages which require the expression of an explicit grammatical subject (e.g., English, French). However, *it* in 1.4 contains an implied referent – most likely some kind of mechanical device previously mentioned in the context. Although the semantic information and/or contextual inference related to 'it' is essential for understanding these two utterances, UG fails to account for the referential information in this analysis. In short, as a model for communicative teaching and testing, the syntactocentric perspective has much to contribute; however, used alone, it may not be appropriate for all situations, and must, therefore, be adopted judiciously.

Another example of the theoretical limitations of applying a purely syntactocentric approach to L2 educational contexts is seen in the following two pairs of utterances.

> **Context**: A French person, who speaks only French, is having a discussion with two Americans, who both speak English <u>and</u> French fluently. During the discussion, one American (Joe) lapses into English. The other American (Sue) says:
>
> (1.5) Sue: Would you please speak French? [request and perhaps criticism]
> (1.6) Joe: Oh, no problem. [acknowledgment and agreement to comply]
>
> Later, noticing that Joe has not stopped speaking English, Sue repeats:

(1.7) Sue: Would you please speak French? [request and criticism/chastisement]

(1.8) Joe: Sorry, I forgot. [apology and excuse]

Sentences 1.5 and 1.7 are identical in syntactic structure. However, these sentences convey very different pragmatic information. Sentence 1.5 was intended as a polite request. It may also have encoded a hint of criticism in this context. Joe's response in 1.6 showed that he interpreted the question as a request, and if the criticism was understood, it was ignored. However, sentence 1.7 was an exact repetition of the initial request (most likely with a moderation in prosody), stated as if Joe had not heard (or heeded) the initial request. This time, the utterance was intended as a criticism or even a chastisement for not speaking French. In 1.8 Joe responded with an apology followed by an excuse, thereby acknowledging that he had heard the sentence in 1.7 as a criticism.

In order for Joe to respond accurately, meaningfully and appropriately in each exchange, Joe had to understand the **grammatical form** (yes/no question) of the utterance; he had to understand the **literal meaning** of the words in syntax and their **intended meaning** in context (Speak French!), and he had to understand any additional **pragmatic meanings** being communicated without actually being said (criticism, annoyance). An analysis of the syntax alone would not have been able to account for the differences in the two sentences with regard to meaning.

To highlight further a need to account for meaning on a **lexico-grammatical** level, consider the different interpretations of the modal auxiliary 'can' in the following sentences:

Can you speak Kurdish?	(ability or potential)
Can I have some milk, please?	(request)
Can I go to the movies tonight, please?	(request for permission)
Can I buy you a beer?	(offer)
Can we talk at 10?	(suggestion)
Can they still be at work?	(speculation)
Can it get any warmer?	(theoretical possibility)

As can be seen, the modal auxiliary *can* has the same basic syntax in these instances, but the semantic representation changes. If further contextual information were provided, a host of pragmatic interpretations could be also derived from these utterances. For example, 'Can you speak Kurdish?' could be used (or interpreted) as a way of discrediting someone who thinks she knows a lot about the Kurdish people. In this context, a layer of pragmatic meaning involving negative affect and attitudinal stance could be superimposed on the linguistic forms and literal meanings. In other words, a focus on grammatical form alone may not be enough in L2 educational contexts to determine if L2 learners have sufficiently acquired a structure to communicate effectively.

UG, like other syntactocentric theories of language, has contributed enormously to how language teachers and testers understand language and linguistic forms. Many L2 educators continue to draw on syntactocentric theories of language to design language syllabi and teach grammatical forms. In the same way, many language testers have designed tests of grammatical form that are firmly rooted in these theories. In fact, many of the traditional, multiple-choice tests of grammar are heavily influenced by a syntactocentric approach to language. While the syntactocentric theories of language continue to inform our understanding of language structures and the principles underlying them, these theories have fallen short on issues of meaningfulness, appropriateness, acceptability and naturalness – for that we might turn to corpus linguistics and to functional grammar.

Form- and use-based perspectives of language

The three theories of linguistic analysis described thus far have provided insights to L2 educators on several grammatical forms. These insights provide information to explain what structures are theoretically possible in a language. Other linguistic theories, however, are better equipped to examine how speakers and writers actually exploit linguistic forms during language use. For example, if we wish to explain how seemingly similar structures like *I like to read* and *I like reading* connote different meanings, we might turn to those theories that study grammatical form and use interfaces. This would address questions such as: Why does a language need two or more structures that are similar in meaning? Are similar forms used to convey different specialized meanings? To what degree are similar forms a function of written versus spoken language, or to what degree are these forms characteristic of a particular social group or a specific situation? It is important for us to discuss these questions briefly if we ultimately wish to test grammatical forms along with their meanings and uses in context.

One approach to linguistic analysis that has contributed greatly to our understanding of the grammatical forms found in language use, as well as the contextual factors that influence the variability of these forms, is **corpus linguistics**. I will briefly describe corpus linguistics along with how findings from this approach can be useful for assessing grammar.

The common practice of compiling linguistic **corpora**, or large and principled collections of natural spoken and written texts, in order to analyze by computer patterns of language use in large databases of authentic texts has led to a relatively new field known as 'corpus linguistics'. Not a theory of language per se, corpus linguistics embodies a suite of tools and methods designed to provide a source of evidence so that linguistic data can be analyzed distributionally – that is, to show how often and where a linguistic form occurs in spoken or written text. According to Biber, Conrad and Reppen (1998), these analyses typically focus on two concerns. One type of study examines the use of one linguistic feature (i.e., a lexical item or grammatical structure) in comparison with another. For example, corpus-based studies might examine the different uses of *would*. These studies might also compare the word *wish* with *that*-clauses and *to*-infinitives, or they might examine a linguistic feature with a non-linguistic feature, such as gender, dialect or setting.

Katz and Fodor (1963) looked at the connections between lexical forms and grammatical forms by examining the features of words that encode grammar. They found that in addition to encoding semantic features and restrictions, a word also contains a number of syntactic features including the part of speech (noun, verb, adjective), countability (singular, plural), gender (masculine, feminine), and it can mark prepositional co-occurrence restrictions such as when the word *think* is followed by a preposition (about, of, over) or is followed by a *that*-clause. Katz and Fodor called this 'the grammatical dimension of lexis'. I will refer to this as **lexical form**, as opposed to **lexical meaning**.

Biber et al. (1998) identified a second kind of corpus-based study that relates grammatical forms to different types of texts. For example, how do academic texts differ from informal conversations in terms of the passive voice? Besides showing which linguistic features are possible in texts, corpus linguistics strives to identify which are probable. In other words, to what degree are linguistic features likely to occur in certain texts and in what circumstances? For example, in physical descriptions of objects the majority of the verbs are non-progressive or **stative**. Unlike descriptive linguistics or UG, corpus linguistics is not primarily concerned with syntax; rather, it focuses on how words co-occur with other words in a single sentence or text. In this respect, the findings from corpus-based studies provide valuable information on how lexical items and grammar relate, and how they relate to meaning or use.

Based on large amounts of data, corpus linguists have begun to supply information on patterns of variation in language use, language change, and varieties of language. One type of information relates to the frequency and distribution of grammatical forms. For example, Grabowski and Mindt's (1995) study of 4,240 regular verb types found in the *Brown Corpus* (Francis and Kučera, 1964) and *Lancaster-Oslo-Bergen Corpus* (Johansson et al., 1978) discovered that regular verbs accounted for only 42.3% of the total English verb tokens, with irregular verbs making up the rest. Moreover, of these irregular verbs, 60% were accounted for by *be, have,* or *do,* and 23.6% by *say, make, go, take, come, see, know, get, give, find, think, tell, become, show, leave, feel, put.* In sum, these 20 verbs constituted an amazing 83.6% of the irregular verbs in the corpora. In testing grammar at different proficiency levels, this information can be very useful in helping to select appropriate content.

Besides frequency of occurrence and the distribution of forms, corpus linguistics has provided information on the different semantic functions of lexical items. For example, a corpus linguist could examine the distribution and frequency of occurrence of the word *black* and discover that it relates to color, race, profit, cleanliness, amount of light and so forth. Besides lexical items, corpus linguistics provides distributional and frequency information on the lexico-grammatical features of the language or those features that could be taken as both lexical and grammatical. For example, the word *since* has a lexical dimension given its semantic encodings and a grammatical dimension given its role as a clause marker or a preposition. This corpus-based information is of great interest to language educators because information on the distribution and frequency of grammar points helps provide an empirical basis for determining which learning points to teach or to test. (See Biber et al., 2004, for a detailed description of the spoken and written languages used at American Universities.)

With new perspectives on language use, corpus linguistics has begun to challenge language teachers to rethink how they view the content of a language curriculum and the manner in which this curriculum is presented to students. For example, instead of asking beginning and intermediate students to learn a large number of tenses and verb forms, as is done in a structural syllabus, language teachers might promote L2 vocabulary development or introduce students to features of the L2 that allow them to function appropriately in social contexts (Kennedy, 1998).

In fact, some researchers (Sinclair and Renouf, 1988) strongly advocate corpus-based lexical syllabi, where lexical-use patterns occupy a central role in the curriculum.

In spite of this renewed interest in corpora, corpus-based lexical syllabi have not replaced theme-based syllabi organized around grammatical structures in communicative language instruction; nor have they yet had a widespread impact on communicative language teaching theory. This is perhaps due to an over-dependence on frequency of occurrence, which may be in conflict with the developmental needs of our students, or it may be a result of questions related to the corpus as a true and unbiased representation of the language. Nonetheless, corpus linguistics has much to offer L2 educators regarding linguistic forms and the uses associated with them, and L2 assessment experts have already begun to draw on corpus-based information for decisions about test content (e.g., Biber et al., 2004).

Communication-based perspectives of language

Other theories have provided grammatical insights from a communication-based perspective. Such a perspective expresses the notion that language involves more than linguistic form. It moves beyond the view of language as patterns of morphosyntax observed within relatively decontextualized sentences or sentences found within natural-occurring corpora. Rather, a communication-based perspective views grammar as a set of linguistic norms, preferences and expectations that an individual invokes to convey a host of pragmatic meanings that are appropriate, acceptable and natural depending on the situation. The assumption here is that linguistic form has no absolute, fixed meaning in language use (as seen in sentences 1.5 and 1.7 above), but is mutable and open to interpretation by those who use it in a given circumstance. Grammar in this context is often co-terminous with language itself, and stands not only for form, but also for meaningfulness and pragmatic appropriacy, acceptability or naturalness – a topic I will return to later since I believe that a blurring of these concepts is misleading and potentially problematic for language educators.

Many of the communication-based approaches to language have had an extensive impact on how L2 teachers and testers currently view grammar. Given the goals of this book, I will look at only Austin's (1962) speech act theory and Halliday and Hasan's (1976) systemic-functional grammar as they might relate to a definition of grammar for assessment.

While structural linguists restricted their focus to grammatical form in the early 1960s, linguistic philosophers looked at issues of language and meaning. Austin (1962) proposed that the action performed by pronouncing an utterance during interaction involved more than the literal conveyance of information. Utterances are also said to 'do' things in a language context; they have a **language function**. For example, when a person being invited to a dinner party says 'I'll be there at eight', that person is not only conveying information on his or her expected arrival time (literal meaning), but also accepting the invitation and committing to do something (language function). Austin (1962) maintained that an utterance involves three related **speech acts**. First, the action of an utterance involves the production of a meaningful proposition, a **locutionary act** – the person's arrival at eight. This conveys the **literal meaning** or **locutionary meaning** of the utterance, terms that I will use synonymously in this book. Second, the action of an utterance communicates the speaker's intention of an utterance in a particular context, an **illocutionary act** – accepting the invitation and committing to go. This conveys the **intended** or **illocutionary meaning** of a speaker's utterance. The intended meaning of an utterance may sometimes, but not always, be unclear to the interlocutor until context is taken into account. This co-occurrence of literal and intended meaning represents the illocutionary force of the utterance. For example, by saying, 'I'll be there at eight', the speaker's response to the request was interpretable as, 'I accept the invitation, and I'll be there at eight.' In my opinion, the literal meaning of an utterance expressed by lexico-grammatical forms is inextricably associated with the intention that a speaker has in generating a proposition in context, and this association of form and meaning is the essence of grammatical ability.

Given the unelaborated state of the context in this utterance, the person's understanding of the offer and his or her response to it can be derived mostly from the words in the sentence used in syntax, and to a much lesser degree from the conditions of the context itself. However, had the person's utterance ('I'll be there at eight') been made in reference to a dinner in Spain, where it is not uncommon to invite friends to your house at 10 pm, this same message could have assumed a very different set of meanings. For example, his or her response could have been intended as: 'I'll be there early to help you prepare things' – an offer of help. In this context, a whole new layer of sociocultural or interpersonal meanings might be encoded in the linguistic forms – something that speech act theory does not account for per se. In this case, the relationship between what was said and what was implied was much more indirect, since the meaning and function of the utterance were mostly derived from the context and not from the words arranged in syntax.

Finally, Austin (1962) maintained that the action of an utterance produces an effect on the interlocutor, a **perlocutionary act** – perhaps a feeling of satisfaction on the part of the host that the invitation was accepted.

Speech act theory did not address how interlocutors jointly construct meaning as they seek to communicate with each other; rather, it focused on the effect that an utterance would have on an interlocutor. At the time, speech act theory did not have a strong influence on language teaching or testing, but it did contribute to a deeper theoretical understanding of the meanings underlying communication. Nonetheless, speech act theory offers useful insights for those wishing to assess grammatical ability at different levels of proficiency, a point I will elaborate on in the next chapters.

Moving beyond both speech act theory and UG, Hymes (1972) proposed a much more complete theory of communication in which effective communication was not simply perceived as a function of linguistic accuracy or acceptable grammar to convey literal and intended meaning. Rather, he argued that utterances in communication must also be *appropriate* for the context. In short, speakers must have both 'linguistic competence' and 'communicative competence'. To illustrate the difference, consider the following example. I once had a student in Kuwait who missed the previous class. She came to see me during office hours and the following exchange ensued:

(1.9) Me: Hi, Samira, what can I do for you?
(1.10) Samira: Excuse me, Your Excellency, correct my homework!

Even though I secretly enjoyed being referred to as 'Your Excellency', I realized that Samira did not know how to address a teacher *appropriately*, nor did she know how to make a polite request. Her English was grammatically accurate and propositionally meaningful, but lacking in sociocultural and sociolinguistic appropriacy.

Hymes (1967) related appropriacy of context to situational factors involving the participants and their roles, the setting (i.e., time and space), the actual form of the message (i.e., the grammatical form of the message), the topic (i.e., what the message is about), the purpose (i.e., its goal or intention), the key (i.e., serious, sarcastic), the channel (i.e., oral), the norms of interaction (i.e., loudness, interruptions), the norms of interpretation (i.e., how violations of the norms of interaction are viewed) and the genre (i.e., informal letter, speech, lab report). Hymes' (1967) theory of communication has had an enormous impact on L2 teaching and assessment. For example, many of these same situational factors have been used as a theoretical basis for identifying task characteristics and variables in the current *Test of Spoken English* (Douglas and Smith, 1997), a test produced by the Educational Testing Service in Princeton, New Jersey.

Another very influential theory of linguistic analysis supporting a com-munication-based view of language is **systemic-functional linguistics**. According to Halliday (1994) and Halliday and Hasan (1976, 1989), this approach views language primarily as a tool for human communication. In this respect, communication is manifested in language by meaning or semantics, and grammar is available as one of the many resources to express meanings. One of the main tenets of systemic-functional gram-mar holds that context and meaning take precedence over linguistic form. It follows, then, that systemic-functional grammar typically describes features of grammatical form that are used to express meaning beyond a single, context-free utterance. Rather, grammatical form is seen as having a symbiotic relationship with meaning and pragmatic use, where each influences and shapes the other within and across utter-ances.

From a communication perspective, Halliday (1994) argued that although language can be used to express meaning for a number of social purposes, the language system itself can be reduced to a small set of **lan-guage functions** that allow us to 'do' things with language. Among these are **experiential** functions used to express experience, **interpersonal** functions used to establish and maintain social ties, and **textual** func-tions used to structure information in oral and written texts. Within each functional component are numerous subfunctions (e.g., socializing) and several ways of realizing those functions grammatically (e.g., introducing people → *This is Carmen and Paulino*).

Unlike Hymes (1967), Halliday and Hasan (1976, 1989) articulated a clear relationship between syntax and semantics. This was done through cohesion theory, where they demonstrated how certain words link gram-matical forms to meaning and contextual use. **Cohesion**, as described by Halliday and Hasan (1976, 1989), refers to 'a set of resources that every language has . . . for linking one part of a text to another' (1989, p. 48). **Cohesive ties** may be used on a sentential level through **grammatical cohesive devices** such as *the boy* linked with *he*, or through **lexical**

cohesive devices such as the replacement of certain lexical items by other lexical items from the same lexical class – for example, *happy, sad,* and *angry* replaced with *these emotions.* Cohesive ties can also be utilized on a suprasentential or discourse level through the organization of given and new information in a text, through parallelism within a paragraph, or, interestingly, through two related language functions occurring in an exchange (e.g., an offer followed by an acceptance; or an accusal followed by a denial). Finally, Halliday and Hasan (1976, 1989) examined the relationship between syntax and social meaning in their treatment of registers (formal and informal language) and dialects. In short, systemic-functional grammar took stock of contextual evidence to propose a means of relating context to both form and meaning.

Influenced by speech act theory and systemic-functional linguistics, van Ek (1975) and Wilkins (1976) proposed a method of organizing language teaching around *functions* and *notions.* Language functions are what people 'do' with language, such as agreeing or disagreeing; **language notions** refer to semantic concepts such as time (e.g., duration, sequence), space (e.g., location, direction) and quantification (number, degree). In the functional–notional syllabus, teachers typically organize instructional input around situations that require students to express specific situational needs by means of language functions (agreeing/disagreeing) and notions (point of time → *since last year;* period of time → *for a year).* The functions and notions are represented by a range of grammatical and lexical forms which display several literal meanings. These functions can also carry pragmatic meanings depending on the context. In this approach, form, meaning and pragmatic use are all important, and success is based on the assumption that learners at the beginning level are able to produce at least one grammatical form to represent the function or notion, while more advanced learners might be able to produce a range depending on the context.

Speech act theory and systemic-functional linguistics, as mediated through the functional–notional categories, have had a considerable impact on L2 syllabus design, teaching and testing, and are credited for shifting the emphasis of language classrooms from a formal grammatical focus to a communication-based one. More recently, research in second language acquisition theory has motivated language educators to consider the role of grammar as it is deployed in interaction and the negotiation of meaning (Pica, 1994).

The theories discussed thus far have shaped how language teachers conceptualize grammar in their work. However, even though these theories have provided coherent systems for describing how language is organized, few teachers draw exclusively on any one theory to implement grammar instruction. Rather, they use both the syntactocentric and the communication-based approaches to language as resources for tailoring grammar instruction to the specific needs of their students.

The assessment of grammatical ability, however, is a different story. Until recently, grammatical ability was typically assessed from a purely syntactocentric perspective with an emphasis on grammatical form. This can be attributed to a long tradition of testing isolated features of grammatical form. In fact, I have known language teachers who go to great lengths to teach grammar communicatively with a concern for both form and meaning, but when it comes to testing, they rely exclusively on traditional, multiple-choice or blank-completion tasks of grammatical form, ignoring the meanings these forms may convey or their appropriate use in a given context. Recently, language teachers and testers have begun to approach the assessment of grammatical ability from a communication-based perspective. Just as the different linguistic theories have enriched what language instructors teach, so are they relevant to how grammatical ability might be assessed.

What is pedagogical grammar?

Many language teachers who have taken courses in linguistic analysis and learned to examine language within the frameworks of formal, grammatical theories have often felt that these courses did not adequately meet their immediate needs. This is often because courses in linguistic analysis rarely address classroom concerns such as what grammar to teach, how to teach it and how to test it. Furthermore, it is unlikely that language teachers would attempt to teach phrase-structure rules, parameter-setting conditions or abstract notions of time and space, and certainly, they would never test students on these principles. As a result, many language teachers feel that knowledge of formal grammatical theory has little to offer their practice, and they have some misgivings as to how relevant this is for language assessment. Instead, in my experience, they prefer to draw on an experiential knowledge base derived from a familiarity with language textbooks, from their own hands-on experience of what actually works in classrooms, from a critical reflection of their practice and from informal discussions of their practice with colleagues.

However, if we as L2 educators are to have the necessary background knowledge to customize grammatical instruction to the needs of our students, we must be able to draw on more than experience or reflection. We must consult pedagogical grammars for information we might otherwise have ignored. A **pedagogical grammar** represents an eclectic, but principled description of the target-language forms, created for the express purpose of helping teachers understand the linguistic resources of communication. These grammars provide information about how language is organized and offer relatively accessible ways of describing complex, linguistic phenomena for pedagogical purposes. The more L2 teachers understand how the grammatical system works, the better they will be able to tailor this information to their specific instructional contexts.

Recently, there have been some comprehensive, formal attempts at interpreting linguistic theories for the purposes of teaching (or testing) grammar. One of these **formal pedagogical grammars** of English is *The Grammar Book*, published by Celce-Murcia and Larsen-Freeman (1999). These authors used transformational-generative grammar as an organizing framework for the study of the English language. However, in the tradition of pedagogical grammars, they also invoked other linguistic theories and methods of analysis to explain the workings of grammatical form, meaning and use when a specific grammar point was not amenable to a transformational-generative analysis. For example, to explain the form and meanings of prepositions, they drew upon case grammar (Fillmore, 1968) and to describe the English tense-aspect system at the semantic level, they referred to Bull's (1960) framework relating tense to time. Celce-Murcia and Larsen-Freeman's (1999) book and other useful pedagogical English grammars (e.g., Swan, 1995; Azar, 1998) provide teachers and testers alike with pedagogically oriented grammars that are an invaluable resource for organizing grammar content for instruction and assessment.

Besides formal pedagogical grammars (and, of course, SLA theory), language teachers would be advised to consult language textbooks when put to the task of specifying grammatical content for instruction or assessment. These books not only provide descriptions, albeit less comprehensive, of the target grammar, but they also inform teachers of the scope with which a grammar point might be treated at a particular proficiency level or the sequence with which grammar points might be introduced. They show teachers how specific grammar points might be evoked by certain themes or how grammar might be taught to English-language learners studying school subjects like science or social studies.

By consulting these resources and relating them to L2 learning processes, teachers should have the information they need to create viable lesson plans that suit their students' needs and to construct assessments of how students are progressing.

Summary

In this chapter, I have attempted to answer the question 'What do we mean by grammar?' In this respect, I have differentiated between language and language analysis or linguistics. I have also discussed several schools of linguistics and have shown how each has broadened our understanding of what is meant by 'grammar'. Finally, I have shown how these different notions of grammar provide complementary information that could be drawn on for purposes of teaching or assessing grammar.

   In the next chapter I will discuss how second language grammatical knowledge is acquired. In this respect, we will examine how grammatical ability has been conceptualized in L2 grammar teaching and learning, and how L2 grammar teaching and learning are intrinsically linked to assessment.

CHAPTER TWO

Research on L2 grammar teaching, learning and assessment

Introduction

As we saw in the last chapter, second and foreign language educators have looked to different schools of linguistics for insights about language. This has considerably broadened our notion of grammar and has led to a deeper understanding of the role that grammar plays in conveying meaning in communication. However, although linguistic analysis can tell us what the language system is and how it works, it still cannot tell us how second or foreign languages are best learned or what teaching practices most effectively promote L2 learning. With respect to learning to use grammar communicatively, several questions arise. First, do learners best learn an L2 naturalistically surrounded by other speakers of the target language, or does L2 learning require instruction? If it does, what type of instruction makes a difference? Does the explicit presentation of grammar rules lead to improved L2 communicative ability, or do rules just confuse students and raise their level of anxiety? And if instruction makes a difference, when should it be implemented? Does timing make a difference? Also, if instruction works for some and not for others, under what conditions is instruction most effective? What, in fact, are the cognitive underpinnings of grammar learning and how does this influence students' rate of learning, their ultimate level of achievement and the ease with which they acquire the grammar? Finally, the assessment question – how do we know that grammar learning has occurred? What claims are we asserting about the learner's grammatical knowledge on the basis of assessment? How much of the knowledge must students demonstrate to support claims of learning? What evidence do we have of grammatical knowledge and is that evidence credible enough to support the claims? What kinds of tasks must students perform to provide the necessary evidence to substantiate these claims? In this chapter, I will discuss the research on L2 grammar teaching and learning and show how this research has important insights for language teachers and testers wanting to assess L2 grammatical ability. Similarly, I will discuss the critical role that assessment has played in empirical inquiry on L2 grammar teaching and learning.

Research on L2 teaching and learning

Over the years, several of the questions mentioned above have intrigued language teachers, inspiring them to experiment with different methods, approaches and techniques in the teaching of grammar. To determine if students had actually learned under the different conditions, teachers have used diverse forms of assessment and drawn their own conclusions about their students. In so doing, these teachers have acquired a considerable amount of anecdotal evidence on the strengths and weaknesses of using different practices to implement L2 grammar instruction. These experiences have led most teachers nowadays to ascribe to an eclectic approach to grammar instruction, whereby they draw upon a variety of different instructional techniques, depending on the individual needs, goals and learning styles of their students.

In recent years, some of these same questions have been addressed by second language acquisition (SLA) researchers in a variety of empirically based studies. These studies have principally focused on a description of how a learner's **interlanguage** (Selinker, 1972), or how a learner's L2, develops over time and on the effects that L2 instruction may have on this progression. In most of these studies, researchers have investigated the effects of learning grammatical forms by means of one or more assessment tasks. Based on the conclusions drawn from these assessments, SLA researchers have gained a much better understanding of how grammar instruction impacts both language learning in general and grammar learning in particular. However, in far too many SLA studies, the ability under investigation has been poorly defined or defined with no relation to a model of L2 grammatical ability. Also, the empirical evidence to support the learning claims have sometimes lacked credibility or generalizability, and the scoring of the tasks or the reliability of the measuring instruments have often not been reported. Nonetheless, given the importance of this research and the implications of its findings for those who wish to assess L2 grammatical ability, I will summarize it, highlighting how assessment was used to support claims about grammatical knowledge.

I might add that this research is especially important for language testers, who have, over the years, overlooked many of the findings obtained in SLA research related to the acquisition of L2 grammatical ability. In fact, language testers can be criticized in many cases for perpetuating the testing of grammar with discrete-point tasks of grammatical form; for constructing scoring rubrics with descriptors of grammatical development that have little support from SLA findings (Savignon, 1985; Pienemann, Johnston and Brindley, 1988) or from a coherent model of grammatical ability; and for downplaying the role of grammatical accuracy in favor of 'communicative effectiveness' in performance assessments of speaking and writing (McNamara, 1996). They might also be faulted for ignoring the role that grammatical knowledge often plays in articulating the different levels of language ability or the role it plays in formulating rater's judgments of student performance (Homburg, 1984). Finally, language testers can be questioned for intimating that grammatical knowledge is impossible to isolate and assess in communicative situations (e.g., Douglas, 1997). In examining rater scoring behaviors while using communicatively oriented criteria in judging speaking performance, McNamara (1996, p. 222) concluded that: 'Given what Savignon (1985:131) says about the pervasiveness of a structural orientation in the language-teaching profession, even among progressive and communicatively oriented teachers, it is likely that accuracy, including structural accuracy, is a strong determinant of scores given in this category.'

Findings from SLA research, according to Bachman and Cohen (1998), Skehan (1998), Tarone (1998) and Ellis (2001a, 2001b), could be useful in providing language testers with new considerations in the design, development and analysis of grammar tests. This information might be helpful to language teachers who wish to measure grammatical development in classroom settings, as well as to those who need to make decisions, for example, about where a new student should be placed in a program of study or whether a student has achieved an adequate level of language proficiency for some real-life purpose.

The SLA research looking at the role of grammar instruction in SLA might be categorized into three strands. One set of studies has looked at the relationship between the acquisition of L2 grammatical knowledge and different language-teaching methods. These are referred to as the **comparative methods studies**. A second set of studies has examined the acquisition of L2 grammatical knowledge through what Long and Robinson (1998) call a '**non-interventionist**' approach to instruction. These studies have examined the degree to which grammatical ability could be acquired **incidentally** (while doing something else) or **implicitly** (without awareness), and not through **explicit** (with awareness) grammar instruction. A third set of studies has investigated the relationship between explicit grammar instruction and the acquisition of L2 grammatical ability. These are referred to as the **interventionist studies**, and are a topic of particular interest to language teachers and testers.

Comparative methods studies

The comparative methods studies sought to compare the effects of different language-teaching methods on the acquisition of an L2. These studies occurred principally in the 1960s and 1970s, and stemmed from a reaction to the grammar-translation method, which had dominated language instruction during the first half of the twentieth century. More generally, these studies were in reaction to **form-focused instruction** (referred to as 'focus on forms' by Long, 1991), which used a traditional structural syllabus of grammatical forms as the organizing principle for L2 instruction. According to Ellis (1997), form-focused instruction contrasts with meaning-focused instruction in that **meaning-focused instruction** emphasizes the communication of messages (i.e., the act of making a suggestion and the content of such a suggestion) while form-focused instruction stresses the learning of linguistic forms. These can be further contrasted with **form-and-meaning focused instruction** (referred to by Long (1991) as 'focus-on-form'), where grammar instruction occurs in a meaning-based environment and where learners strive to communicate meaning while paying attention to form. (Note that Long's version of 'focus-on-form' stresses a meaning orientation with an incidental focus on forms.) These comparative methods studies all shared the theoretical premise that grammar has a central place in the curriculum, and that successful learning depends on the teaching method and the degree to which that promotes grammar processing.

One early comparative methods study, carried out by Scherer and Wertheimer (1964), compared the effects of using the 'traditional' grammar-translation method to teach German as a foreign language with the effects of using the audio-lingual method. At the end of the first and second years, students were tested in reading, writing, listening and speaking. It must be noted, however, that these skill-based tests were essentially form-focused grammar tests designed to measure knowledge of linguistic forms while performing one of the language skills. For example, the following speaking task provided students with a spoken present tense sentence, and students were asked to say the same sentence in the past.

A: Er spielt mit seinem Freund.   (He plays with his friend.)
B: *Er spielte mit seinem Freund.*   (*He played with his friend.*)

The study results showed that those students who studied in the grammar-translation group outperformed those studying in the audio-lingual group in both reading and writing, while those studying in the audio-lingual group outperformed those in other groups in both listening and speaking. In short, student test scores were a reflection of the instructional method they had studied under, and no superiority of one method over another was established.

In a later study, referred to as the Pennsylvania (Foreign Language) Project, Smith (1970) compared the effects of three methods on the acquisition of two foreign languages (French and German) at two different proficiency levels (beginning and intermediate). The methods included the 'traditional' or the grammar-translation method, the 'functional skills' or the audiolingual method and the 'functional skills plus grammar' method. In short, this study compared three different approaches to teaching grammar. At the beginning and end of the study, students were administered a battery of standardized tests (e.g., The MLA Cooperative Classroom Tests) which measured listening, speaking, reading and writing ability. Again of note is that these skill-based tests were, for all practical purposes, measures to assess knowledge of grammatical forms in a skill context. The results showed no statistically significant differences among the scores from the three methods. However, the traditional group outperformed the functional group on the reading test in the first year, and the functional group outperformed the traditional group on the speaking test in the second year. Again, no one method provided the magic answer to L2 learning. However, we might wonder what conclusions might have been drawn had the assessments been more than tests of grammatical forms based on a coherent model of L2 grammatical ability.

Much later, Hammond (1988) investigated the effects of two methods on the learning of Spanish in a university setting. This study compared the grammar-translation approach, where grammar was taught deductively, with the Natural Approach (Krashen and Terrell, 1983), where no explicit grammar instruction is used, on the acquisition of Spanish. Again, no one method was favored. However, this study underscored the fact that grammar learning could occur in the absence of grammar instruction.

Allen, Swain, Harley and Cummins (1990) studied the effects of teaching French to grade 6 students in Canada by means of a 'communicative' versus a 'non-communicative' approach. They used a classroom interaction analysis schedule to characterize classes as 'communicative' or 'non-communicative' and a battery of language tests to measure grammatical, discourse and sociolinguistic knowledge. These tests involved multiple-choice tasks of grammatical forms (morphology and syntax), discourse and sociolinguistics, and oral production and written production tasks, both measuring grammatical, discourse and sociolinguistic competence. Allen et al. (1990) expected students in the non-communicative classes to perform better on the written and grammatical accuracy tests, and students in the communicative classes to score better on the sociolinguistic and discourse competence tests. However, again, no conclusive evidence was observed to privilege one method over another.

One of the criticisms of this study according to Bachman (1990a) related to the language tests used to measure the grammatical, discourse and sociolinguistic competence. Bachman states, 'the measures include a wider range of test method facets, and may well tap a richer variety of language abilities than were hypothesized by the theoretical model. It is this unplanned complexity that may explain, to some extent, why attempts to fit the data to the model were not successful' (pp. 30–1).

The vast majority of studies attempting to show that one method of teaching grammar was superior to another failed to do so. In each case, the assessment of grammatical ability played a crucial role in helping researchers draw these conclusions. However, the assessment procedures were as much a part of the problem as they were a facilitator in reaching conclusions, since students obviously do better on tests that cover what they have been taught. In the end, researchers realized that the method studies produced inconclusive results. From this one might conclude that 'global method' as a variable for investigating SLA involves far too many interacting dimensions for researchers to seek simple answers to second language acquisition – such as the superiority of one method over another. SLA is simply too complex to attribute L2 learning uniquely to method.

Celce-Murcia (1991) identified two broad categories of variables critical to making informed decisions about learning grammar. One involves learner variables (e.g., age, proficiency level, educational background) and the other instructional variables (e.g., skill, register, need or use for the language). Besides these two variables, we could mention a host of other variables such as (1) typological distance between the first language and the L2, (2) the socio-psychological characteristics of learners (i.e., strategy use or processing attributes, motivational attributes, or levels of anxiety), (3) teacher characteristics (e.g., beliefs about language learning, formal training), (4) task characteristics and (5) contextual characteristics (e.g., input-poor versus input-rich environments). In the end, method may not be the most feasible unit by which to examine L2 grammar learning. For this reason, most researchers now utilize 'pedagogical techniques' as a more refined level of analysis (Doughty, 2002).

In sum, the investigation of the effects of teaching method on SLA is extremely complex. First of all, method is not a monolithic concept as the early researchers might have us believe. Rather, instruction involves numerous variables that may interact with each other and that may contribute differentially to SLA. Furthermore, a comprehensive approach to examining the relationships between L2 teaching and learning requires the use of multiple assessments (e.g., tests, self-rating measures, observation schedules, questionnaires, interview protocols) to examine this multifaceted phenomenon, and assessment needs to track development over time. Until a multidimensional, recursive approach to investigating methods can be devised, we would be wise to follow Ellis' (1990) conclusion: 'Method may not be the most appropriate unit for investigating the effect that language teaching has on L2 learning' (pp. 572–3).

Non-interventionist studies

While some language educators were examining different methods of teaching grammar in the 1960s, others were feeling a growing sense of dissatisfaction with the central role of grammar in the L2 curriculum. As a result, questions regarding the centrality of grammar were again raised by a small group of L2 teachers and syllabus designers who felt that the teaching of grammar in any form simply did not produce the desired classroom results. Newmark (1966), in fact, asserted that grammatical analysis and the systematic practice of grammatical forms were actually interfering with the process of L2 learning, rather than promoting it, and if left uninterrupted, second language acquisition, similar to first language acquisition, would proceed naturally.

At the same time, the role of grammar in the L2 curriculum was also being questioned by some SLA researchers (e.g., Dulay and Burt, 1973; Bailey, Madden and Krashen, 1974) who had been studying L2 learning in instructed and naturalistic settings. In their attempts to characterize the L2 learner's interlanguage at one or more points along the path toward target-like proficiency, several researchers came to similar conclusions about L2 development. They found that instead of making incremental leaps in grammatical ability through an accumulation of grammatical forms, as presented in a traditional grammar syllabus, learners in both instructed and naturalistic settings acquired the target structures in a relatively **fixed order** (Ellis, 1994) regardless of when they were introduced. For example, Krashen (1977) claimed that, in general, ESL learners first acquire the -*ing* affix, plural markings and the copula (stage 1), and then the auxiliary and the articles (stage 2). This is followed by the irregular past verb forms (stage 3) and finally, the regular past, the third-person singular affix and the possessive -*s* affix (stage 4). While this information is interesting, research findings involve only a skeletal list of the possible grammar points that any typical curriculum would encompass. As a result, we might wonder how this order will change if other grammar points are investigated at the same time. Also, we have no idea how this order would hold for many other languages.

Many interlanguage studies also showed that learners acquiring any individual grammatical feature such as negatives, interrogatives, relative clauses, word order, or pronouns appeared to pass through a relatively **fixed developmental sequence** toward mastering that form (Ellis, 1994). For example, ESL learners learning the interrogatives would first use word(s) plus rising intonation (*You going?*). They would then use non-inverted word order (*You are going?*), then inverted word order (*Are you going?*). After that, they would incorporate *do*-support into their interlanguage (*Did you go?*). Finally, they would develop embedding (*We know when you are going*). These stages are characterized as 'transitional' since learners exhibit a high degree of variability in the production of grammatical forms as they pass from one developmental stage to the next.

The findings from these studies provided compelling evidence of a relatively predictable order and sequence of acquisition. As a result, several

SLA researchers concluded that L2 learners had a built-in syllabus for grammar acquisition (Corder, 1967), or as many theorists (e.g., Eckman, 1977; White, 1989) now claim, the order and sequence in which these forms are acquired are largely universal and, in fact, form part of Universal Grammar.

The empirical evidence of ordered acquisitional patterns coupled with dissatisfaction with the results obtained from grammar teaching led a few SLA researchers to call for the total abandonment of traditional grammar instruction in the L2 classroom. Drastic as this was, researchers supporting this position (e.g., Krashen, 1982; Prabhu, 1987) argued that an L2 is not actually acquired through formal instruction; rather, it is learned incidentally and implicitly through exposure to the target language, as long as the input that learners are exposed to is made comprehensible. These researchers further claimed that in input-rich settings, the learner's attention is focused solely on meaning in natural communication, and any form of explicit error correction is harmful to the acquisitional process. Supporters of this position further maintained that grammar acquisition was impervious to form-focused instruction, since the 'natural' processes of acquisition were at work. In other words, learners progress toward native-like proficiency in a predetermined order, making a number of predictable interlanguage errors, regardless of any instructional intervention. Finally, some researchers (e.g., Pica, 1983) found that learners who, in fact, did receive form-focused instruction showed an order of acquisition of grammatical features similar to that seen with the naturalistic learners, lending further support to the non-interventionist position.

Empirical studies in support of non-intervention

The non-interventionist position was examined empirically by Prabhu (1987) in a project known as the Communicational Teaching Project (CTP) in southern India. This study sought to demonstrate that the development of grammatical ability could be achieved through a task-based, rather than a form-focused, approach to language teaching, provided that the tasks required learners to engage in meaningful communication. In the CTP, Prabhu (1987) argued against the notion that the development of grammatical ability depended on a systematic presentation of grammar followed by planned practice. However, in an effort to evaluate the CTP program, Beretta and Davies (1985) compared classes involved in the CTP with classes outside the project taught with a structural-oral-situational method. They administered a battery of tests to the students, and found that the CTP learners outperformed the control group on a task-based test, whereas the non-CTP learners did better on a traditional structure test. These results lent partial support to the non-interventionist position by showing that task-based classrooms based on meaningful communication can also be effective in promoting SLA. However, these results also showed that again students do best when they are taught and tested in similar ways.

Similar results have been observed in other studies (e.g., Terrell, Gomez and Mariscal, 1980; Lightbown, 1992), which also demonstrated the effectiveness of communicative classrooms in promoting SLA. In terms of language testing, Beretta and Davies' (1985) results also raise questions as to the underlying model of grammatical ability that served as a basis for test development of both the traditional structure test and the task-based test. Was performance on the test more an indicator of method familiarity than of L2 ability?

In contrast to Prabhu's claims, researchers such as Harley and Swain (1984) and Genesee (1987) found that after several decades of French immersion classes in Canada, students were indeed able to understand French and get their message across fairly well, but even at the highest grade levels, they had not reached target-like levels of proficiency, especially with certain morphological and syntactic features. In other words, input-rich language classrooms with ample opportunities for meaningful interaction proved to be insufficient for pushing learners from developing a communicatively effective command to a target-like command of the L2.

While current research, theory and practice overwhelmingly favor an interventionist position to grammar teaching, as we will see in the next section, the non-interventionist position can be credited with showing us (1) that learners appear to acquire *different* grammatical structures in a fixed 'acquisitional order' and the *same* structure in a fixed 'acquisitional sequence', (2) that meaning-focused classrooms can promote the development of L2 fluency provided there are plenty of opportunities for meaningful communication and (3) that meaning-focused classrooms can promote the development of grammatical ability no less than traditional classrooms, although, as we see, this may be inadequate for promoting high levels of SLA in a timely and efficient manner. Finally, Seliger (1979) and Lightbown (1985) note that although L2 grammar instruction may not 'cause' acquisition, it might raise the learner's awareness of grammar so that this information can be used later when the learner is 'developmentally ready' for acquisition.

Possible implications of fixed developmental order to language assessment

The notion that structures appear to be acquired in a fixed developmental order and in a fixed developmental sequence might conceivably have some relevance to the assessment of grammatical ability. First of all, these findings could give language testers an empirical basis for constructing grammar tests that would account for the variability inherent in a learner's interlanguage. In other words, information on the acquisitional order of grammatical items could conceivably serve as a basis for selecting grammatical content for tests that aim to measure different levels of developmental progression, such as Chang (2002, 2004) did in examining the underlying structure of a test that attempted to measure knowledge of the relative clauses. These findings also suggest a substantive approach to defining test tasks according to developmental order and sequence on the basis of how grammatical features are acquired over time (Ellis, 2001b). In other words, one task could potentially tap into developmental level one, while another taps into developmental level two, and so forth.

To illustrate, grammar tests targeting beginning English-language learners often include questions on the articles and the third-person singular -s affix, two features considered to be 'very challenging' from an acquisitional perspective. Since, according to these findings, no beginning learner would be expected to have target-like control of these particular grammatical items, the inclusion of these grammatical features in a beginning classroom achievement test might be questionable. However, the inclusion of these items in a placement test would be highly appropriate since the goal of placement assessment is to identify a wide range of ability levels so that developmentally homogeneous groups can be formed.

In addition to acquisitional orders, information on the acquisitional sequence of items could hypothetically serve as a basis for test construction in certain limited contexts. For example, teachers wishing to measure the developmental proficiency of learners with regard to question formation might base their assessment on Pienemann and Johnston's (1986) six-stage sequence as cited in Spada and Lightbown (1993, p. 222) below:

Stage	Examples
1. Single words or sentence fragments	Go there?
2. Canonical word order	You like it?
3. *Wh*-fronting and *do*-fronting	Where you are going?
	Do you like it there?
4. Pseudo inversion	Where is the salt?
	The salt is it on the stove?
5. *Do*-second: Inversion with *do* in *wh*-questions	What do you want?
Aux-second: Inversion with other auxiliaries	What is he making?
in *wh*-questions	What can he do?
6. Tag questions, negative questions and	It's late, isn't it?
embedded questions	Can't you go?
	Do you know what time it is?

If grammatical assessment tasks could be constructed with developmental proficiency levels in mind, then the scores from these tests could have been used not only to infer grammatical accuracy, as we have always done, but also to make inferences about the underlying acquisitional development of the L2 learners. Consider, for example, a teacher wishing to determine a learner's level of target-like accuracy in forming questions. We would consider all test items in a test as potentially right (1 point) or wrong (0 points). The sum of the right answers would indicate the extent to which a student has mastered that feature. This accuracy-based score, however, might be somewhat misleading. If high beginners were given an English language test on question formation, they might produce eight sentences depicted by Pienemann and Johnston (1986) at stage 3 (*Where you are going?*), one at stage 2 (*You are John?*) and one at stage 4 (*What is this?*). They would end up with an accuracy score of 10, indicating that the student's target-like performance with regard to question formation would be at the extreme low end of the interlanguage continuum. However, from an acquisitional perspective, the target-like score provides no reflection of the student's acquisitional development, or their internalization of the target feature. In other words, the different types of sentences are not equal from an acquisitional perspective, and it would be misleading to characterize a student who can communicate grammatical meaning without accurate grammatical forms as 'absolute beginner'. Therefore, in addition to accuracy scores, we might possibly wish to assess the learner's developmental level of question formation by scoring different types of responses on a 1 to 6 scale corresponding to Pienemann and Johnston's (1986) acquisitional sequence. As Ellis (2001a) recommends, this would weight the scores to reflect the developmental level of a given structure. In this case, we could say that the student mentioned above produced level 3 questions 80% of the time. Then, if a student produces the feature at some developmental stage a criterion number of times (e.g., 70% or greater), it would be possible to attribute a level of developmental progression to that student with regard to that feature.

In a study on the effects of form-focused instruction and corrective feedback on the acquisition of questions, Spada and Lightbown (1993) did just that. They assessed the students' target-like accuracy by calculating the percentage of well-formed questions – 'accuracy' for interrogatives being defined in terms of word order with the placement of the *wh*-word, the auxiliary verb and the subject. They then categorized each learner's questions according to Pienemann and Johnston's (1986) six-stage developmental sequence. They found that from pre- to post-test, all students showed improvement in the production of interrogatives; however, the comparison group, receiving periodic but sustained interrogative instruction and corrective feedback over several months, showed higher levels of target-like performance (accuracy-based score) than the experimental group, which received two weeks of intensive interrogative instruction, exposure and corrective feedback. They also found that on a pre-test, all students produced interrogatives at stages one and two, and most also produced them at stage three or more. On the post- and follow-up tests, the comparison group performed as well or even better in terms of developmental progression. In sum, the provision of scores that reflect both target-like and developmental norms are likely to give a much more complete picture of the students' grammatical knowledge with regard to a single grammatical feature, the interrogatives.

Problems with the use of development sequences as a basis for assessment

Although developmental sequence research offers an intuitively appealing complement to accuracy-based assessments in terms of interpreting test scores, I believe this method is fraught with a number of serious problems, and language educators should use extreme caution in applying this method to language testing. This is because our understanding of natural acquisitional sequences is incomplete and at too early a stage of research to be the basis for concrete assessment recommendations (Lightbown, 1985; Hudson, 1993). First, the number of grammatical sequences that show a fixed order of acquisition is very limited, far too limited for all but the most restricted types of grammar tests. For example, what is the order for acquiring the modals, the conditionals, or the infinitive or gerund complements? Second, much of the research on acquisitional sequences is based on data from naturalistic settings, where students are provided with considerable exposure to the language. We have yet to learn about how these sequences hold for students whose only exposure to a language is an L2 classroom. Furthermore, acquisitional sequences make reference only to linguistic forms; no reference is made to how these forms interact with the conveyance of literal and implied meanings associated with a specific context. Third, as the rate (not the route) of acquisition appears to be influenced by the learner's first language and by exposure to other languages, we need to understand how these factors might impact on development rates and how we would reconcile this if we wished to test heterogeneous groups of language learners. Finally, as the developmental levels represent an ordering of grammatical rules during acquisition, this may or may not be on the same measurement scale as accuracy scores. Thus, until further research demonstrates the precise relationship between these scales, we should be careful about comparisons between proficiency levels based on accuracy scales and levels of interlanguage development. In the end, it is premature to apply the findings from acquisitional sequences research to language assessment given our current level of understanding of developmental sequences.

Despite these shortcomings, however, research on the interface between SLA and language testing should continue. Fairly stable routes of development have been identified for negation, questions, relative clauses and word order, and when instruction on non-contiguous stages was implemented, it proved ineffective (Lightbown, 1998). Therefore, the investigation of one or more language structures approached from both accuracy-based and developmental-based perspectives, similar to what Chang (2002, 2004) has done with respect to the relative-clause test, would greatly increase our understanding of this important interface.

Until further research has been done with regard to acquisitional sequences, we could address the problem of right/wrong accuracy scores by assigning partial credit to scores, thereby taking account of interlanguage development. Instead of using a 1 to 6 scale and linking the measurement directly to the sequence, we might use a 1 to 3 partial credit scale, where 1 refers to the lowest stage of accuracy, depicting 'very limited knowledge of the structure' (and, by extension, development) and where 3 indicates the highest level of accuracy (or target-like development). In this way, accuracy-based scores that show different levels of mastery might provide a more complete picture of the students' proficiency with regard to specific grammatical features, especially if these scores were accompanied by verbal descriptions or by a profile of scores. I will discuss this in more detail in later chapters.

Interventionist studies

Not all L2 educators are in agreement with the non-interventionist position to grammar instruction. In fact, several (e.g., Schmidt, 1983; Swain, 1991) have maintained that although some L2 learners are successful in acquiring selected linguistic features without explicit grammar instruction, the majority fail to do so. Testimony to this is the large number of non-native speakers who emigrate to countries around the world, live there all their lives and fail to learn the target language, or fail to learn it well enough to realize their personal, social and long-term career goals. In these situations, language teachers affirm that formal grammar instruction of some sort can be of benefit. Furthermore, most language teachers would contend that explicit grammar instruction, including systematic error correction and other instructional techniques, contributes immensely to their students' linguistic development. Finally, despite the non-interventionist recommendations toward grammar teaching, I believe grammar still plays an important role in most L2 classrooms around the world.

Empirical studies in support of intervention

Aside from anecdotal evidence, the non-interventionist position has come under intense attack on both theoretical and empirical grounds with several SLA researchers affirming that efforts to teach L2 grammar typically results in the development of L2 grammatical ability. Hulstijn (1989) and Alanen (1995) investigated the effectiveness of L2 grammar instruction on SLA in comparison with no formal instruction. They found that when coupled with meaning-focused instruction, the formal instruction of grammar appears to be more effective than exposure to meaning or form alone. Long (1991) also argued for a focus on both meaning and form in classrooms that are organized around meaningful and sustained communicative interaction. He maintained that the focus on grammar in communicative interaction serves as an aid to clarity and precision.

Similar results were found by Doughty (1991), who compared the effectiveness of naturalistic exposure to the target language with different types of instruction in the acquisition of relative clauses. Using intermediate-level ESL students, she asked one group, the control group, to read passages on the computer that contained relative clauses. A second group, the meaning-oriented group, was asked to read the same passages, except these students were also provided with highlighted or capitalized lexical and semantic rephrasings of the relative clauses, so the forms would potentially become salient and 'noticed'. A third group, the rule-oriented group, read the same passages, except they were also given explicit rule statements below each relative clause so that the rules would become salient. Knowledge of the relatives was measured by written grammaticality-judgment, sentence-combination and gap-filling tasks, and by sentence-level oral tasks based on pictures. Although no attempt was made to measure literal, intended, or pragmatic meaning independent of the relative clause forms, Doughty found that on the post-tests, the rule and meaning-oriented groups outperformed the control group in their ability to use relative clauses. However, the meaning-oriented group performed better than the other two groups on the overall comprehension of the text. In short, this study showed that naturalistic exposure *alone* was less effective than form-and-meaning-based instruction in promoting the acquisition of relative clause forms. In later studies, Doughty and Williams (1998) showed that form-and-meaning-based instruction which focused on meaning while attending to form had both a short- and often a long-term impact on performance, especially if the learners wished to move beyond simple communicative effectiveness to target-like performance. However, in a comprehensive survey of studies looking at interventions, Norris and Ortega (2000) found that instruction incorporating an explicit focus on form and meaning together would result in higher gains than instruction incorporating an explicit focus on forms alone. However, this would produce higher gains than instruction which encompasses an implicit focus on form and meaning together or, worse yet, an implicit focus on forms alone.

In attempts to explain differences in grammar learning, several SLA researchers (e.g., Lightbown, Spada and White, 1993; Ellis, 1997; Doughty and Williams, 1998) have moved beyond monolithic methods of grammar instruction to individual teaching techniques which are said to promote grammatical development. In an effort to understand those

conditions which enhance learning, several researchers have investigated how different instructional techniques could be used to present
grammatical features so that the properties of grammar would be made
more salient, and would thereby be more likely to be 'noticed' by the
learners in the input. By directing the learners' attention to the promi-
nent features of the input, they claim that further processing will occur or
will occur more rapidly.

Research on instructional techniques and their effects on acquisition

Much of the recent research on teaching grammar has focused on four
types of instructional techniques and their effects on acquisition.
Although a complete discussion of teaching interventions is outside the
purview of this book (see Ellis, 1997; Doughty and Williams, 1998), these
techniques include form- or rule-based techniques, input-based techniques, feedback-based techniques and practice-based techniques
(Norris and Ortega, 2000).

Form- or rule-based techniques revolve around the instruction of
grammatical forms. They can involve implicit, inductive grammar teaching, where the focus is on meaning, but the goal is to attract the learner's
attention to the form without using grammatical metatalk, or linguistic
terminology. Form-based techniques might also involve explicit, deductive grammar teaching, where the goal is to provide learners with the rule
purposefully. The teacher may or may not use grammatical metatalk.
Form-based techniques could also involve consciousness-raising activities. Inductive consciousness-raising activities provide learners with L2
data, and ask them to derive an explicit rule from the target structure,
while deductive consciousness-raising activities provide learners with a
grammar rule, and ask them to apply it to L2 data. Finally, another form-
based technique is the dictogloss, where a carefully selected passage is
read to learners while they listen and take notes. Then, in groups, learners are asked to reconstruct the passage and compare it with the original.

Input-based techniques deal with how input is used in grammar
instruction. One such technique is input flooding, where learners are presented with large amounts of input in which the targeted feature is
present. Another involves typographical input enhancement, where
input is manipulated by means of capitalization, printing in boldface and
so forth. Comprehension practice is an input-based technique, where

learners are asked to relate grammatical form to meaning – often by means of pictures or meaning-focused questions. Input-based techniques have been successfully used in assessment to measure grammatical meaning (see VanPatten and Cadierno, 1993a, 1993b; Lee and VanPatten, 2003), as we will see in Chapter 8.

Feedback-based techniques involve ways of providing negative evidence of grammar performance. For example, 'recast' is a feedback-based technique, where an utterance containing an error is repeated without the error. Another is referred to as 'garden path' since learners are explicitly shown the linguistic rule and allowed to generalize with other examples; however, when the generalization does not hold (negative evidence), further instruction is provided. Finally, metalinguistic feedback involves the use of linguistic terminology to promote 'noticing'.

A final set of instructional techniques mentioned by Norris and Ortega (2000) are practice-based techniques of grammar instruction. These involve input-processing instruction and output practice (Lee and VanPatten, 2003).

Other researchers (e.g., Sharwood Smith, 1981, 1988; Schmidt, 1990, 1993; DeKeyser, 1995) have sought to explain L2 grammar learning by examining how explicit instructional techniques lead learners to attend to and process different aspects of the L2 (i.e., the message of the interaction; the formal properties of the language), so that explicit grammatical knowledge can be converted into implicit knowledge. Arguing against Krashen's (1981) claim that no relationship exists between explicit and implicit knowledge, Lee and VanPatten (2003) described SLA as the construction of an unconscious or implicit system of language consisting of several components (e.g., lexis, syntax) interacting in language use. More specifically, they proposed a set of three acquisitional processes: input processing, system change, and output processing. Input processing describes how learners understand the grammatical information they hear or see. This is where input is converted into intake by strategies that promote form–meaning associations during comprehension. VanPatten used grammatical comprehension tasks in an attempt to measure this process. System change describes how new grammatical information is incorporated or accommodated into the developing system of language and how this new information restructures the implicit system of language. The final process involves output processing. This accounts for how learners learn to use the newly acquired grammar to produce meaningful utterances spontaneously. These processes are depicted in Figure 2.1.

		I		II		III	
input	→	intake	→	developing system	→		output

Figure 2.1 Three processes in SLA and use (VanPatten, 1996, p. 154)

Grammar processing and second language development

It is important for language teachers and testers to understand these processes, especially for classroom assessments. As we will see in Chapter 8, we might need to design assessments to determine which stage of the learning process students need help with. For example, I have had students fake their way through an entire lesson on the second conditional. They knew the form and could produce it well enough, but it was not until the end of the lesson that I realized they had not really understood the meaning of the hypothetical or counterfactual conditional. In other words, meaning was not mapped onto the form. A short comprehension test earlier in the lesson might have allowed me to re-teach the meaning of the conditionals before moving ahead.

In the grammar-learning process, **explicit grammatical knowledge** refers to a conscious knowledge of grammatical forms and their meanings. Explicit knowledge is usually accessed slowly, even when it is almost fully automatized (Ellis, 2001b). DeKeyser (1995) characterizes grammatical instruction as 'explicit' when it involves the explanation of a rule or the request to focus on a grammatical feature. Instruction can be **explicitly deductive**, where learners are given rules and asked to apply them, or **explicitly inductive**, where they are given samples of language from which to generate rules and make generalizations. Similarly, many types of language test tasks (i.e., gap-filling tasks) seem to measure explicit grammatical knowledge.

Implicit grammatical knowledge refers to 'the knowledge of a language that is typically manifest in some form of naturally occurring language behavior such as conversation' (Ellis, 2001b, p. 252). In terms of processing time, it is unconscious and is accessed quickly. DeKeyser (1995) classifies grammatical instruction as implicit when it does *not* involve rule presentation or a request to focus on form in the input; rather, implicit grammatical instruction involves semantic processing of the input with any degree of awareness of grammatical form. The hope, of course, is that learners will 'notice' the grammatical forms and identify form–meaning relationships so that the forms are recognized in the input and eventually incorporated into the interlanguage. This type of instruction occurs when learners are asked to listen to a passage containing a specific grammatical feature. They are then asked to answer comprehension questions, but not asked to attend to the feature. Similarly, language test tasks that require examinees to engage in interactive talk might also be said to measure implicit grammatical knowledge.

Among the many studies that examined the benefits of explicit instruction on SLA, one set of studies examined issues related to whether and when grammatical forms are actually 'teachable' or whether and when they are 'learnable' (Pienemann, 1989). In other studies, researchers attempted to investigate learning in terms of the innate, linguistic predispositions humans have for learning language (e.g., Eckman, Bell and Nelson, 1988; White, 1989). Still another set of studies examined instruction by focusing on the relationship between structure and meaning (Garrett, 1986). Some findings from these studies have shown that pedagogical interventions are beneficial provided they do not interrupt the learner processing constraints which underlie certain developmental orders; that the use of a variety of techniques in instruction can promote form–meaning connections and trigger acquisitional processes; and that instruction can help learners develop higher levels of attainment in an L2 more efficiently and at a quicker pace.

Given the vast number of studies examining the effectiveness of grammar instruction on SLA, several researchers (e.g., Ellis, 1990; Norris and Ortega, 2000; Hinkel and Fotos, 2002) have attempted to make sense of this work by surveying the relevant empirical studies and by summarizing the findings. Interestingly, these reviews have shown that the empirical research on how grammar is learned and taught has provided no one simple, best answer to grammatical development. However, there is sufficient evidence to conclude that when students are asked to focus on grammar points that are more or less appropriate for their developmental level, they usually learn. In fact, 'focused instructional treatments of whatever sort far surpass non- or minimally-focused exposure to the L2' (Norris and Ortega, 2000, p. 463), and this result holds in both the short and the long term (Doughty and Williams, 1998). These summaries have also shown that comprehensible input, together with meaningful interaction, appear to contribute to grammar learning in both instructed and non-instructed settings. However, a focus *solely* on meaning presented limitations on what could ultimately be learned and, therefore, did not seem to provide a context in which learners could achieve high levels of grammatical ability in a timely and efficient fashion. Finally, in cases where input, interaction and multiple forms of explicit grammar instruction were included in the curriculum, students generally outperformed those who did not receive all three instructional components. These results are summarized in Figure 2.2.

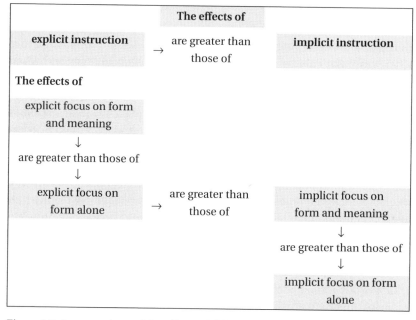

Figure 2.2 A comparison of the effects of different types of instruction on SLA

In sum, the majority of studies surveyed showed a clear advantage for learners receiving explicit grammar instruction. Formal, explicit grammar instruction seemed to help L2 learners develop their interlanguage at a more rapid pace; it helped them achieve higher ultimate levels of grammatical ability; and it helped them reduce instances of language fossilization.

In the end, the ensuing debates on grammar teaching and learning have had a positive impact on the field of applied linguistics. They have prompted researchers to take a much closer look at what it actually means to teach grammar and what influence this has on the acquisition of grammatical ability. They have also provoked researchers to seek ways of explaining the underlying acquisitional process. Because of this research, our understanding of this complex topic has been considerably expanded.

Implications for assessing grammar

The studies investigating the effects of teaching and learning on grammatical performance present a number of challenges for language assessment. First of all, the notion that grammatical knowledge structures can be differentiated according to whether they are fully automatized (i.e., implicit) or not (i.e., explicit) raises important questions for the testing of grammatical ability (Ellis, 2001b). Given the many purposes of assessment, we might wish to test explicit knowledge of grammar, implicit knowledge of grammar or both. For example, in certain classroom contexts, we might want to assess the learners' explicit knowledge of one or more grammatical forms, and could, therefore, ask learners to answer multiple-choice or short-answer questions related to these forms. The information from these assessments would show how well students could apply the forms in contexts where fluent and spontaneous language use is *not* required and where time could be taken to figure out the answers. Inferences from the results of these assessments could be useful for teachers wishing to determine if their students have mastered certain grammatical forms. However, as teachers are well aware, this type of assessment would not necessarily show that the students had actually internalized the grammatical forms so as to be able to use them automatically in spontaneous or unplanned discourse. To obtain information on the students' implicit knowledge of grammatical forms, testers would need to create tasks designed to elicit the fluent and spontaneous use of grammatical forms in situations where automatic language use was required. In other words, to infer that students could understand and produce grammar in spontaneous speech, testers would need to present students with tasks that elicit comprehension or full production in real time (e.g., listening and speaking). Ellis (2001b) suggests that we also need to utilize time pressure as a means of ensuring that implicit knowledge is being tested. Although this idea is interesting, the introduction of speed into an assessment should be done with caution since it is often difficult to determine the impact of speed on the test taker. In effect, speed may simply produce a heightened sense of test anxiety, thereby introducing irrelevant variability in the test scores. If this were the case, speed would not necessarily provide an effective means of eliciting automatic grammatical ability. In my opinion, comprehensive assessments of grammatical ability should attempt to test students on both their explicit and their implicit knowledge of grammar.

At the same time, the research in SLA on the effectiveness of instructional treatments highlights the critical role that grammatical assessment plays in how language educators decide if learners are able to recognize and produce the target-language structures. Assessment is used not only to determine the state of a learner's interlanguage, but also to ascertain the impact of instructional treatments. It is thus surprising how little attention has been devoted to ensuring that outcome instruments provide valid and reliable measures of grammatical ability in SLA research. Because of this lack of rigor, readers are often left questioning the viability of the research. Thus, SLA researchers need to inform readers about how the tests used in their research were conceptualized, developed and scored. They also need to provide technical information on the quality of the assessments used to make inferences about learning (e.g., evidence of test reliability and validity) and should follow the 'best practices' for test development and use.

The studies I have reviewed used a wide variety of outcome measures to assess the learners' grammatical ability at one or more points in time. However, a model of grammatical ability upon which these assessments were based was never overtly specified. Nor was grammatical ability related to a more comprehensive model of communicative language ability. As a result, the components of grammatical knowledge being assessed by the outcome measures were often difficult to identify. The lack of a clear theoretical definition of what is being measured presents a serious problem for language assessment, since the goal of assessment is to use assessment scores to make inferences about what learners know. Failure to articulate what is being measured in an assessment instrument allows no means by which to determine if the instrument is actually assessing what it was intended to assess.

For example, many studies set out to investigate form-and-meaning-based teaching practices; however, no theoretical definition of grammatical form or grammatical meaning was presented. Instead, grammatical forms were treated as isolated linguistic features of language ability, with no clear discussion to how these forms might relate to other forms, to meaning, or how they might be used in discourse. Furthermore, I have rarely seen an attempt to assess grammatical meaning, even though meaning is an integral part of the research, and inferences and generalizations about meaning are often offered. An obvious exception to this was VanPatten (1996), who in conjunction with his colleagues sought to examine grammatical meaning by asking learners to match pictures with texts in which the grammatical forms were used. The students' ability to recognize form–function mappings on these 'comprehension measures' allowed for inferences to be drawn on the students' ability to recognize forms that convey meaning. Even though meaning is assessed, I have not seen it characterized as literal meaning within a model of communicative competence in the studies, and I have found few instances of grammatical meaning being scored separately on grammatical assessments.

Instead of articulating what aspects of grammatical knowledge were being assessed by certain tasks, the majority of studies discussed in this chapter simply described the tasks used to measure grammatical knowledge (i.e., multiple-choice, open-ended), thereby providing an operational, but not a theoretical, description of grammatical ability. Other studies depended heavily on grammaticality-judgment tasks as a means of measuring grammatical knowledge, even though it is well documented that these tasks may present some reliability or validity concerns (Chaudron, 1983; Ellis, 1994, Gass, 1994; Gass and Selinker, 1994). Grammaticality-judgment tasks ask learners to judge from intuition whether an utterance can be generated from the target language grammar and, if so, whether it is grammatically accurate, meaningful, acceptable, appropriate or natural. However, in using these tasks, Hinkel (2002) found that non-native speakers of English with high TOEFL scores do not necessarily share the same grammaticality judgments for certain linguistic features as native speakers do, even after years of language instruction and exposure. Also, Schachter, Tyson and Diffley (1976) found that in utilizing these tasks with learners of different language backgrounds in order to measure knowledge of English relative clauses, the Farsi speakers in their study viewed typical errors made by Farsi speakers as grammatical, while the Japanese speakers responded randomly to errors typically made by Japanese speakers, thereby casting some doubt on the validity of these measures.

In sum, no matter how narrow the focus of our tests, I believe it is important for language educators to be able to define the abilities they are measuring in terms that will distinguish them from other components of language ability. Furthermore, the development and use of language tests, no matter how limited in scope, need to be informed by a broad conceptualization of language ability. Given the importance of this notion, I will devote the next chapter to the description of a model of L2 grammatical ability that could be used as a framework for the development and use of L2 grammatical assessments. This framework will be the basis for test development throughout the rest of the book.

Summary

In this chapter, I have demonstrated how the teaching, learning and assessment of L2 grammatical ability are intrinsically related. Language educators depend on linguists for information on the nature of language, so that teaching, learning and assessment can reflect current notions of language. Language educators also depend on experience, other language teachers and SLA researchers for insights on teaching and learning, so that the processes underlying instruction and acquisition can be obtained and so that information on how learning can be maximized can be generated. Finally, both language educators and SLA researchers depend on language testers for expertise in the design and development of assessments so that samples of learner performance can be consistently elicited, and so that the information observed from assessments can be used to make claims about what a learner does or does not know.

In the next two chapters I will discuss how grammar has been defined in models of language proficiency and will argue for a coherent model of grammatical ability – one that could be used for test development and test validation purposes.

CHAPTER THREE

The role of grammar in models of communicative language ability

Introduction

In the previous chapters I reviewed several theories of grammar and we saw how language teachers and SLA researchers drew on these theories to define 'grammar' in their work. I also discussed how different instructional practices influenced how learners acquire knowledge of a second or foreign language grammar. Implicit in this discussion was the notion that knowledge of the L2 grammatical system can be demonstrated by a learner on some outcome measure, whatever form that might take, and that teaching can potentially influence the results obtained on this measure. From the results of these assessments, we can then make inferences about the students' grammatical ability, which would subsequently provide an empirical basis for decision-making. For example, language teachers use test results to make decisions about student placement in a language program or about the degree to which their students have mastered the material in a course, and SLA researchers use test results to make decisions about whether young learners acquire grammatical features better than older learners. Implicit was also the notion that if more than one assessment of grammatical ability was obtained over time, inferences related to grammatical learning or even the effectiveness of instruction could be determined based on the observed changes in what learners demonstrate on these measures. This information is of particular concern to language teachers, testers and SLA researchers for making instructional recommendations and for theory-building. In short, language assessment is clearly an integral part of language teaching and learning, as it provides an empirical basis for making a variety of educational decisions, both on practical and theoretical levels. Therefore, it is crucial that the assessments we use to measure grammatical ability reflect the best practices available in the field; otherwise, the inferences we make from assessment scores may be neither meaningful nor appropriate, and potentially unfair.

Although, over the years, grammar instruction has changed considerably in communicative language classrooms and research on how best to teach and learn it has proliferated, this has had surprisingly little impact on how grammatical ability is assessed in second and foreign language educational contexts. Far too many language educators still use only multiple-choice tests of grammar and vocabulary in assessing grammatical ability, or they use grammaticality judgments – if, in fact, grammatical ability is assessed at all! Also, most language educators remain wedded to a definition of grammatical knowledge that is limited to sentence-level morphosyntactic form, even though in their classrooms, meaning and grammar in discourse contexts are emphasized.

In this chapter I will discuss the role that grammar plays in models of communicative competence. I will then endeavor to define grammar for assessment purposes. In this discussion I will describe in some detail the relationships among grammatical form, grammatical meaning and pragmatic meaning. Finally, I will present a theoretical model of grammar that will be used in this book as a basis for a model of grammatical knowledge. This will, in turn, be the basis for grammar-test construction and validation. In the following chapter I will discuss what it means for L2 learners to have grammatical ability.

The role of grammar in models of communicative competence

Every language educator who has ever attempted to measure a student's communicative language ability has wondered: 'What exactly does a student need to "know" in terms of grammar to be able to use it well enough for some real-world purpose?' In other words, they have been faced with the challenge of defining grammar for communicative purposes. To complicate matters further, linguistic notions of grammar have changed over time, as we have seen, and this has significantly increased the number of components that could be called 'grammar'. In short, definitions of grammar and grammatical knowledge have changed over time and across context, and I expect this will be no different in the future. So how has grammatical knowledge been conceptualized and defined in the major models of communicative competence over the last few decades?

In the early 1960s, Lado (1961), having been influenced by structuralist theory, proposed a 'skills-and-elements' model of language proficiency that viewed language ability as three more or less independent, yet related, dimensions of language knowledge, interpreted rather narrowly as phonology, structure and the lexicon – all aspects of linguistic form. The underlying assumption was that 'proficient' second or foreign language learners would be able to demonstrate their knowledge of the elements (i.e., phonology, structure and the lexicon) in the context of the language skills (i.e., listening, reading, speaking and writing). Grammatical knowledge for Lado consisted solely of morphosyntactic form. Lado's model is presented in Figure 3.1.

	Phonology	Structure	Lexicon
Listening			
Reading			
Speaking			
Writing			

Figure 3.1 Lado's skills-and-elements model of language knowledge

Building on Lado's (1961) notion of language proficiency, Carroll (1968) defined language competence in terms of phonology and orthography, grammar, and the lexicon. For Carroll, however, grammatical competence incorporated both the morphosyntax and semantic components of grammar, whereas lexical competence included morphemes, words and idioms on the one hand, and the semantic and grammatical components of the lexicon on the other. In this view, Carroll recognized the overlap between form and meaning in instances of language use.

Carroll (1968) expanded Lado's (1961) model of language knowledge by arguing that tests should be designed to predict the use of language elements and skills in future social situations or future tasks that the learners might encounter in life. By relating tests to target language use contexts, Carroll (1961) challenged the **discrete-point** approach to measuring one point of grammar at a time, as seen in Lado's (1961) skills-and-elements model, and proposed that discrete-point tasks be complemented by **integrative** tasks that would also assess the learner's capacity to use several components of language at the same time. In other words, Carroll (1961, 1968) characterized grammatical knowledge as being intrinsically associated with use, thereby redefining language proficiency as the degree to which the learner can demonstrate control of phonology or orthography, grammar (morphology, syntax) and the lexicon, while using one of the language skills in some real-life task.

Influenced by Carroll's (1961, 1968) ideas on grammar and language use, Oller (1979) rejected the elements-and-skills approach to proficiency, proposing instead a view of second or foreign language proficiency in terms of an individual's 'pragmatic expectancy grammar'. He defined **pragmatic expectancy grammar** as a psychologically real system that 'causes the learner to process sequences of elements in a language that conform to the normal contextual constraints of that language, and . . . requires the learner to relate sequences of linguistic elements via pragmatic mappings to the extralinguistic context' (Oller, 1979, p. 38). In other words, pragmatic expectancy grammar attributes the shape of linguistic forms to contextual meanings, which reflect the prototypical norms, preferences and expectations of language in communicating real-life messages.

To illustrate the notion of pragmatic expectancy grammar, consider the gap-filling task. In this task, the test-taker reads a passage with periodic gaps in the text. Reading the passage introduces the test-taker to the context of the passage, allowing him or her to relate the information to 'extralinguistic context' and to interpret it accordingly. This provides a basis for the test-taker to predict information for the gap, invoking the notion of 'expectancy'. The type of information the test-taker might be expected to supply could relate to linguistic form, semantic meaning and/or pragmatic use, or could, in some way, tap into the test-taker's rhetorical, sociocultural or topical knowledge. For example, a test-taker might examine the linguistic environment of the gap and determine from the sequential organization of language (i.e., expectancy grammar) that a verb best completes the gap. He or she might also decide that the verb needs to carry past meaning and embody a specific lexical form. Finally, in realizing that the contextual focus of the sentence is on the action and not on the agent, the test-taker uses a passive voice construction (pragmatic use). In sum, pragmatic expectancy grammar forces the test-taker to integrate his or her knowledge of grammar, meaning and pragmatic use to complete the task.

Oller's (1979) definition of 'grammar' involves more than what had previously been subsumed under the rubric of grammar. Interestingly enough, 'grammar' in this view embraces not only grammatical form (involving phonology, morphosyntax and the lexicon) on the sentential level, but also grammatical form on the suprasentential or discourse level through cohesion and coherence. It also involves grammatical form on a pragmatic level through extralinguistic reference that might be invoked by the suppliance of a contextually appropriate word. Oller's (1979) notion of pragmatic expectancy grammar can thus be credited as the first serious attempt in language testing to define grammar as an integration of linguistic form and pragmatic use as this relates to context.

Although Oller's (1979) notion of pragmatic expectancy grammar suggested a radically different and more complex definition of what was generally understood by grammatical knowledge, he did not identify or clearly define the distinct components of expectancy grammar. Nor did he clearly specify how these components might be measured separately or how they might relate to a coherent model of language proficiency. On the contrary, Oller hypothesized that pragmatic expectancy constituted a single, unitary ability. Subsequent research in language testing (e.g., Bachman and Palmer, 1982) clearly demonstrated, however, that this hypothesis was not supported by research data and that language ability was, indeed, multi-componential. As a result, research on pragmatic expectancy grammar was, unfortunately, short-lived.

In 1980, the notion of grammatical competence as a component distinct from other components of language competence was proposed in an influential paper published by Canale and Swain. Inspired by the theoretical descriptions of language in use proposed by Hymes (1971, 1972), they argued that Chomsky's (1965) notion of competence had failed to account for sociolinguistic appropriateness expressed by an utterance in context. They maintained that this failing had serious implications since an utterance might be grammatically correct, but sociolinguistically inappropriate. As a result, Canale and Swain (1980) and later Canale (1983) proposed a model of communicative competence consisting of grammatical competence, sociolinguistic competence, discourse competence and strategic competence. This model has significantly broadened our understanding of communicative competence by specifying features of linguistic form alongside other features of language use.

In their model, Canale and Swain (1980) defined grammatical competence as knowledge of the rules of phonology, the lexicon, syntax and semantics. Grammatical competence embodied the lexico-grammatical or semantico-grammatical features of the language. However, even though Canale and Swain acknowledged that both form and meaning constituted interrelated features of grammatical competence, they failed to distinguish how the two were associated. Similarly, they failed to articulate the relationship between grammatical competence and the other competencies in their framework. In other words, no explanation was provided on how their framework accounted for cases in which grammar was used to encode meanings beyond the sentence level or meanings that were implied without being said. Finally, when put to the test of validation, Canale and Swain's (1980) model was only partially supported by research data (e.g., Harley, Allen, Cummins and Swain, 1990).

In spite of these caveats, Canale and Swain's (1980) model of communicative competence, with its broadened view of language, has had an enormous impact on the field of second or foreign language education. It is credited for having provided the main theoretical framework underlying communicative language teaching and materials development, and it has succeeded in generating considerable discussion and research activity.

Building on this work and that of many others, Bachman (1990b) and later Bachman and Palmer (1996) proposed a multi-componential model of communicative language ability which has provided the most comprehensive conceptualization of language ability to date. Instead of limiting their model to components of language knowledge, Bachman and Palmer also specified non-linguistic components of communicative language ability invoked in test-taking and language use. For example, in their model of language use, a test-taker's language knowledge, along with her topical knowledge and personal characteristics, is hypothesized to interact with her strategic competence (i.e., metacognitive strategies) and affect (i.e., anxiety, motivation). This, in turn, is said to interact with the characteristics of the language-use or test-task situation. In short, this model views language ability as an internal construct, consisting of language knowledge and strategic competence, that interacts with the language user's topical knowledge and other internal characteristics (e.g., affect), as well as with the characteristics of the context. Language use thus consists of internal interactions among learner attributes (e.g., language knowledge, strategic competence, topical knowledge, affect) together with external interactions between these attributes and features of the language-use context.

In describing language knowledge, Bachman and Palmer (1996) specified two general components: (1) organizational knowledge or how individuals control language structure to produce grammatically correct utterances or sentences and texts, and (2) pragmatic knowledge or how individuals communicate meaning and how they produce contextually appropriate utterances, sentences or texts.

Organizational knowledge is further divided into grammatical knowledge, or 'how individual utterances or sentences are organized', and textual knowledge, or 'how utterances or sentences are organized into texts' (ibid., p. 68). Grammatical knowledge is defined as an individual's knowledge of vocabulary, syntax and phonology/graphology, while textual knowledge refers to an individual's knowledge of cohesion (e.g., pronouns, lexical repetition), rhetorical organization (e.g., logical connectors) and conversational organization (e.g., turn-taking strategies, topic nomination). In short, grammatical knowledge in this model accounts for grammar on the subsentential and sentential levels, while textual knowledge accounts for language on a suprasentential or discourse level.

Pragmatic knowledge is then defined in terms of functional knowledge and sociolinguistic knowledge. Functional knowledge refers to 'how utterances or sentences and texts are related to the communicative goals of language users' (p. 68). In other words, functional knowledge enables individuals to use organizational knowledge to express or interpret language functions in communicative settings. Sociolinguistic knowledge refers to 'how utterances or sentences and texts are related to features of the language use setting' (p. 68). In other words, it enables individuals to understand situation-specific language and to tailor language to a particular language-use setting.

In Bachman and Palmer's (1996) view, grammatical knowledge refers to several components of linguistic form relating strictly to sentence-based phonology, graphology, vocabulary and syntax. From an assessment perspective, this depiction is useful if our goal is to measure linguistic forms alone – and in fact, there are many instances in which one might wish to do just that. For example, if we want to determine an individual's knowledge of the present perfect tense forms, we could construct a discrete-point test of grammar, targeting aspects of the verb form (*have/has* + past participle), or we could develop a test targeting word order in question formation. This view of grammatical knowledge defined as form, however, does not account for situations where a student might know the form, but be unclear about the meaning. Nor does it differentiate between the different types of meanings that grammatical forms encode.

To illustrate, imagine we wanted to determine a student's grammatical knowledge of the simple present, the simple past and the present perfect tenses as used in conversational narratives. This is a case in which we might wish to test for both grammatical form and meaning, in order to ask questions such as: What makes the three tenses different in terms of time? Does the learner know to use the present perfect to communicate the notion of current relevance in announcing that a story is about to be told? (*I've never been more embarrassed!*)? Once the story begins, does the learner know to use the past tense to set the scene and the present to tell the sequence of events (*We were talking when this waiter appears and uncorks the cava . . .*)? At the end of the story, does the learner know to revert back to the present perfect to convey again the notion of current relevance (*I've never seen him again.*)? All along, the learners could make mistakes that relate to grammatical form and/or grammatical meaning, an analysis of which could inform teachers on how to refocus their teaching and learners on how to direct their learning.

Bachman and Palmer's (1996) definition of language knowledge encompasses the grammatical, textual, functional and sociolinguistic components of language knowledge, but it is unclear how these components relate in actual language use or how grammatical knowledge might provide a resource for the interactions to occur. In other words, their model could benefit from a more detailed description of how grammar is used to encode meaning at the sentential and suprasentential levels. It addresses meaning to some degree under the rubric of organizational knowledge (vocabulary), textual knowledge (cohesion), functional knowledge and sociolinguistic knowledge; however, given the central role of meaning in language instruction and communicative language use, a more explicit depiction of this aspect of language knowledge would be helpful.

In sum, many different models of communicative competence have emerged over the years. The more recent depictions have presented much broader conceptualizations of communicative language ability; however, definitions of grammatical knowledge have remained more or less the same – morphosyntax. Also, within these expanded models, more detailed specifications are needed for how grammatical form might interact with grammatical meaning to communicate literal and intended meanings, and how form and meaning relate to the ability to convey pragmatic meanings. If our assessment goal were limited to an understanding of how learners have mastered grammatical forms, then the current models of grammatical knowledge would suffice. However, if we hope to understand how learners use grammatical forms as a resource for conveying a variety of meanings in language-acquisition, -assessment and -use situations, as I think we do, then a definition of grammatical knowledge which addresses these other dimensions of grammatical ability is needed.

Rea-Dickins' definition of grammar

In discussing more specifically how grammatical knowledge might be tested within a communicative framework, Rea-Dickins (1991) defined 'grammar' as the single embodiment of syntax, semantics and pragmatics. She argued against Canale and Swain's (1980) and Bachman's (1990b) multi-componential view of communicative competence on the grounds that componential representations overlook the interdependence and interaction between and among the various components. She further stated that in Canale and Swain's (1980) model, the notion of grammatical competence was limited since it defined grammar as 'structure' on the one hand and as 'structure and semantics' on the other, but ignored the notion of 'structure as pragmatics'. Similarly, she added that in Bachman's (1990b) model, grammar was defined as structure at the sentence level and as cohesion at the suprasentential level, but this model failed to account for the pragmatic dimension of communicative grammar. Instead, Rea-Dickins (1991) argued that for grammar to be truly 'communicative', it had to 'allow for the processing of semantically acceptable syntactic forms, which are in turn governed by pragmatic principles' (p. 114), and not be solely an embodiment of morphosyntax.

Although Rea-Dickins' emphasis on grammar as pragmatics offers an important perspective, her view of 'communicative grammar' is controversial. First, neither Canale and Swain (1980) nor Bachman (1990b) left pragmatics 'unspecified'. Rather, they saw it as a separate component of language ability in which all components were hypothesized to interact. More importantly, Rea-Dickins' conceptualization of 'communicative grammar' failed to distinguish between grammar and language. In her model, grammar constitutes one unifying linguistic representation that encodes three dimensions, similar to Oller (1979). However, if grammar encompasses syntax, semantics and pragmatics, what then is language? Empirical studies on the nature of language proficiency have repeatedly found that language proficiency consists of several *distinct*, but related, components (Bachman and Palmer, 1982). In other words, a test-taker can have different levels of knowledge when it comes to syntax, semantics and pragmatics, such that he or she may be able to express an idea with perfect syntax, but in a totally inappropriate or unintelligible way. The question here, then, relates to naming and definition, which according to

Davies (1991) is not trivial, as this may have serious implications in the design of tests and the application of test results to teaching and learning. In short, we need to define the domain of grammatical knowledge so that it can be distinguished from the domains of semantic and pragmatic knowledge, while at the same time, the obvious interrelationships can be recognized. Finally, we must also bear in mind the fact that even though two components of language ability may be highly correlated, this does not necessarily mean they are identical or they can be combined. In the end, score-based information on both may be useful.

Rea-Dickins (1991) further stated that the goal of communicative grammar tests is to provide an 'opportunity for the test-taker to create his or her own message and to produce grammatical responses as appropriate to a given context' (p. 125). This underscores the notion that pragmatic appropriateness or acceptability can add a crucial dimension to communication, and must not be ignored. We must remember, however, that communication can occur on a literal level and, at the same time, on a number of pragmatic levels. In fact, all language teachers are keenly aware that literal meanings can be conveyed in a given context through grammatical forms with a total *lack* of appropriateness and with no awareness of the range of pragmatic inferences that might be ascribed to their utterances. Consequently, the position taken in this book is that the essence of communication is the expression of a speaker's literal and intentional meanings through grammatical forms. Once expressed, these propositions are then ratified by an interlocutor's understanding of the message, and communication ensues. If the message is not understood as intended, the message can be repaired or misunderstandings can persist. When other implied interpersonal, sociocultural, sociolinguistic, psychological or rhetorical meanings are extrapolated from grammatical forms and meanings, we have moved out of the domain of grammatical knowledge and into the domain of pragmatic knowledge – both components constitute communicative language ability. Nonetheless, Rea-Dickins' emphasis on grammar as pragmatics correctly reminds us of the close relationship among grammar, semantics and pragmatics. She also reminds us that the distinctions between these levels are at times fuzzy at best.

Larsen-Freeman's definition of grammar

Another conceptualization of grammar that merits attention is Larsen-Freeman's (1991, 1997) framework for the teaching of grammar in communicative language teaching contexts. Drawing on several linguistic theories and influenced by language teaching pedagogy, she has also characterized grammatical knowledge along three dimensions: linguistic form, semantic meaning and pragmatic use. Form is defined as both morphology, or how words are formed, and syntactic patterns, or how words are strung together. This dimension is primarily concerned with linguistic **accuracy**. The meaning dimension describes the inherent or literal message conveyed by a lexical item or a lexico-grammatical feature. This dimension is mainly concerned with the **meaningfulness** of an utterance. The use dimension refers to the lexico-grammatical *choices* a learner makes to communicate appropriately within a specific context. Pragmatic use describes *when* and *why* one linguistic feature is used in a given context instead of another, especially when the two choices convey a similar literal meaning. In this respect, pragmatic use is said to embody presuppositions about situational context, linguistic context, discourse context, and sociocultural context. This dimension is mainly concerned with making the right choice of forms in order to convey an **appropriate** message for the context.

According to Larsen-Freeman (1991), these three dimensions may be viewed as independent or interconnected. For example, a linguistic form such as the articles in English displays a syntactic, semantic and pragmatic dimension, even though, perhaps in the classroom, it might be necessary to focus more on the pragmatic aspect, which can pose the greatest challenge to learners. While Celce-Murcia and Larsen-Freeman (1999) admit that the boundaries among the dimensions are not always distinct, they argue that this framework can be useful in determining how to specify grammatical content for instruction. Although Larsen-Freeman's (1991) depiction is helpful in many ways, from an assessment perspective, the notion of pragmatic choice presents an interesting challenge. When a student produces a correct sentence on a test, we might assume that she is choosing from several possible alternatives that she knows and has chosen the one that she feels is accurate, meaningful and appropriate for the context. Unfortunately, we often have no data to examine the alternatives that she has not chosen to produce. In fact, it may be that the student knows only one way of expressing the message.

In sum, the models proposed by Canale and Swain (1980) and Bachman and Palmer (1996) on the one hand, and those proposed by Rea-Dickins (1991) and Larsen-Freeman (1997) on the other are similar in many respects. Both groups deal with linguistic form, semantic meaning and pragmatic use on some level. Certainly, Larsen-Freeman's model is the most explicit in describing how a single linguistic form can encode different meanings. It is simple and it is intuitive, but in her view and in that proposed by Rea-Dickins (1991), grammar is, in essence, co-terminous with language. I believe, however, that there is a fundamental difference in how grammatical forms and meanings are used to evoke literal and intended messages, and then how they are used to convey implied meanings that require pragmatic inference. For example, I may understand the literal meaning of a joke, but may completely fail to see the double meaning (pragmatic inference) that makes it funny. To view all three components as 'grammar' is, in my opinion, misleading. If these dimensions constitute 'grammar', what then is 'language'? Nonetheless, I agree that the boundaries among the three components, with certain forms, are at times blurred.

From both an instructional and an assessment perspective, there are times, especially for beginning and intermediate learners, when we might only expect students to demonstrate their ability to use correct forms to express fairly transparent, literal meanings in a given context. For example, we might expect a beginning student to say or understand: 'Close the window' (literal meaning embodying a context-transparent directive), whereas we might expect this learner to understand, but perhaps not say: 'It feels like winter', meaning 'Close the window.' In this case, the relationship between the words used and the intended meaning was indirect and highly dependent upon contextual clues. To expect learners to use a broad range of linguistic devices to express contextual subtleties of meaning with native-like appropriateness at lower proficiency levels may be beyond their capability, especially when the subtleties relate to complex interpersonal, sociolinguistic, sociocultural, psychological, or rhetorical nuances. For this reason, I will treat grammatical knowledge and pragmatic knowledge as separate components of language ability, knowing full well that in order to communicate certain meanings, these two components are inextricably related.

What is meant by 'grammar' for assessment purposes?

Now with a better understanding of how grammar has been conceptualized in models of language ability, how might we define 'grammar' for assessment purposes? It should be obvious from the previous discussion that there is no one 'right' way to define grammar. In one testing situation the assessment goal might be to obtain information on students' knowledge of linguistic forms in minimally contextualized sentences, while in another, it might be to determine how well learners can use linguistic forms to express a wide range of communicative meanings. Regardless of the assessment purpose, if we wish to make inferences about grammatical ability on the basis of a grammar test or some other form of assessment, it is important to know what we mean by 'grammar' when attempting to specify components of grammatical knowledge for measurement purposes. With this goal in mind, we need a definition of grammatical knowledge that is broad enough to provide a theoretical basis for the construction and validation of tests in a number of contexts. At the same time, we need our definition to be precise enough to distinguish it from other areas of language ability.

From a theoretical perspective, the main goal of language use is communication, whether it be used to transmit information, to perform transactions, to establish and maintain social relations, to construct one's identity or to communicate one's intentions, attitudes or hypotheses. Being the primary resource for communication, language knowledge consists of grammatical knowledge and pragmatic knowledge. Therefore, I propose a theoretical definition of language knowledge that consists of two distinct, but related, components. I will refer to one component as grammatical knowledge and to the other as pragmatic knowledge.

In this section, I will discuss grammatical knowledge in terms of grammatical forms and grammatical meanings (both literal and intended) at the sentential and suprasentential levels. I will then discuss pragmatic knowledge in terms of how grammatical forms and meanings can use context to extend the meaning of an utterance. An overview of the concepts to be discussed in this section appears in Figure 3.2.

Grammatical knowledge embodies two highly related components: grammatical form and grammatical meaning. I will use the term **grammatical form** to refer to linguistic forms on the subsentential, sentential and suprasentential levels, as described in the syntactocentric approaches to language discussed previously. Grammatical form includes a host of forms, for example, on the phonological, lexical, morphosyntactic, cohesive, information management, and interactional levels. Knowledge of grammatical form, therefore, refers to the knowledge of one or more of these linguistic forms. Grammatical meaning is sometimes used to refer to the literal meaning expressed by sounds, words, phrases and sentences, where the meaning of an utterance is derived from its component parts or the ways in which these parts are ordered in syntactic structure. Some linguists have referred to this as

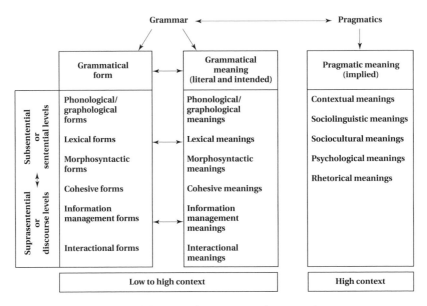

Figure 3.2 A theoretical definition of grammar and pragmatics

semantic meaning, utterance meaning or the compositionality of an utterance (Jaszczolt, 2002). Others (e.g., Grice, 1957; Levinson, 1983) have referred to it as literal meaning, sentence meaning or conventional meaning. I will refer to this as **literal meaning.**

Although literal meaning allows us to identify what is said by a speaker, Jaszczolt (2002) notes that some utterances may not be sufficiently informative for the speaker's meaning to be fully conveyed (p. 54). In these cases, we must resort to contextual clues, including the speaker's intentions, to interpret the meaning of an utterance in relation to a real or possible situation. For example, in a story about painting, ladders and buckets, if someone says, 'she kicked the bucket', this could be taken literally to mean an action that might result in the paint spilling or it could be taken idiomatically to mean that she died. Therefore, in addition to literal meaning, grammatical meaning encodes the meaning associated with the propositional intention that the speaker has in mind while conveying a message. Some linguists have referred to this as speaker meaning, conveyed meaning, locutionary meaning, communicative intent, or propositional intent. I will refer to it as **intended meaning.** To summarize, knowledge of **grammatical meaning** refers to knowledge of the meaning associated with an utterance as the sum of its parts and how these parts are arranged in syntax (literal meaning), as well as how these parts are used to convey the speaker's intended meaning in context (intended meaning). I believe that the literal meaning of an utterance and its intended meaning cannot be separated when a speaker is trying to communicate a proposition in context. Also, more importantly, the literal meaning of a sentence, while informative, may prove rather useless when a speaker's intended meaning of that same utterance differs widely from the literal meaning. Therefore, it is important to include both literal and intended meaning in a definition of grammatical meaning if we wish to account for meaning in both context-impoverished (e.g., multiple-choice tasks) and context-rich (e.g., problem-solving tasks) testing situations. Finally, I acknowledge that the inclusion of speaker intention along with literal meaning in a definition of grammatical meaning might blur the traditional lines among grammatical, semantic and pragmatic meaning; however, my intention is to construct a view of grammatical meaning for assessment purposes, where the unit of analysis is the utterance, said as intended. This is notably a much broader depiction of grammar than has been traditional in applied linguistics. Reasons for this definition will, I hope, become clear as the discussion ensues.

Since meaning is a critical component in the assessment of grammatical knowledge, let us examine this notion in much greater detail. Grammatical meaning refers to instances of language use in which what is said is what is meant literally and is closely related to what the speaker intends to communicate. First, the notion of 'conveying literal meaning' is important since in many cases, the primary assessment goal is to determine if learners are able to use forms to get their basic point across accurately and *meaningfully*. This is especially true for test-takers who need to express literal meaning in a particular situation or who, due to the decontextualized nature of the task or their level of proficiency, are able to express only literal meaning. This depiction of grammatical meaning allows us to identify and assess individual forms and their literal meanings, especially in contexts where the characteristics of the communicative event are either reduced or unknown (e.g., a fill-in-the-blank or a complete-the-sentence task). Secondly, the notion of 'conveying the speaker's intended meaning' is also important, since, as we will see, the literal meaning of an utterance can be used by a speaker in a given context to convey an intention that is different from what the literal meaning might suggest. Therefore, this definition of grammatical meaning allows us also to assess both literal and intended meanings, where the characteristics of the communicative event are rich or impoverished. In rich communicative contexts, the range of meanings associated with grammatical forms is much broader than in impoverished communicative contexts, and the probability of meaning extension or even the probability of multiple meanings occurring simultaneously is much greater, as we will see.

In order to illustrate the relationships between grammatical form and meaning, I will use the context of a father (F) talking to his daughter (D) about straightening up her room before relatives arrive for a visit. As seen in column 1 of Table 3.1, I present five different ways in which the father could make this request. Although all the examples are situated within the same general communicative event, each presents language that is slightly different based on what the speaker is trying to communicate. The sentences are ordered from the most to the least direct way of making the request. Each utterance is followed by an interlocutor's response to illustrate how the father's utterance could be understood and responded to by the daughter.

In example 1 (column 1), the father says, 'Straighten up your room', and the daughter responds, 'OK.' The grammatical forms (sounds, words, morphosyntax) arranged in an imperative sentence encode the literal meaning of the father's utterance. The literal meaning is, 'Clean up your room', as seen in column 2, and can be derived solely from the meaning of the words arranged in syntax. The form–meaning relationship can, therefore, be characterized as direct and explicit.

Note that I could also refer to the literal meaning of a word, an intonation pattern or verb tense. In those cases, I will use the more specific terms **lexical meaning**, **phonological meaning** and **morphosyntactic meaning** to refer to the individual components of grammatical meaning. The combined meaning associated with all these forms in a given utterance, however, incorporates grammatical meaning.

In addition to expressing literal meaning, the utterance 'Straighten up your room' could be used for the communicative purpose of expressing a directive. In other words, the forms in the utterance can be used to express the **language function** 'giving an order', as seen in column 3. Just as we cannot disassociate the grammatical forms in an utterance from the literal meaning of the utterance, we also cannot disassociate literal meaning from the language function(s) evoked by the words in the utterance. In short, the grammatical forms encode both the literal meaning of an utterance and the possible communicative function(s) associated with that utterance outside of any specific context.

However, in addition to the words arranged in syntactic structure, the form–meaning relationship of an utterance is also determined by the speaker's intention or locutionary meaning (Searle, 1975), and to some degree by information in the context that exists beyond what can be derived from the words alone. For example, in the context of a father talking to his daughter about her room, the literal meaning ('Clean up your room') and the father's intended meaning in this context ('Clean up your room') are the same, as seen in column 4. Intended meaning is derived primarily from the speaker's communicative intention and from the forms used to express this intention. Thus, every utterance expressed in context encodes both literal and intended meaning. Sometimes literal and intended meanings are similar, as seen in example 1; other times, they are different.

Out of context, the literal meaning of an utterance can evoke one or more possible language functions. The speaker's intended meaning in context, however, is usually associated with one primary function. The language function associated with intended meaning in example 1 is a directive in the form of 'giving an order', as seen in column 5. Thus, the functions associated with both literal and intended meaning in this example are similar. In order to assess the meaning of grammatical forms expressed in context, grammatical meaning thus embodies the literal and intended meanings of the utterance and the language functions associated with these meanings.

In addition to the intended meaning of an utterance and the function associated with that meaning, an utterance may simultaneously encode other layers of pragmatic meaning (e.g., sociolinguistic meaning, sociocultural meaning) in a given context. For example, the father's use of the imperative in this utterance conveys sociolinguistic or sociocultural meaning related to his power to order his daughter to clean her room ('As your father, I have the right to order you around and I'm ordering you to clean up your room'). These extensions of meaning are derived primarily from context and may be intentional or unintentional on the part of the speaker. They are highly dependent upon an understanding of the shared norms, assumptions, expectations and presuppositions of the interlocutors in the communicative context. Thus, while grammatical meaning is defined as the literal and intended meanings of an utterance along with the function, **pragmatic meaning** is defined in terms of the other implied meanings (e.g., sociolinguistic, sociocultural) that an utterance can encode.

In the father's utterance in example 1, the literal meaning of the utterance ('Clean up your room') is primarily derived from the meaning of the words arranged in syntax. In other words, what is said is similar to what is meant. Also, as what is meant literally is similar to what is intended, we

Table 3.1 *Relationships among grammatical form, grammatical meaning and pragmatic meaning*

	Grammatical form		Grammatical meaning		Pragmatic meaning
Different forms of expression	**Literal meaning** (derived from the words in syntax)	**Language function(s)** (associated with literal meaning)	**Intended meaning** (derived from speaker's intention)	**Language function(s)** (associated with intended meaning)	**Other implied meanings** (derived primarily from context)
1. **F: Straighten up your room.** D: OK.	F: Clean up your room. D: I'll clean up my room.	F: Directive: order D: Agreement to do as ordered	F: Clean up your room! D: I'll clean up my room.	F: Directive: order D: Agreement to do as ordered	**SL/SC meaning:** F: Expression of power D: Acceptance of power relationship
2. **F: Could you straighten up your room?** D: OK.	F: Is it possible for you to clean up your room? D: (Yes) I'll clean up my room.	F: Representative: request for information F: Directive: request for action D: Agreement to do as asked	F: Clean up your room! D: I'll clean up my room.	F: Directive: request for action D: Agreement to do as asked	**SL/SC meaning:** F: Expression of politeness D: Agreement to maintain harmony or to obey parent
3. **F: Would you mind straightening up your room?** D: OK.	F: Would it trouble you to clean up your room? D: (I don't mind) I'll clean up my room.	F: Representative: request for information F: Directive: request for action D: Agreement to do as asked	F: Clean up your room! D: I'll clean up my room.	F: Directive: request for action acknowledging imposition D: Agreement to do as asked	**SL/SC meaning:** F: Expression of politeness and respect given the imposition D: Agreement to maintain harmony or to obey parent

4. **F: Your room's a mess!** D: OK. I'll clean it up.	F: You have a disorderly room. D: I hear the request. I'll clean up my room.	F: Representative: imparting information D: Acknowledgment of request and agreement to do what's needed	F: Clean up your room! D: I'll clean up my room.	F: Directive: request for action D: Agreement to do something	**Psych. meaning:** F: Expression of negative affect (criticism or complaint); **SL/SC meaning:** F: Expression of rudeness D: Acknowledgment of problem; agreement to comply and maintain harmony and obey parent
5. **F: How can you live like this?** D: OK. I'll clean it up.	F: How can you live under these conditions? D: I hear the request. I'll clean up my room.	F: Representative: seeking factual information D: Acknowledgment of request and agreement to do what's needed	F: Clean up your room! D: I'll clean up my room.	F: Directive: request for action D: Agreement to do something	**Psych. meaning:** F: Expression of negative affect (expression of disgust/outrage) **SL/SC meaning:** F: Expression of rudeness D: Acknowledgment of problem and agreement to maintain harmony and obey parent

Notes:

F = father; D = daughter; SL = sociolinguistic; SC = sociocultural; Psych: psychological can say that the literal and the intended meanings of the utterance are, in this situation, closely related. Similarly, the literal and intended meanings both express a directive in the form of 'giving an order'. In this situation, the relationships among form, meaning, and the associated functions are **direct**. In other words, the literal meaning of the forms and their intended meaning, as used in context, are the same. This is not the case when the intended meaning of a speaker's utterance is derived more from the information in the context than from the actual words used in the utterance.

Finally, in example 1, the daughter responds to the father by saying, 'OK.' In so doing, she shows that she has heard the utterance as an order to clean up her room (literal and intended meaning) and agrees to follow the order. The literal and intended meaning of 'OK' is 'I'll clean up my room.' The daughter's response implicitly ratifies his right to order her around by expressing her willingness to comply. Obviously, the daughter could have understood the utterance and responded to it in many different ways, conveying a range of pragmatic meanings. If she had replied, 'Who are you to order me around?' she would have shown that she had heard the literal and intended meaning of her father's utterance (Clean up your room), but is reacting to the pragmatic assumption that her father has the authority to order her around. Similarly, if she responds, 'It looks fine', this response indicates that she has heard her father's literal and intended meaning, but contests his judgment of the condition of her room. In sum, the addition of an interlocutor in interaction determines if the grammatical meaning of a speaker's utterance is understood and ratified. If so, communication transpires smoothly; if not, a complex negotiation of grammatical and pragmatic meanings by the interlocutors is entertained. For assessment purposes, the addition of an interlocutor, while authentic, significantly complicates the measurement of meaning.

In example 2, the father expresses the same request of his daughter, but this time by means of a modal question with *could* ('Could you straighten up your room?'). The literal meaning of this question is 'I'm asking if it is possible for you to clean up your room.' Hypothetically, the meaning expressed by this utterance could possibly serve to communicate a representative (a request for information) or a directive (a request for action). Given the context, the father is not interested in knowing about his daughter's ability to clean up the room (a representative); he is more concerned with the room being cleaned up (a directive). Although the literal meaning of the utterance can be used to accomplish more than one communicative purpose, the speaker has an intended meaning in mind when expressing an utterance in context. Thus, the literal and intended meanings associated with grammatical forms work together to create a speaker's message in communication.

In example 2, the daughter replies, 'OK', which shows that she has heard her father's utterance as intended – a directive. In this case, an explicit response to the request for information ('Yes') was unexpressed, but understood by her agreement to his request. The function associated with the daughter's literal and intended meaning encodes her willingness to do as asked. Obviously, the daughter could also have responded with a representative by saying, 'Well, I could . . .' in which case a more direct form of the request would likely have been forthcoming.

Beyond the intended request for action, this response might also encode a desire on the daughter's part to maintain family harmony or it might reflect the daughter's obligation to obey her father. In short, the response simultaneously conveys sociolinguistic, sociocultural and, perhaps, psychological meanings. To illustrate, the subtext of the father's utterance might be, 'I'm going to treat you how you should treat others, so I'd like to ask you politely if it would be possible for you to clean up your room.' What is different in example 2 is that the force of the father's request is considerably softened by the use of 'could', thereby indicating that the expectation of compliance was not as fully assumed as it was in example 1, but the daughter could, in fact, refuse to comply. A refusal might be seen as rude, and the father could address that behavior and still get his way, but the possibility of a refusal is open. Therefore, while the relationship between form, meaning and function is still relatively direct in example 2, it is less so than in example 1. According to Hatch (1992), the degree of directness seems to be in direct relation to the degree to which we expect that a person will comply with a request we have made. In other words, as the risk of refusal increases, so does the indirectness of the request.

In example 3, the father makes the same request, this time by means of a question with *would you mind* + *Ving*. Sentence stress is placed on the gerund, 'straightening up your room', and not on 'would you mind'. The literal meaning of this utterance is, 'Would it trouble you to clean up your room?' Similar to example 2, this utterance can be interpreted both as a representative in the form of a request for information (would you mind?) and as a directive in the form of a request for action. However, given the context, the father's intended meaning is for his daughter to clean up her room – a request for action. The request in example 3 uses the verb *mind* to acknowledge the potential imposition on the daughter. Given the possibility of a refusal due to the imposing nature of the request, the form of this utterance is even less direct than in example 2. Pragmatically, the father's utterance could also encode the sociocultural assumption of 'I know this is an imposition, but I am your father and I would like you to clean up your room, so I'm asking you politely to do this for me.'

The daughter replied to the father's request with 'OK', thereby responding to the intended meaning, but not to the literal meaning. Had she replied, 'No problem. I'll do it in a minute', she would be responding explicitly to both the literal meaning ('No problem' = I don't mind) and the intended meaning. Her response represents an agreement to comply with his request. Pragmatically, the daughter's response might convey sociocultural meaning since the response serves to maintain family harmony and it shows the daughter's willingness to comply with her father's request even though this may be an imposition.

In these three examples, the relationship between grammatical form and the meanings they convey can be characterized as increasingly less direct and explicit. Also, the relationship between literal and intended meaning is increasingly less direct. Nonetheless, it is still possible, for the most part, to derive the intended meaning of the utterance principally from the words expressed. The contextual contribution to meaning is minimal.

These three examples provide a relatively good illustration of how grammatical meaning, when assessed explicitly in language tests, has been conceptualized. In other words, grammatical meaning is assessed in terms of the degree to which test-takers are able to use linguistic resources to convey literal and intended meanings, predominantly when the relationships between form and literal and intended meanings, along with their associated functions, are relatively direct, and minimally dependent upon context. In some language tests, grammatical meaning has been characterized in terms of the communicative success or effectiveness of test-takers to complete some task – in other words, their ability to get their point across effectively. Restricting the measurement of meaning in terms of form–meaning directness provides testers with the advantage of having control over responses. However, communication is also full of instances of language use where the relationships between form, meaning and function are indirect. In these instances, a more complete depiction of grammatical meaning might be useful for the assessment of grammatical ability. Table 3.2 provides a depiction of how form, meaning and function relate with regard to context.

Let us now consider examples in which the intended meaning of an utterance cannot be interpreted primarily from the meaning of the words

Table 3.2 *Relationships among form, meaning, function and context*

Grammatical form	Grammatical meaning		
Different forms of expression	Relationship between literal and intended meaning	Relationship between language function(s) associated with literal and intended meaning	Context
1. Straighten up your room.	very direct	very direct	very low
2. Could you straighten up your room?	relatively direct	relatively direct	low
3. Would you mind straightening up your room?	relatively direct	relatively direct	low
4. Your room's a mess!	somewhat indirect	somewhat indirect	high
5. How can you live like this?	very indirect	very indirect	very high

arranged in syntax but, rather, requires a considerable amount of contextual information to decipher the speaker's intended meaning. In other words, the intended meaning of the speaker's utterance is derived primarily from how the forms and their literal meanings are used in context.

In example 4 of Table 3.1, the father uses a declarative sentence about the room to request that his daughter clean it up. He says, 'Your room's a mess!' The literal meaning of this utterance makes explicit the disorderliness of the room. This utterance out of context functions as a representative, communicating a description of factual information. However, in the current context, the father's *primary* intention is not simply to describe the orderliness of the room or even to express his negative feelings about this orderliness (pragmatic meaning); rather, the father's *main* intention is to get his daughter to clean up her room before the relatives arrive. In other words, the literal and intended meanings of the utterance are very different. Also, the primary language function of the father's utterance is to communicate a directive (a request for action) and not a representative (description of factual information). Thus, unlike the previous three examples, the intended meaning of the utterance here is derived primarily from the context and secondarily from the way in which the meaning of the words are arranged in syntax. In other words, the relationship between the literal meaning of the forms and the intended meaning of the utterance is indirect, and the match between the functions associated with the literal and intended meanings is uneven. These relationships in terms of context are depicted in Table 3.2.

Pragmatically, the father's utterance contains several other layers of meaning that can be simultaneously superimposed upon the utterance. For example, beyond conveying a directive (and a representative), the father might simultaneously have wished to communicate psychological meaning in the form of negative affect toward the disorderliness of his daughter's room. Used as an expressive, this utterance serves to convey a complaint or criticism. Then, in terms of sociolinguistic/sociocultural meaning, this utterance's on-record evaluation of the room, and by implication, the daughter's responsibility for the condition, presents a face-threatening act of impoliteness.

The daughter's response to her father is, 'OK. I'll clean it up.' By saying 'OK', the daughter acknowledges her father's request for action and responds with a promise to comply at a later time (I'll clean it up). In short, the daughter responds, as expected, to the father's intended meaning. Pragmatically, her response acknowledges what is perceived to be a problem and offers a solution to the problem, thereby maintaining family harmony and recognizing the parent's sociocultural right to make a request and to criticize.

However, had the daughter responded to the messy room comment with, 'No, it's not', this response would have shown that she had heard her father's utterance as a representative, and not as a directive. This way of responding contests the truth value of her father's assessment of her room. Such a response might have led to further discussion of the room and a more direct way of communicating the directive. The daughter could also have heard the utterance as an expressive, and responded, 'Dad, that's mean', or she could have interpreted this response as an expression of power, in which case she might have asked, 'Dad, why are you always picking on me?'

The father's request for a neater room in example 4 is indirect in that the intended meaning of the utterance is not derivable solely from the literal meaning of the forms arranged in syntax. Rather, much more context is needed to disambiguate the father's intention. Following Hatch (1992), the father's indirectness is probably motivated by the high risk that his daughter might not have granted his request.

In example 5 of Table 3.1, the father uses an information question to make his request ('How can you live like this?'). The literal meaning of this question is, 'How can you live under these conditions?' Taken literally, this utterance has the function of a representative (seeking information).

In this context, however, the father's intended meaning is again, 'Clean up your room', a directive. Similar to example 4, the relationship between the literal and intended meanings is very indirect, as is the relationship between the associated functions. These relationships with regard to context are characterized in Table 3.2. Again, in this utterance, the speaker's intended meaning could not be fully derived from the meaning of the words arranged in syntax; rather, information from the context was needed. Pragmatically, the father's request encodes a layer of psychological meaning in the form of an emotive response to the room. As an expression of disgust, it communicates the notion that 'Your room is so disgusting I don't know how you or any other human being can tolerate it. So, clean it up!' Socioculturally, this utterance also conveys notions of family order, power and rudeness.

As in example 4, the daughter's response ('OK. I'll clean it up.') shows acknowledgment of her father's question as a directive and a promise of compliance. Had she replied, 'It's easy', she would be addressing the representative function of the utterance, and in so doing risk sounding sarcastic or impertinent. Finally, had she asked, 'Why are you always yelling at me?' she could be responding to the sociocultural or psychological meaning encoded in the utterance.

In sum, Table 3.1 illustrates the potential complications associated with assessing meaning. As seen in the five examples, grammatical forms encode the literal meaning of an utterance and one or more potential language functions. They also encode the speaker's intended meaning in context and any number of pragmatic meanings associated with the utterance expressed in context. These examples also show that the language forms can have a relationship that ranges from direct to indirect with both the meanings and the functions they express in context (see Table 3.2). In other words, the meaning and functions of some grammatical forms are derived primarily from the meaning of the words arranged in syntax, while others stem primarily from information in the context.

These examples also show that while a single utterance can potentially be used to express several language functions, speakers usually have one primary communicative intention in mind – their intended meaning. Beyond that, several pragmatic meanings can be communicated (intentionally or unintentionally) within a given context, especially if speakers wish to be funny, sarcastic, condescending, and so forth. For example, the father wants to tell the daughter to clean up the room (primary intended message), and he wants to communicate some psychological meaning in the form of criticism, and possibly some sociocultural meaning in the form of a display of authority. From the daughter's possible responses, we see that the hearer needs to identify which meaning best represents the speaker's intention, so that a meaningful and appropriate response can be made. These distinctions in meaning and function are important to make in assessing second or foreign language performance so that we can make the best possible inferences about how learners are able to understand and use grammatical forms to express different kinds of meaning in a variety of contexts. In grammar assessment, we are primarily interested in the degree to which test-takers are able to use grammatical forms precisely to get their point across meaningfully in a given context. If the task requires test-takers to be polite or show compassion and if it is successful in eliciting other pragmatic meanings consistently, we might also be able to assess for the pragmatic meanings expressed by utterances in those contexts.

In language tests where the context is sometimes highly reduced or unknown, such as in a discrete-point multiple-choice task, we might be constrained to some degree in that the forms that are typically assessed have a fairly direct relationship with meaning and function. However, in assessment situations where the context is elaborated, such as in a role-play or a problem-solving simulation task, we can assess grammatical forms that have both a direct and an indirect relationship with meaning and function, thereby providing a more complete assessment of the learner's grammatical ability. Obviously, in language tests, we are concerned with both grammatical and pragmatic meaning; however, much of what is typically tested under the rubric of grammar testing involves the assessment of forms along with their literal and intended meanings.

To recap, **grammatical meaning** embodies the literal and intended meanings of an utterance derived both from the meaning of the words arranged in syntax and the way in which the words are used to convey the speaker's intention. Phonological meaning, lexical meaning and the morphosyntactic meaning of an utterance are all components of grammatical meaning. The current depiction of grammatical knowledge involves grammatical forms together with the literal and intended meanings they encode as well as the language functions they are used to express. **Pragmatic meaning** embodies a host of other implied meanings that derive from context relating to the interpersonal relationship of the interlocutors, their emotional or attitudinal stance, their presuppositions about what is known and the sociocultural setting of the interaction. These meanings occur simultaneously. Sometimes they are intentional and sometime not. In short, **pragmatics** refers to a domain of extended meanings which are superimposed upon forms in association with the literal and intended meanings of an utterance. The source of pragmatic meanings, as seen in Figure 3.2, may be contextual, sociolinguistic, sociocultural, psychological or rhetorical. Grammar in this book, therefore, encompasses grammatical forms and grammatical meanings (literal and intended), but views pragmatics as separate. For the purpose of assessing grammatical ability, it is important, to the extent possible, to keep what is 'grammatical' distinct from what is 'pragmatic', so that inferences about grammatical ability can be made.

Before describing the theoretical definition of grammar to be used in this book, I will attempt to describe what I mean by 'pragmatics' so that the boundaries between grammar and pragmatics can be better drawn. Consider what is actually said, what is intended, and what can be extrapolated in the following exchange:

Dick: Can I have another doughnut, honey?
Jane: You keep it up and you're gonna look like one.
Dick: Just gimme the box.
Jane: [hands him the box] Go ahead. Kill yourself.

Dick uses grammatical forms (phonology, lexis and syntax) to communicate his desire for an additional doughnut (intended meaning = Give me another doughnut). This utterance is used to make a request (a directive), rather than to inquire about Jane's ability to give Dick a doughnut (a representative). The relationship between the grammatical forms and the literal meaning of this sentence is, thus, relatively direct. The use of the informal register with the word 'honey' conveys pragmatic information about the interlocutors' social relationship – they are partnered or related to each other (sociocultural meaning). It simultaneously communicates a sense of endearment (sociocultural meaning). Similarly, the use of 'honey' could also be used to convey sarcasm (psychological meaning), especially if Jane had already given Dick a hard time about doughnuts in a prior situation. This could have led Dick to emphasize 'honey' sarcastically, in a way that shows he does not really mean it as a term of endearment.

Instead of explicitly granting Dick's request (e.g., 'Sure. Have another one, dear'), Jane responds with an implied conditional sentence ([if] 'You keep it up, you're gonna look like one') to convey the literal meaning that if Dick persists in eating doughnuts, he will become fat and round like a doughnut. Jane's intention in comparing his appearance to that of a doughnut is to dissuade him from eating something that she perceives as being bad for his health. Jane's intended meaning is 'Don't eat another!' She might simultaneously wish to humiliate him (psychological meaning) or remind him about his weight (contextual meaning). Then again, on the darker side, the intended meaning might be to encourage him to endanger his health by eating more doughnuts so she can bid him a 'sweet' good-bye. The sociocultural sensitivity of the message (i.e., a discussion of weight and overeating) also carries pragmatic information about their close personal relationship.

Allowing no further opportunity for an indirect response, Dick reformulates his polite request as a directive with the use of an imperative verb form. The literal and intended meaning of the utterance is, 'Just hand me a doughnut.' Pragmatically, the switch from a polite request to a directive could encode a number of implied meanings (e.g., exasperation, aggression, authority).

In the following turn, Jane correctly interprets Dick's response as a directive and complies by handing him the box. However, knowing that her first attempt to dissuade him from having another doughnut has failed, she utters two directives (Go ahead. Kill yourself.). The intended meaning might be, 'If you want to die, be my guest. I can't stop you.' This utterance is ostensibly not what Jane wants, but is said sarcastically to discourage him from having another doughnut (psychological meaning – sarcasm). Although Jane might appear openly rude towards Dick (sociocultural meaning), she obviously feels close enough to him to know this will probably not damage their relationship (shared assumptions about their interpersonal relationship).

From a cultural perspective, this exchange encodes pragmatic information about how men and woman can interact with one another within the culture of this relationship and within a larger national culture, and about how discussions about health and weight can transpire. In sum, each utterance in this exchange uses grammatical forms to convey literal and intended meanings for the purpose of some communicative goal. Each also conveys a number of pragmatic meanings deriving from contextual, sociocultural, and psychological presuppositions.

To summarize, pragmatics refers not so much to the literal meaning of the utterance (What did you say?) or to the intended meaning (What did you want to say?), but to the *implied* or *pragmatic* meaning of the utterance interpreted by another person (What did you mean by that?). It can also refer to the relative *appropriateness* of the utterance within a given context (Why did you say it that way in this context?), to the relative *acceptability* of the utterance within the general norms of interaction (Is it OK to say that?), or to the *naturalness* of the utterance in terms of how native speakers might say it (Does this sound like something native speakers would say?). Finally, pragmatics refers to the *conventionality* of the utterance in terms of how speakers from a certain regional or social language variety might express it (Does it sound like something that someone from my social or regional dialect would say?). The determination of what is meaningful or pragmatically appropriate, acceptable, natural or conventional depends on the underlying contextual, sociocultural, sociolinguistic, psychological or rhetorical norms, assumptions, expectations and presuppositions of the interlocutors in a given situation.

From an assessment perspective, the measurement of pragmatic knowledge presents a major challenge for test developers given that one utterance can simultaneously encode multiple pragmatic meanings, and many times, without asking the speaker, it is difficult to determine which meanings were implied, and in fact, without asking the interlocutor, it is difficult to determine which meanings were actually understood. However, I believe it is possible to craft test tasks that require examinees to use linguistic forms to communicate one or more specific pragmatic meanings in a consistent fashion. For example, one of the tasks in the *Test of Spoken English* (TSE Program Office, 2003) requires examinees to listen to a phone message in which a complaint about a product or service is being made. The examinee must assume the role of someone who can solve the problem and then leave a message that addresses the problem in a grammatically precise, meaningful and pragmatically appropriate manner. 'Pragmatically appropriate' might be determined by the examinee's ability to sound empathetic to the customer's concerns (i.e., correct use of apologies) and willing to compensate for the problem, and sincere in ensuring that the problem will not reoccur.

A comprehensive approach to the assessment of pragmatic knowledge and how this may complement the assessment of grammatical knowledge is beyond the purview of this book. This is by no means intended to downplay the importance of pragmatics in language use or the need to devise useful assessments of pragmatic knowledge in language tests. In fact, it would be an interesting challenge to devise assessments of pragmatic ability that measure a wide range of pragmatic meanings. However, the focus of this book is on the assessment of the grammatical component. At the same time, I do recognize that, sometimes, the distinction between grammatical and pragmatic knowledge is difficult to discern, and I will, therefore, continue to discuss the assessment of pragmatic knowledge in some detail at times in order to differentiate it from grammatical knowledge.

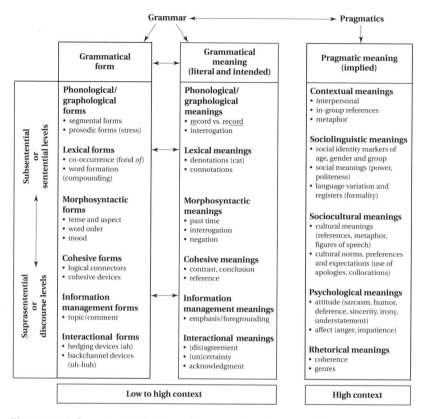

Figure 3.3 A theoretical definition of grammar (and pragmatics)

Figure 3.3 presents the theoretical definition of grammar (and pragmatics) for the purposes of assessment in this book. This depiction of grammar will also be used as a basis for defining grammatical knowledge in much greater detail in the next chapter.

In Figure 3.3, grammar encompasses both subsentential- and sentential-level forms and meanings on the one hand, and suprasentential- or discourse-level forms and meanings on the other. (The interactions are depicted by double-headed arrows.) The subsentential- and sentential-level depiction of grammatical form includes **phonological forms** (e.g., intonation), **lexical forms** (e.g., derivational affixation – -*tion*) and **morphosyntactic forms** (e.g., voice, tense, word order). The subsentential- and sentential-level depiction of meaning embodies **phonological meanings** (e.g., contrast, interrogation) associated with phonological forms (e.g., word stress, intonation); **lexical meanings** (e.g., denotations) associated with lexical forms (e.g., *book* = pages bound together*)*; and

morphosyntactic meanings (e.g., past time reference) associated with morphosyntactic forms (e.g., *-ed* affix – work*ed*). Morphosyntactic meaning referring to the syntax of an entire sentence might embody the notion of interrogation or passivization. When phonological forms, lexical forms and morphosyntactic forms work together to create meaning in syntactic structure, they embody the grammatical meaning (literal and intended) of the utterance.

The theoretical framework of grammar in Figure 3.3 also accounts for grammar used beyond the sentence level. As seen in Halliday (1994) and Halliday and Hasan (1976), grammar also encompasses grammatical form and meaning at the suprasentential or discourse level. In this book, **discourse** is defined as an instance of spoken or written language whose internal relationships can be identified through forms and meanings on a textual level. This notion of discourse is much narrower than is commonly discussed in the applied linguistics literature, where discourse also includes negotiation or the co-construction of meaning. Discourse here also differs from pragmatics in that pragmatics involves the use of grammatical resources to encode a host of other meanings based on external context, extrapolation and presuppositions.

Suprasentential- or discourse-level grammatical form includes **cohesive forms** (e.g., pronominals), **information management forms** (e.g., changes to canonical word order to express contrast – *The old one I know* ...) and **interactional forms** (e.g., the discourse marker 'ah' to signal disagreement). Suprasentential-level grammatical forms use many of the same sentential forms (pronominals), but on a discourse level. The grammatical forms also encode discourse-level grammatical meanings. These include **cohesive meanings** (e.g., the tie between a pronoun and its referent – *she* linked to *the female kitten*), **information management meanings** (e.g., subject–verb inversion in a declarative sentence to place emphasis on or foreground the subject of the sentence: *In the abandoned tower hid the embittered old Queen*) and **interactional meanings** (e.g., the conveyance of shared knowledge and conversational alignment signaled by backchannel devices such as 'ya, ya' in Spanish or 'uh-huh' in English).

The framework of grammar in Figure 3.3 is also designed to represent the grammar, expressed in forms, of more than one interlocutor. This is important for communicative grammar assessment, where interaction is typically organized around **exchanges** or pairs of utterances. These exchanges are usually, but not always, adjacent and express a mutually dependent relationship. For example, an apology (the first pair part) is followed by an acceptance (the second pair part).

A: Sorry about that.   [apology]

B: No problem.   [acceptance of apology]

Other mutually dependent **adjacency pairs** include: offer/refusal, summons/response, blame/denial, request/granting, and so forth. Halliday and Hasan (1976, 1989) maintain that these exchanges add a sense of cohesion to interaction. Although interaction has not traditionally been viewed from a grammatical perspective, grammatical forms on the discourse level (e.g., cohesive, information management and interactional forms) provide a critical resource for the communication of grammatical meanings, and these forms can be a source of consternation to second or foreign language learners. For this reason, I have included a discourse perspective to grammar in the current model to account for grammar in tests used beyond the sentence level.

Finally, on the pragmatic level, grammatical forms and meanings may carry one or more implied meanings depending on the context of language use. These can involve a range of **contextual meanings** (e.g., meanings that are highly contextualized and mutually understandable to individuals or insiders), **sociolinguistic meanings** (e.g., meanings that convey social identity, politeness, formality), **sociocultural meanings** (e.g., meanings associated with a specific culture such as the use of apologizing strategies to thank someone in Japanese), **psychological meanings** (e.g., meanings derived from the use of description to convey sarcasm, humor, irony, criticism, anger or understatement) and **rhetorical meanings** (e.g., meanings associated with the use of genre – chairing a business meeting by following an accepted protocol). Given a certain context, one speaker may use a set of grammatical forms to convey one set of meanings, while the hearer may use the same set of forms to hear the same or a very different set of meanings. Larsen-Freeman (2002) describes these 'choices' as the result of knowing when to use one grammatical form over another 'to convey meanings that match our intentions in particular contexts' (p. 105). However, the possibility of ascribing multiple meanings to the same grammatical forms increases the potential for misunderstandings, but also allows for humor and poetry. The grammatical choices we make and the meanings they convey display meaningfulness on a number of levels, which can then be viewed as more or less appropriate, acceptable, natural or conventional (for native speakers) in given situations.

To illustrate how this model of grammar might be used to identify what grammar a learner knows, consider the following exchange:

Jack:	I really love San Francisco.	[expression of preference]
Mary:	*So I do. I'd love to move	
	there some day.	[agreement and wish]
	* = ungrammatical	

Jack communicates his love for San Francisco and Mary wishes to communicate her love for San Francisco as well (literal and intended meaning). As Jack had done so first, Mary chooses to agree with Jack (language function). She avoids repeating 'really love San Francisco' by using the elliptical form 'so'. Although Mary knows which cohesive form to use and which meaning, she does not know the grammatical constraints on 'so' in clause-initial position in English. Therefore, she does not invert the subject and auxiliary (So do I). From this error, we might conclude that Mary needs more instruction with cohesive form. Interactionally, from what little context there is, we might also be able to infer that Mary knows that it is appropriate to use agreement in order to align herself with Jack and that 'so' allows her to avoid redundancy. Pragmatically, other meanings could also be superimposed on Mary's response; however, given the paucity of contextual information, all such extrapolations may be pure speculation.

For language educators seeking to develop second or foreign language grammar tests, the model of grammar presented in Figure 3.3 provides a flexible framework for specifying grammar on the sentence or discourse levels, and it accounts for the form and meaning dimensions. It also provides a distinction between grammar (grammatical form and meaning) and pragmatics. In the next chapter, I will describe this framework in much more detail, showing how it relates to what a student 'knows' about grammar. Finally, although we as language educators might decide to measure the individual components of grammar separately, we must understand that these components inevitably interact in language use, and that we might be measuring other components at the same time. Nonetheless, it remains important to specify, to the best of our ability, what component(s) of grammar we are attempting to measure.

Summary

Given the central role that construct definition plays in test development and validation, my intention in this chapter has been to discuss the 'what' of grammar assessment. I have examined how grammar has been depicted in models of communicative language ability over the years, and have argued that for assessment purposes grammar should be clearly differentiated from pragmatics. Grammar should also be defined to include a form and meaning component on both the sentence and discourse levels. I have also argued that meaning can be characterized as literal and intended. Also the pragmatic dimension of language constitutes an extrapolation of both the literal meaning and the speaker's intended meaning, while using contextual information beyond what is expressed in grammatical forms. I have argued that pragmatic meanings may be simultaneously superimposed upon grammatical forms and their meanings (e.g., as in a joke). In short, grammar should not be viewed solely in terms of linguistic form, but should also include the role that literal and intended meaning plays in providing resources for all types of communication. Although forms and meanings are highly related, it is important for testers to make distinctions among these components, when possible, so that assessments can be used to provide more precise information to users of test results. In the next chapter, I will use this model of grammar as a basis for defining second or foreign language grammatical ability for assessment.

CHAPTER FOUR

Towards a definition of grammatical ability

Introduction

In the previous chapter, I discussed the role of grammar in models of communicative competence and showed how a more detailed depiction of grammar was needed in order to assess how learners use grammatical forms as a resource for conveying a variety of meanings. I argued, as many others have, that language consists of grammar and pragmatics, and these two components should be clearly differentiated. Finally, I presented a theoretical model of language in which grammar is defined in terms of both form and meaning, and where pragmatics refers to a variety of implied meanings superimposed upon the grammatical forms and meanings of an utterance.

In the current chapter, I will discuss how the proposed model of grammar can be used to define what it means to have second language grammatical ability. In so doing, I will describe a theoretical model of grammatical knowledge that can serve as a basis for grammar-test construction and validation. Before describing this model in much greater detail and applying it more specifically to assessment, I will clarify the many terms that are used in this discussion.

What is meant by grammatical ability?

Having described how grammar has been conceptualized, we are now faced with the challenge of defining what it means to 'know' the grammar of a language so that it can be used to achieve some communicative goal. In other words, what does it mean to have 'grammatical ability'?

Defining grammatical constructs

Although our basic underlying model of grammar will remain the same in all testing situations (i.e., grammatical form and meaning), what it means to 'know' grammar for different contexts will most likely change (see Chapelle, 1998). In other words, the type, range and scope of grammatical features required to communicate accurately and meaningfully will vary from one situation to another. For example, the type of grammatical knowledge needed to write a formal academic essay would be very different from that needed to make a train reservation. Given the many possible ways of interpreting what it means to 'know' grammar, it is important that we define what we mean by 'grammatical knowledge' for any given testing situation. A clear definition of what we believe it means to 'know' grammar for a particular testing context will then allow us to construct tests that measure grammatical ability.

The many possible ways of interpreting what it means to 'know' grammar' or to have 'grammatical ability' highlight the importance in language assessment of defining key terms. Some of the same terms used by different testers reflect a wide range of theoretical positions in the field of applied linguistics. In this book, I will use several theoretical terms from the domain of language testing. These include *knowledge, competence, ability, proficiency* and *performance*, to name a few. These concepts are abstract, not *directly* observable in tests and open to multiple definitions and interpretations. Therefore, before we use abstract terms such as *knowledge* or *ability*, we need to 'construct' a definition of them that will both suit our assessment goals and be theoretically viable. I will refer to these abstract, theoretical concepts generically as **constructs** or **theoretical constructs**.

One of the first steps in designing a test, aside from identifying the need for a test, its purpose and audience, is to provide a clear **theoretical definition** of the construct(s) to be measured. If we have a theoretically sound, as well as a clear and precise definition of grammatical knowledge, we can then design tasks to elicit performance samples of grammatical ability. By having the test-takers complete grammar tasks, we can observe – and score – their answers with relation to specific grammatical criteria for correctness. If these performance samples reflect the underlying grammatical constructs – an empirical question – we can then use the test results to make inferences about the test-takers' grammatical ability. These inferences, in turn, may be used to make decisions about the test-takers (e.g., pass the course). However, we need first to provide evidence that the tasks on a test have measured the grammatical constructs we have designed them to measure (Messick, 1993). The process of providing arguments in support of this evidence is called **validation**, and this begins with a clear definition of the constructs.

Language educators thus need to define carefully the constructs to be measured when creating tasks for tests. They must provide clear definitions of the constructs, bearing in mind that each time a test is designed, it should reflect the different components of grammatical knowledge, the purpose of the assessment, the group of learners about which we like to make inferences and the language-use contexts to which, we hope, the results will ultimately generalize.

Definition of key terms

Before continuing this discussion, it might be helpful if I clarified some of the key terms.

Grammatical knowledge

Knowledge refers to a set of informational structures that are built up through experience and stored in long-term memory. These structures include knowledge of facts that are stored in concepts, images, networks, production-like structures, propositions, schemata and representations (Pressley, 1995). **Language knowledge** is then a mental representation of informational structures related to language. The exact components of language knowledge, like any other construct, need to be defined. In this book, **grammar** refers to a system of language whereas **grammatical knowledge** is defined as a set of internalized informational structures related to the theoretical model of grammar proposed in Figure 3.2 (p. 62). In this model, grammar is defined in terms of grammatical form and meaning, which are available to be accessed in language use.

To illustrate, suppose a student learning French knows that the passive voice is constructed with a form of the verb *être* (to be) plus a past participle, and is able to produce this form accurately and with ease. She may also know intuitively from her first language that the passive is used to place greater focus on the action in a sentence. However, she is still unclear when to use the passive or the active with the indefinite pronoun *on* (one). For example, to say: *Then the olives are washed,* she is unsure whether to use the impersonal form: *Puis, on lave les olives* (Then one washes the olives) or the passive form: *Puis les olives sont lavées* (Then the olives are washed). As a result, she defaults to her first language and mistakenly overuses the passive. Based on this observation, we might infer that this student has knowledge of passive grammatical forms, reflected in her ability to access passive forms accurately. She also has knowledge of grammatical meaning, since she knows what message she wants to convey. However, from a pragmatic perspective, she is uncertain how to choose the forms *appropriately* in different contexts (i.e., language-use norms or discourse constraints); she seems unaware that the French would probably prefer the impersonal construction on most occasions, based on what we know from corpus linguistics studies.

Grammatical ability

Although some researchers have defined knowledge and ability similarly, I use these terms differently. 'Knowledge' refers to a set of informational structures available for use in long-term memory. **Ability**, however, encompasses more than just a domain of information in memory; it also involves the capacity to *use* these informational structures in some way. Therefore, **language ability**, sometimes called **communicative competence** or **language proficiency**, refers to an individual's capacity to utilize mental representations of language knowledge built up through practice or experience in order to convey meaning. Given this definition, language ability, by its very nature, involves more than just language knowledge. Bachman and Palmer (1996) characterize language ability as a combination of language knowledge and **strategic competence**, defined as a set of **metacognitive strategies** (e.g., planning, evaluating) and, I might add, **cognitive strategies** (e.g., associating, clarifying), for the purpose of 'creating and interpreting discourse in both testing and non-testing situations' (p. 67).

Grammatical ability is, then, the combination of grammatical knowledge and strategic competence; it is specifically defined as the capacity to realize grammatical knowledge accurately and meaningfully in testing or other language-use situations.

Grammatical performance

Hymes (1972) distinguished between competence and performance, stating that communicative competence includes the underlying potential of realizing language ability in instances of language use, whereas **language performance** refers to the use of language in actual language events. Carroll (1968) refers to language performance as 'the actual manifestation of linguistic competence . . . in behavior' (p. 50).

For example, imagine that a student in Brazil is for all practical purposes fluent in English. He uses English at work, and has no problems communicating with native speakers. When given an English placement test, however, he has to describe the relationships between population growth and economic tendencies over the past fifty years based on a graph. Not used to analyzing graphs, he gets confused and makes grammar mistakes in the process. This student has the potential to communicate accurately in English; however, due to non-linguistic factors such as his inability to interpret a graph and the anxiety that this caused in a testing situation, he was unable to demonstrate his true grammatical ability. In short, the student's grammatical performance may not have been a good representation of his underlying grammatical knowledge.

A reality that all language educators must face is the fact that a test-taker's language ability is always in danger of being clouded by sources of variation which are independent of language knowledge and which can severely diminish the validity of our interpretations about language ability. Carroll (1968) refers to these 'extraneous sources of variation' as 'non-linguistic factors in performance'. In other words, performance is observed as a result of the test-taker's language knowledge interacting with the characteristics of the test task and other non-linguistic characteristics of the test-taker (i.e., his or her strategic competence, knowledge of the topic, affect and personal attributes) (Bachman, 1990b).

In this book, **grammatical performance** is defined as the observable manifestation of grammatical ability in language use. In grammatical performance, the underlying grammatical ability of a test-taker may be masked by interactions with other attributes of the examinee or the test task. In other words, each time we perform language, we use our language knowledge. At the same time, our use of this knowledge may be influenced by interactions with other factors, such as the attributes of test-takers or characteristics of the test task. Thus, every instance of grammar use is a manifestation of grammatical performance, taking into account that the underlying ability may be masked by interactions with other attributes of the test-taker or the test task. Although a grammar test elicits instances of grammatical performance, the primary goal of testing is to make inferences about test-takers' underlying grammatical ability, or how they are able to use their grammatical knowledge to convey meaning. This, of course, must be done on the basis of test performance.

The relationships among grammatical knowledge, ability, and performance are presented in Figure 4.1.

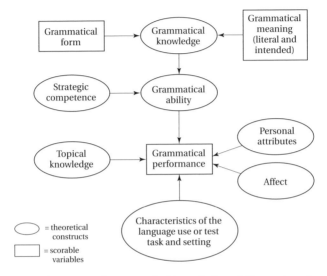

Figure 4.1 A depiction of grammatical knowledge, ability and performance

Metalinguistic knowledge

Finally, **metalanguage** is the language used to describe a language. It generally consists of technical linguistic or grammatical terms (e.g., noun, verb). **Metalinguistic knowledge**, therefore, refers to informational structures related to linguistic terminology. We must be clear that metalinguistic knowledge is not a component of grammatical ability; rather, the knowledge of linguistic terms would more aptly be classified as a kind of specific topical knowledge that might be useful for language teachers to possess.

Some teachers almost never present metalinguistic terminology to their students, while others find it useful as a means of discussing the language and learning the grammar. It is important to remember that knowing the grammatical terms of a language does not necessarily mean knowing how to communicate in the language.

What is 'grammatical ability' for assessment purposes?

The approach to the assessment of grammatical ability in this book is based on several specific definitions. First, grammar encompasses grammatical form and meaning, whereas pragmatics is a separate, but related, component of language. A second is that grammatical knowledge, along with strategic competence, constitutes grammatical ability. A third is that grammatical ability involves the capacity to realize grammatical knowledge accurately and meaningfully in test-taking or other language-use contexts. The capacity to access grammatical knowledge to understand and convey meaning is related to a person's strategic competence. It is this interaction that enables examinees to implement their grammatical ability in language use. Next, in tests and other language-use contexts, grammatical ability may interact with pragmatic ability (i.e., pragmatic knowledge and strategic competence) on the one hand, and with a host of non-linguistic factors such as the test-taker's topical knowledge, personal attributes, affective schemata and the characteristics of the task on the other. Finally, in cases where grammatical ability is assessed by means of an interactive test task involving two or more interlocutors, the way grammatical ability is realized will be significantly impacted by both the contextual and the interpretative demands of the interaction.

Having argued for the importance of providing clear, theoretical definitions of test constructs, we now return to the question 'What exactly does it mean to have second or foreign language grammatical ability?' or 'What does a person have to "know" in terms of grammar to be able to use it for some real-life purpose?' Generally speaking, grammatical knowledge is involved when examinees understand or produce utterances that are grammatically precise and contextually meaningful. Based on the definition of grammar in Figure 3.2, knowledge of grammatical form relates to phonology, lexis, morphosyntax, cohesion, information management and interaction. Given that many of the same grammatical forms are used on both the (sub)sentential and the suprasentential levels, it is obvious that knowledge of grammatical forms overlap especially when tests involve more than single sentences. Similarly, knowledge of grammatical meaning relates to the meanings associated with phonological, lexical, morphosyntactic, cohesive, information management and interactional forms. These meanings appear in sentence and discourse level utterances. Finally, these meanings can be viewed separately or taken together to form the literal and intended meaning of a speaker's utterance.

From an assessment perspective, we can construct tasks that target individual or combined features of grammatical form or meaning. For example, VanPatten (1996) tested the meaning associated with object pronouns and word order in Spanish by providing students with a sentence *Les invita Manuel al cine* (Manuel invites them to the movies = treats them to the movies; pays for their tickets). He then asked them to select the picture that best corresponded to the sentence: one in which Manuel was inviting them or one in which Manuel was being invited by them. In this case, students were given the form and had to select the meaning. However, in many instances, the boundaries between the components of form and meaning may be difficult to specify. In these cases, we can design tasks to measure form and meaning simultaneously. In these instances, learners might demonstrate complete mastery of the form, but incomplete mastery of the meanings. Of course, whether the tests actually do measure these constructs separately or together is an empirical question to be answered as part of a test validation argument, but it is nonetheless important in the test-design process that test developers attempt to provide a clear definition of the components of grammatical knowledge to which they hope to make inferences. The definition of these constructs can then be used as the basis for creating tasks to measure these constructs.

Figure 4.2 presents the components of grammatical knowledge along with a list of possible grammatical points that could be used to measure each component. This list is not meant to be exhaustive; nor does it suggest that these categories must all be tested in any one grammar test. Rather, this framework is offered simply as an illustrative guide for defining the construct of grammatical knowledge, and is offered with the full understanding that it will need to be tailored to a given test-development situation.

In the remaining part of this chapter, I will describe the components of grammatical knowledge in light of how they might be used for assessment.

Knowledge of phonological or graphological form and meaning

Knowledge of **phonological/graphological form** enables us to understand and produce features of the sound or writing system, with the exception of meaning-based orthographies such as Chinese characters, as they are used to convey meaning in testing or language-use situations. Phonological form includes the segmentals (i.e., vowels and consonants)

Figure 4.2 Components of grammatical and pragmatic knowledge

and prosody (i.e., stress, rhythm, intonation contours, volume, tempo). These forms can be used alone or in conjunction with other grammatical forms to encode **phonological meaning**. For example, the ability to hear or pronounce meaning-distinguishing sounds such as the /b/ vs. /v/ could be used to differentiate the meaning between different nouns (boat/vote), and the ability to hear or pronounce the prosodic features of the language (e.g., intonation) could allow students to understand or convey the notion that a sentence is an interrogative (You're staying?).

For example, imagine where you could end up if you were told to meet someone at the _greenhouse_ (= glass house for growing plants) instead of the _green house_ (house painted green). Here, the student's inability to use stress to differentiate noun compounds from nouns modified by adjectives and the changes in meaning that result shows that he or she knows lexical form and meaning, but still has difficulty with phonological form. From the confusion and misunderstanding that could ensue, mistakes in phonological form are not trivial since they affect intelligibility and interpretability.

Knowledge of **graphological form** enables us to understand and produce features of the writing system as they are used to convey meaning in testing or language-use situations. Graphological form includes sound–spelling correspondences (bear/bare), and other orthographical conventions.

On a pragmatic level, phonological forms can encode several pragmatic meanings. For example, they can encode sociocultural information regarding the speaker's identity (e.g., their ethnicity, race, gender or sexual orientation) or psychological information by his or her use of affective stance (sarcasm, anger, joy).

Knowledge of lexical form and meaning

Knowledge of **lexical form** enables us to understand and produce those features of words that encode grammar rather than those that reveal meaning. This includes words that mark gender (e.g., waitress), countability (e.g., people) or part of speech (e.g., relate, relation). For example, when the word _think_ in English is followed by the preposition _about_ before a noun, this is considered the grammatical dimension of lexis, representing a co-occurrence restriction with prepositions. One area of lexical form that poses a challenge to learners of some languages is word formation. This includes compounding in English with a noun + noun or a verb + particle pattern (e.g., fire escape; breakup) or derivational affixation in Italian (e.g., *ragazz**ino*** 'little kid', *ragazz**one*** 'big kid'). For example, a student who says 'a teacher of chemistry' instead of 'chemistry teacher' or '*this people' would need further instruction in lexical form.

Knowledge of **lexical meaning** allows us to interpret and use words based on their **literal meanings**. Lexical meaning here does not encompass the suggested or implied meanings of words based on contextual, sociocultural, psychological or rhetorical associations. For example, the literal meaning of a rose is a kind of flower, whereas a rose can also be used in a non-literal sense to imply a number of sociocultural meanings depending on the context. These include love, beauty, passion and still a host of other cultural meanings (e.g., the Rose Bowl, a rose window). Lexical meaning also accounts for the literal meaning of formulaic or lexicalized expressions (e.g., *You're welcome*). Although it is possible to test lexical form or meaning separately, we must recognize that lexical form and meaning are very closely associated.

An example of knowing the lexical form and not the other meanings is seen in my own language learning. When I was learning Arabic in Kuwait, I had learned that the word *ma'a'lesh*, an adverb (lexical form), meant roughly 'it doesn't matter, no problem', or 'never mind'. I did not know that *ma'a'lesh* could also mean 'sorry' (lexical meaning) in the context of an apology. So when a Kuwaiti salesman innocently said *ma'a'lesh* when he realized he had mistakenly shortchanged me. My response was, 'Why is it no problem? – It's a BIG problem!' Later I regretfully understood why the salesman looked confused at my response.

From a pragmatic perspective, lexical forms and meanings often encode cultural meaning by means of metaphor or figurative speech. 'Metaphor' is used here as an instance in which literal meaning is extended through a transfer of meaning from one area to another. For example, Lakoff and Johnson (1980), in *Metaphors We Live By*, discuss the underlying relationship between food (the source) and ideas (the target) to explain metaphors such as *food for thought, a half-baked idea* or *that idea smells fishy*. Metaphor is an integral part of every language and, in many cases, inseparable from the language itself. Metaphors that encode realities specific to one culture and not to another often lack the sufficient transparency for second language learners to understand the meaning being communicated. Lexical forms and meanings that encode pragmatic meanings often pose enormous problems for second and foreign language learners and for children in their native language (L1).

Finally, the choice of some lexical forms is based purely on usage norms, preferences or expectations, and not solely on grammatical grounds. One example of this is collocation and the restrictions imposed on words when juxtaposed. For example, we can express the meaning of contentment with words such as *happy, glad, merry,* or *jolly*; however, collocational restrictions prevent us from saying '*Merry Hanukkah' or '*Glad Fourth-of-July'. Again, this taps into the pragmatic aspect of the lexicon.

Knowledge of morphosyntactic form and meaning

Knowledge of **morphosyntactic form** permits us to understand and produce both the morphological and syntactic forms of the language. This includes the articles, prepositions, pronouns, affixes (e.g., -est), syntactic structures, word order, simple, compound and complex sentences, mood, voice and modality. A learner who knows the morphosyntactic form of the English conditionals would know that: (1) an *if*-clause sets up a condition and a result clause expresses the outcome; (2) both clauses can be in the sentence-initial position in English; (3) *if* can be deleted under certain conditions as long as the subject and operator are inverted; and (4) certain tense restrictions are imposed on *if* and result clauses.

Morphosyntactic forms carry **morphosyntactic meanings** which allow us to interpret and express meanings from inflections such as aspect and time, meanings from derivations such as negation and agency, and meanings from syntax such as those used to express attitudes (e.g., subjunctive mood) or show focus, emphasis or contrast (e.g., voice and word order). For example, a student who knows the morphosyntactic meaning of the English conditionals would know how to express a factual conditional relationship (*If this happens, that happens*), a predictive conditional relationship (*If this happens, that will happen*), or a hypothetical conditional relationship (*If this happened, that would happen*). On the sentential level, the individual morphosyntactic forms and meanings taken together allow us to interpret and express the literal or grammatical meaning of an utterance and they allow us to identify the direct language function associated with language use.

Morphosyntactic forms and meanings can also encode a wide range of pragmatic meanings, where the literal meaning of an utterance has an interpretation beyond the actual words expressed. For example, when a friend asks the question: 'Is that cake any good?' the speaker's intent may be to elicit an evaluation of the cake (literal meaning). Given the reduced context, the interlocutor would most likely hear it as intended – as a request for an evaluation (direct language function) and respond, 'It's fantastic.' However, the hearer could also have heard the question as a request for some cake (indirect language function – pragmatic meaning), and respond with an offer, 'You want a bite?' Given a much richer context, the same question could be heard as a criticism about the person's manners for not offering the food (sociocultural meaning), or in certain contexts as a criticism (Oh, you're eating cake again. Enjoy it while you're still young and thin) (psychological meaning).

Knowledge of cohesive form and meaning

Knowledge of **cohesive form** enables us to use the phonological, lexical and morphosyntactic features of the language in order to interpret and express cohesion on both the sentence and the discourse levels. Cohesive form is directly related to **cohesive meaning** through cohesive devices (e.g., *she, this, here*) which create links between cohesive forms and their referential meanings within the linguistic environment or the surrounding co-text. Halliday and Hasan (1976, 1989) list a number of grammatical forms for displaying cohesive meaning. This can be achieved through the use of personal referents to convey possession or reciprocity; demonstrative referents to display spatial, temporal or psychological links; comparative referents to encode similarity, difference and equality; and logical connectors to signal a wide range of meanings such as addition, logical conclusion and contrast. Cohesive meaning is also conveyed through ellipsis (e.g., *When* [should I arrive at your house]?), substitution (e.g., *I hope so*) and lexical ties in the form of synonymy and repetition. Finally, cohesive meaning can be communicated through the internal relationship between pair parts in an adjacency pair (e.g., invitation/ acceptance). When the interpretation source of a cohesive form is within the linguistic environment, the interpretation is said to be **endophoric** (Halliday and Hasan, 1989).

To understand cohesive form and meaning, imagine that a Catalan student speaking English says *the her dog* (*el seu gos*) instead of *her dog*. In this case, the student is unaware that English personal adjectives cannot be preceded by a determiner (the). However, she did know that an English personal adjective (her) encodes the biological sex of the owner, and not the grammatical gender of the noun head (dog) as in Catalan. As a result, she used *her* for the masculine personal adjective *seu*. This is a clear example of a student knowing cohesive meaning, but not form.

Cohesive form on a phonological level (common literary terms called assonance and alliteration) can be seen in an excerpt from a poem by Paul Verlaine (1866) in *Poèmes saturniens*:

Les sanglots longs de l'automne	(The long sobs of the autumn)
blessent mon cœur	(wound my heart)
d'une langueur monotone	(with a monotonous languor)

Here the repetition of the sounds /ã/, /o/, /õ/, /n/, /œ/ and /œ:r/ provides a sense of phonological cohesion. So do the four instances of the /l/ sound in the first line, and the repetition of /l/ in the second and third lines. In my opinion, the phonological forms used in this poem also evoke meaning outside the linguistic environment, what Halliday and Hasan (1989) call **exophoric reference**. The repetition of the l's in the first line seems 'long', 'languorous' and 'monotonous'. And the nasals might be associated with 'sadness'. This is a case where phonological form and meanings convey a host of pragmatic meanings as well, which is the essence of poetry.

The pragmatic dimension of cohesion embodies several meanings. On a lexical level, it can carry cultural meaning. For example, when a New Yorker says 'I live near *the Park*', *the park* is often understood to be Central Park. The reference lies outside the linguistic environment and within the context of the situation. Similarly, cohesive form and meanings can evoke rhetorical meanings. One kind of rhetorical meaning is **coherence**, or the logical organization of ideas in a spoken or written text so that one sentence, paragraph or turn can provide a context for the next. Given that knowledge of coherence conventions can be culturally based, this presents a special challenge to language learners. For example, Ricento (1987) found that Japanese texts translated into English were better understood by Japanese students than by English-speaking students, suggesting that the Japanese rhetorical conventions were different from English ones. Ricento reminded us that topic sentences in Japanese texts often come after several paragraphs, a practice that would signal lack of coherence in English writing.

Knowledge of information management form and meaning

Knowledge of **information management form** allows us to use linguistic forms as a resource for interpreting and expressing the information structure of discourse. Some resources that help manage the presentation of information include, for example, prosody, word order, tense-aspect and parallel structures. These forms are used to create **information manage-ment meaning**. In other words, information can be structured to allow us to organize old and new information (i.e., topic/comment), topicalize, emphasize information and provide information symmetry through par-allelism and tense concordance.

For example, consider how word order can emphasize the new infor-mation variation in the following sentences.

1. Liz gave Steve the wine.
2. Liz gave the wine to Steve.

In sentence 1, barring the use of emphatic stress on *Steve*, the object given (the wine) is placed at the end of the sentence in order to signal new or emphasized information in the sentence. This might be in response to a question like: 'What kind of presents were exchanged?' In sentence 2, the recipient (Steve) is now the new or emphasized information and, accord-ingly, is placed at the end of the sentence. This might answer the ques-tion: 'What happened to the remaining bottles of merlot?'

On a pragmatic level, knowledge of information management forms and meanings interacts with coherence conventions to allow us to struc-ture coherent pieces of spoken and written discourse with respect to certain cultural norms, preferences, and expectations. For example, a Japanese student who does not foreground the main theme but only alludes to it may lack knowledge of information management on a prag-matic level. Or students from two different countries might structure a critique of *Madame Bovary* in very different ways. The organizational pattern is not just a question of information structure, but it also invokes a system of principles regarding coherence. Again, this dimension lies well beyond the conventional sense of the linguistic expressions used in the event to a domain of the implied or pragmatic.

Knowledge of interactional form and meaning

Knowledge of **interactional form** enables us to understand and use lin-guistic forms as a resource for understanding and managing talk-in-interaction. These forms include discourse markers and communication management strategies. Discourse markers consist of a set of adverbs, conjunctions and lexicalized expressions used to signal certain language functions. For example, *well* . . . can signal disagreement, *ya know* or *ah-huh* can signal shared knowledge, and *by the way* can signal topic diversion. Conversation-management strategies include a wide range of linguistic forms that serve to facilitate smooth interaction or to repair interaction when communication breaks down. For example, when interaction stops because a learner does not understand something, one person might try to repair the breakdown by asking, *What means that?* Here the learner knows the interactional meaning, but not the form.

Similar to cohesive forms and information management forms, interactional forms use phonological, lexical and morphosyntactic resources to encode **interactional meaning**. For example, in saying *What means that?*, the learner knows how to repair a conversation by asking for clarification, but does not know the form of the request. Other examples of interactional forms and meanings include: backchannel signals such as *ah-huh*, or *right* in English to signal active listening and engagement; lexicalized expressions like *guess what?* and *you know what?* to indicate the initiation of a story sequence; and others such as *Oh my God, I can't believe it! Oh my God, you're kiddin' me!* or in current Valleyspeak, *Shut up!* (with stress on 'shut' and falling intonation on 'up'), commonly used to express surprise.

Although interactional form and meaning are closely associated, it is possible for students to know the form but not the meaning, and vice versa. For example, a student who says *thanks you* to express gratitude or *you welcome* to respond to an expression of gratitude obviously has knowledge of the interactional meanings, but not the forms.

Finally, from a pragmatic perspective, interactional forms and meanings embody a number of implied meanings. Consider the following examples.

Example 1
A: Sorry. I didn't have money to buy the flowers.
B: **Hello** . . .? Today's her birthday. You could'a told me.

Example 2
A: Wow, those kids're really a handful!
B: **Thank you.**

In Example 1, the typical greeting *Hello* in current American slang can be used to criticize the other person for being mindless: 'What were you thinking? Were you awake?' Similarly, *Thank you* in example 2 is not used as an expression of gratitude, but as an expression of criticism of the other person who recognized the problem so late. *Thank you* means 'Now you understand. Why are you aware of this so late?'

Given that many interactional conventions may differ from culture to culture, interactional forms and meanings can embody important pragmatic ascriptions. For example, the discourse markers *ma no* (but no) in Italian or *que no* (that no) in Spanish can be used to disagree strongly, whereas in English expressions like: *no sir, not even,* or *I don't think so* can be used.

Summary

Given the central role that construct definition plays in test development and validation, my intention in this chapter has been to discuss the 'what' of grammatical knowledge invoked by grammar assessment. After describing grammatical constructs and defining key terms in this book, I have proposed a theoretical model of grammatical ability that relates grammatical knowledge to pragmatic knowledge and that specifies grammatical form and meaning on the sentence and discourse levels. I have provided operational descriptions of each part of the model along with examples that differentiate knowledge of grammatical form and meaning from knowledge of pragmatic meaning. This model aims to provide a broad theoretical basis for the definition of grammatical knowledge in creating and interpreting tests of grammatical ability in a variety of language-use settings. In the next chapter, I will discuss how this model can be used to design tasks that measure one or more components of grammatical ability.

CHAPTER FIVE

Designing test tasks to measure L2 grammatical ability

Introduction

In the previous chapters, we saw that performance on grammar tests can be influenced by many other factors besides grammatical ability. In fact, test scores can vary as a result of the personal attributes of test-takers such as their age (Farhady, 1983; Zeidner, 1987), gender (Kunnan, 1990; Sunderland, 1995) and language background (Zeidner, 1986, 1987). They can also fluctuate due to their strategy use (Cohen, 1994; Purpura, 1999), motivation (Gardner, 1985) and level of anxiety (Gardner, Lalonde, Moorcroft and Evans, 1987). However, some of the most important factors that affect grammar-test scores, aside from grammatical ability, are the characteristics of the test itself. In fact, anyone who has ever taken a grammar test, or any test for that matter, knows that the types of questions on the test can severely impact performance. For example, some test-takers perform better on multiple-choice tasks than on oral interview tasks; others do better on essays than on cloze tasks; and still others score better if asked to write a letter than if asked to interpret a graph. Each of these tasks has a set of unique characteristics, called **test-task characteristics**. These characteristics can potentially interact with the characteristics of the examinee (e.g., his or her grammatical knowledge, personal attributes, topical knowledge, affective schemata) to influence test performance. Given the potential impact of test-task characteristics on performance, it is important for test developers to understand the individual characteristics of the tasks they use and to follow systematic procedures for designing and developing tasks that will elicit the best possible manifestations of grammatical ability. If we understand both the nature of grammatical ability and the nature of the test tasks we use, we will be able to account for the effect of method on how we interpret scores on grammar tests. If not, we run the risk of masking the very constructs we wish to measure by factors in performance that are non-linguistic.

Considerable research evidence (e.g., Ong, 1982; Shohamy, 1983) has demonstrated that the methods we use to elicit test performance, otherwise known as **test method**, significantly impacts how test-takers score on tests. Early studies examining the effect of test method on performance viewed 'method' as a holistic activity such as an interview task or a reporting task. For example, Bachman and Palmer (1982) examined whether the variation in scores obtained from speaking and reading tests was due to the examinees' speaking and reading abilities or to the methods used to elicit speaking and reading performance (i.e., an oral interview, a translation task and self-ratings). Unsurprisingly, they found considerable evidence of a **test-method effect** in the data. In other words, the self-ratings they used seemed to be more a measure of the method than of test-takers' underlying abilities, and the interview task appeared to be more a measure of interviewing than of the students' underlying reading ability.

When the individual characteristics of these holistic activities were described, research has again shown a clear interaction between the specific characteristics of the test tasks and test performance. In this regard, Douglas and Selinker (1985, 1993) investigated the effect of manipulating characteristics such as the instructions, vocabulary, contextualization, distribution of information, level of abstraction, topic and genre on test performance, and found that scores on a 'general' test were different from those on the mathematics and chemistry versions of the speaking tests. Differences were also found in the rhetorical structure of the examinee responses as a function of their different fields of study. These results showed that individual test-task characteristics significantly impact performance.

Similarly, Clapham (1996) found that in studying the relationship between certain characteristics of reading passages and reading comprehension, the examinees' reading scores were not adversely affected – as long as the passages did not present information that was overly specific to a particular subject area. However, when they did, the students' background knowledge contributed as much as, if not more than, language ability to the test scores, thereby demonstrating both the effects of manipulating task characteristics on test performance and the role this plays in obtaining accurate assessments.

Given the importance of understanding the nature of test tasks, this chapter is devoted to the notion of 'task' and to the ways in which grammar tasks can be specified in tests to elicit the type of performance we are mainly interested in measuring. This should serve us well in Chapter 6 when we discuss the design and development of whole grammar tests that are made up of several individual test tasks. In this chapter, I will first discuss the role of task in the test-development process. I will then define the notion of task and present a framework for characterizing grammar-test tasks. Finally, using this framework, I will describe several grammar-test tasks in light of their distinctive characteristics.

How does test development begin?

Every grammar-test development project begins with a desire to obtain (and often provide) information about how well a student knows grammar in order to convey meaning in some situation where the target language is used. The information obtained from this assessment then forms the basis for decision-making. Those situations in which we use the target language to communicate in real life or in which we use it for instruction or testing are referred to as the **target language use** (TLU) **situations** (Bachman and Palmer, 1996). Within these situations, the tasks or activities requiring language to achieve a communicative goal are called the **target language use tasks**. A TLU task is one of many language-use tasks that test-takers might encounter in the **target language use domain**. It is to this domain that language testers would like to make inferences about language ability, or more specifically, about grammatical ability.

To illustrate, suppose we wanted to know if a student with two years of English language instruction at a Saudi Air Force Academy has some requisite level of English language proficiency to begin flight school in English. To obtain this information, we give the student a test in which the tasks are based on helicopter flight-training sessions. In other words, one task requires the student to demonstrate his knowledge of the flight controls by answering cause–effect questions (e.g., *What'll happen if you mistakenly move the cyclic to the left?*). The language being tested involves the future tense in conditional sentences used to express cause–effect relationships related to flight control. Based on the results of all the grammar tasks and our interpretation of the scores, we decide whether the student has some criterion level of English language proficiency for flight school.

In this example, the TLU situation is language instruction at flight school, and the assessment purpose is to measure the student's ability to use grammar as a resource for communication in this setting. Among the competencies to be measured, we include the student's ability to use conditional sentences to express cause–effect relationships. One TLU task requires the student to respond to questions about the flight controls. This is one of many TLU tasks that could have been selected from the TLU domain. The decision to permit or deny the student admission into the program is a **high-stakes** decision given the potential seriousness of its consequences. In other words, to permit him to begin flight training with an insufficient command of English could be dangerous, and to delay him from beginning training could cost time and money.

Given the role that TLU tasks play in the assessment of grammatical ability, it is important that we understand how tasks are characterized, especially if we wish to design test tasks that correspond to the types of tasks we might encounter in the TLU situation. Once we identify the characteristics of the TLU tasks, we can then design test tasks. As we will see later, Bachman and Palmer (1996) have proposed a single framework that allows us to characterize both the features of the language-use task and the features of the test task. The correspondence between the features of language-use tasks and those of test tasks is called **test authenticity**. We might expect that the more authentic our test tasks are, the more confident we can be that the inferences we make from test scores will generalize beyond the actual test to the TLU domain.

In developing grammar assessments, we first articulate the purpose(s) of the test, consider the constructs and identify the situational domain(s) in which we would like to make inferences about the test-takers' grammatical ability. For example, do we want to generalize to a real-life domain where students would need to demonstrate their ability to bargain for a souvenir in a Turkish bazaar? Or do we want to generalize to an instructional domain where students need to demonstrate their ability to edit a French essay? Once we have stated a clear purpose (or clear purposes) of the test, considered the constructs and identified several language-use tasks that occur within the TLU domain, we can then select specific language-use tasks from the domain to serve as a basis for test construction.

In considering the constructs and the tasks together, the first major challenge is to define what grammatical knowledge examinees need to have to perform these tasks successfully (i.e., accurately and meaningfully) in situated contexts. In other words, as Mislevy, Steinberg and Almond (2002) might put it, what claims do we wish to make about the test-takers' grammatical knowledge or about their ability to use grammatical knowledge in this situation and what credible evidence can be gathered by means of test tasks and then scored, that can support each claim? The process of defining constructs for tests is called **construct definition**. Before discussing construct definition and test-task design in more detail, let us illustrate these steps with an example.

When I was teaching in the Faculty of Engineering at Kuwait University, an English-medium faculty, we devoted part of the curriculum to the language used to communicate in a chemical engineering context. For the students' midterm exam, we wanted to measure their ability to communicate in grammatically accurate and meaningful ways about topics they might encounter in this setting. The scores on the test would be used to provide **diagnostic information** for helping to identify areas of further instruction, as well as **achievement information** for determining the degree to which students had mastered the course material. Therefore, in the context of an English for chemical engineering class, the target language use domain for the exam was broadly identified as 'the English used in chemical engineering classes', since it consisted of a range of identifiable language-use activities which could be the basis of test tasks and since it was to this domain to which our inferences about grammatical ability were intended to generalize.

Within this TLU domain we could have selected from several possible language-use tasks including describing the physical properties of certain gases and their interactions with other gases, working in groups to conceptualize an experiment, reading instructions and labels, identifying the materials needed for an experiment, describing the steps of an experiment, and describing the causes and effects of certain procedures. In the end, we decided to design a test that measured the students' ability to write a lab report for a first-year chemistry class in a grammatically accurate and meaningful fashion. This decision was taken because writing lab reports was perceived as critical for chemistry classes at the university and was one of the topics covered in language instruction.

I might also add that we wanted to design test tasks to correspond as closely as possible to 'real' lab reports in an attempt to maximize test authenticity. However, it should be noted that the actual goal of this assessment was not to test the students' knowledge of chemistry per se; consequently, the level of technical background knowledge needed to perform test tasks was geared to be far below the presumed conceptual level of the examinees. In short, to the extent possible, we attempted to reduce the effects of background knowledge on test performance by providing technical cues or hints when necessary. In this way, we were able to focus assessment on the grammatical forms and meanings used to communicate in the chemistry lab, and not on knowledge of chemistry.

After identifying the test purpose and selecting test tasks from the TLU domain, the next challenge was to define what specific areas of grammatical knowledge the examinees needed to display in order to write the lab report and to determine how much knowledge they needed to display to support claims of grammatical ability. In short, what claims did we want to make about the students' grammatical ability from this test? Table 5.1 provides a summary of the steps so far.

Although this process is sequential, identifying the TLU domain and areas of grammatical knowledge to be measured does not necessarily have to be done in this order. This is because the specification of language-use tasks and the definition of the constructs we want to measure is recursive and interactive. Thus, we could just as easily have defined the constructs before identifying the TLU domains and tasks. What is essential is that we include both in our procedures.

In the lab-report test, after describing the target language use tasks, we provided theoretical definitions of the underlying constructs we wanted to measure. In specifying the precise area(s) of grammatical knowledge for measurement, we are providing a **theoretical definition** of the test construct. Based on this definition, we are able to determine what kinds of evidence we would need to observe in the test performance to support claims of grammatical ability in this particular context. This definition also allows us to design test tasks to gather the evidence needed to support our claims and, just as importantly, to examine if our test actually measures what we say it does. In other words, we are able to investigate the **construct validity** of the test by providing empirical evidence that justifies both the claims we make about what examinees know and the inferences we wish to make from the test scores (Mislevy, 1995; Mislevy, Steinberg and Almond, 2002).

There are several ways of making explicit the exact nature of grammatical ability we wish to measure in a theoretical definition. We can derive the theoretical definition of constructs from an overarching theory of grammatical knowledge such as the one presented in Chapter 4. We can also base our definition on a course syllabus, on a language textbook (e.g., *the test will be on chapters one through four*) or on a set of course

Table 5.1 *Lab-report example: initial steps in test-task development*

Steps	Description
• Identify the test purpose(s), the use of the test results, and the potential impact of the test on test-takers and on further instructions	• To measure students' ability to communicate in grammatical and meaningful ways (in a chemistry lab context) • To determine areas of further instruction • To determine degree of course mastery • Medium stakes – midterm grade and diagnostic feedback
• Identify the target language use domain	• English for Engineering (chemical engineering part)
• Identify a range of language use tasks from the target language use domain	• Read instructions and labels • Compare and contrast the physical properties of gases • Write a lab report based on a lab experiment • Hypothesize alternative outcomes
• Select the target language use task(s) for this test	• Write a lab report based on an experiment • Describe lab materials, procedures and cause/effect relationships

• Define the constructs to be measured (i.e., the claims we want to make about what test-takers know and/or can do) by identifying the areas of grammatical knowledge (meanings and forms) needed to complete the task	• Understand the prompt
	• Write a valid and relevant response to the task that is grammatically accurate and meaningful
	• Describe lab materials by using:
	  • noun compounding (test tube)
	• Describe procedures by using:
	  • active and passive voice
	  • logical connectors (chronology, conclusion)
	• Describe cause/effect relationships by using:
	  • *when-* and *if*-clauses
	• Speculate outcomes
	  • modals of logical probability (may, must)
	  • adverbs of probability (probably, most likely)

objectives. Finally, a combination of these methods can be used to define the areas of grammatical knowledge to be included in a test.

In providing a theoretical definition for the test, let us use the model of grammatical knowledge presented in Chapter 4 as a basis for identifying and making explicit the areas of grammatical knowledge to be measured, as seen in Figure 5.1.

On the lab-report test, we would like to make inferences about the students' ability to use lexical forms ('noun + noun' compounding –

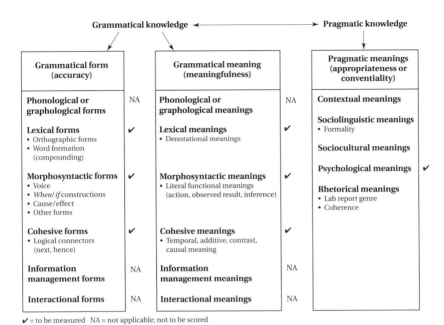

Figure 5.1   Areas of grammatical knowledge for the lab report

litmus paper) and their associated meanings to describe the materials in the experiment. We would also like to make inferences about their ability to use a variety of morphosyntactic forms (e.g., present active and voice, cause–effect statements with *when* and *if)* to express literal meanings while describing the procedures in the experiment and the results of taking certain actions. Finally, inferences could be made about the students' ability to use cohesive forms (e.g., logical connectors) to signal chronology (e.g., *next*), conclusion (e.g., *hence*) and so forth. By stating these components of grammatical knowledge, we are providing a theoretical definition of the construct.

In most classroom testing contexts, the definition of test constructs is relatively straightforward – we test what we teach. In other words, the theoretical definition of our constructs derives from a textbook, syllabus, set of objectives, substantive theory, or any combination of these. However, in instances of language use where the areas of grammatical knowledge are not so clearly identified or described, the job of identifying and defining test constructs becomes much more complicated. For example, how do we define grammatical ability in the context of middle-school children in a social studies class in an ESL environment? Or even primary school children at play during recess? Or what is the nature of grammatical ability in nursing contexts in Australian hospitals? In these cases, we would need to spend time identifying what components of grammatical knowledge examinees need to know to communicate accurately and meaningfully in these real-life language-use domains. This information requires some form of preliminary **needs analysis** to determine the specific characteristics of language use in these contexts. A needs analysis focusing on the language needed to communicate in some TLU situation involves both the gathering of data from the target language use domain (e.g., samples of lab reports) and the analysis of these data from a language-needs perspective spelled out in grammatical terms (e.g., morphosyntactic forms, cohesive forms, literal meanings) or pragmatic terms (e.g., rhetorical structure – chronological organization). In sum, the definition of grammatical ability as it relates to the test purposes, the target language use domain, and the target language use tasks is an essential preliminary step to the specification of test tasks.

Once the grammatical constructs have been defined, we need to consider what types of evidence and how much of it examinees would need to supply in order to demonstrate that they have grammatical ability. To determine this, we could list the claims we want to make in one column and the types of evidence we would need to see to support each claim in another. For example, if we claim that in order to write a lab report examinees needed to have grammatical ability, the evidence associated with this claim might involve the accurate and meaningful use of the past tense, the past passive tense, and logical connectors of chronology and result, and if we claim that pragmatic knowledge defined in terms of rhetorical structure is needed, the evidence associated with this claim might involve the appropriate (i.e., coherent) ordering of the sentences.

Once we know the kinds of evidence we need to observe, we can then design, develop and score the test tasks so as to put the test to operational use. The process of designing tasks to elicit concrete samples of performance to reflect the underlying claims about the constructs, and the process of deciding how to measure or score the responses, is called **operationalization**. In making explicit the kinds of test tasks used to measure the claims about the constructs and in articulating the scoring procedures, we are providing an **operational definition** of the construct. In other words, operationalization lays out a plan for how the test will actually look, and it specifies the individual features of each test task. These steps are summarized in Table 5.2.

Table 5.2 *Lab-report example: further steps in test-task development*

| Steps | Description | |
	Claims	Evidence
• Identify the types of evidence students would need to supply to demonstrate support for the claims we would like to make about what relevant test-takers know and/or can do	• The response demonstrates an understanding of chemistry • The response displays grammatical knowledge (grammatical form and grammatical meaning) • The response displays pragmatic knowledge (rhetorical control – the ability to sequence the steps and outcomes)	• Information in the response is complete, valid and relevant • The response is accurate with respect to the noun compounds, active and passive voice sentences, logical connectors, *when-* clauses and modals • The language conveys a range of literal meanings • The report is coherent and well-organized
• Identify how much of the evidence is needed to support claims about the constructs at different levels of ability (performance levels)	• Specify what constitutes full credit, partial credit and no credit	
• Operationalize test tasks to supply the evidence needed to support claims of grammatical ability, and determine how these tasks will be scored	• Specify test-task characteristics (e.g., the instructions, time allotment, the input, the expected response, the scoring method and so forth)	

An initial step in the operationalization of test constructs is the **specification of test tasks**. This is a process of identifying and describing the characteristics of the individual test tasks. It is also a process of comparing how target language use tasks and test tasks compare. Before we can write test specifications, we need to be familiar with the characteristics of tasks. In the rest of the chapter, I will first discuss the notion of 'task', I will then present a framework for characterizing test tasks. In the next chapter, I will continue the discussion on how to construct an entire grammar test.

What do we mean by 'task'?

The notion of 'task' in language-learning contexts has been conceptualized in many different ways over the years. Traditionally, 'task' has referred to *any* activity that requires students to *do* something for the intent purpose of *learning* the target language. A task then is any activity (i.e., short answers, role-plays) as long as it involves a linguistic or non-linguistic (circle the answer) response to input. Traditional learning or teaching tasks are characterized as having an intended pedagogical purpose – which may or may not be made explicit; they have a set of instructions that control the kind of activity to be performed; they contain input (e.g., questions); and they elicit a response. More recently, learning tasks have been characterized more in terms of their communicative goals, their success in eliciting interaction and negotiation of meaning, and their ability to engage learners in complex meaning-focused activities (Nunan, 1989, 1993; Berwick, 1993; Skehan, 1998).

In a discussion of the degree to which pedagogical tasks are successful in eliciting the specific grammatical structures under investigation, Loschky and Bley-Vroman (1993) identified three types of grammar-to-task relationships. The first involves **task-naturalness**, a condition where 'a grammatical construction may arise naturally during the performance of a particular task, but the task can often be performed perfectly well, even quite easily, without it' (p. 132). For example, in a task designed to elicit past modals in the context of a murder mystery, we expect forms like: *the butler could have done it* or *the maid might have killed her*, but we might get forms like: *Maybe the butler did it* or *I suspect the maid killed her*. The second condition is **task-utility**, where 'it is possible to complete the task [meaningfully] without the structure, but with the structure the task becomes easier' (ibid.). For example, in a comparison task, I once had a student say: **Shiraz is beautiful city, but Esfahan is very, very, very, beautiful city in Iran.* Had he known the comparatives or the superlatives, his message could have been communicated much more easily. The final and most interesting condition for grammar assessment entails **task-essentialness**. This is where the task cannot be completed *unless* the grammatical form is used. For example, in a task intended to distinguish stative from dynamic adjectives, the student would need to know the difference between *I'm really bored* and *I'm really boring* in order to complete the task. Obviously task essentialness is the most difficult, yet the most desirable condition to meet in the construction of grammar tasks.

The notion of task in language tests has also been the subject of much

discussion among language testers given the role that task plays in eliciting samples of performance designed to reflect test constructs. In the
early 1980s, a task in the language testing research was generally treated
as, what Bachman (1990b) termed, a 'monolithic whole'. In other words,
tasks such as a dictation or essay were viewed as holistic entities, where
the individual characteristics of these activities (e.g., types of instructions, stimulus) were virtually ignored. This position, however, provided
no accounting of the different ways in which individual task characteristics might affect performance. For example, a multiple-choice grammar
task could be based on an image, a sentence or a passage, each with a
potentially different impact on performance. For this reason, tasks in language testing are now seen as an aggregation of characteristics, which can
vary on several dimensions.

Addressing the notion of 'communicative tasks' in language testing,
Rea-Dickins (1991) argued that grammar tasks should minimally provide
a realistic situation in which test-takers need to exchange information in
order to complete the task. She specified five design characteristics that
could contribute to the communicative nature of the task. These include
(1) the contextualization of the test items, (2) the identification of a communicative purpose, (3) the identification of interlocutors, (4) instructions that focus on meaning rather than forms and (5) the opportunity for
'the test-taker to create his/her own messages and to produce grammatical responses as appropriate to a given context' (p. 125).

More recently, the notion of task, especially as it relates to task-based
language instruction and assessment, has taken on a much more specific
meaning. Tasks in this literature (e.g., Robinson and Ross, 1996; Norris,
2001) refer to activities that elicit communicative performances similar to
those occurring in some non-test or 'real-life' situation. Good performance is then judged according to criteria that involve the degree to
which examinees have achieved the communicative goal of a specific
task.

In my view, this notion of task is somewhat limiting for grammatical
assessment for two reasons. First, task is seen purely in terms of real-life
situations in which the target language is used to achieve some communicative goal through language-based interaction, which can be judged
'successful' if the communicative goal is achieved. Among the many possible test activities, only those meeting the stated criteria embody the
notion of task. Activities designed to develop an awareness of grammatical forms or to promote the comprehension or internalization of forms
are not considered tasks because they might not involve interpersonal

communication or might not be embedded in 'real-life' contexts. In grammar testing, however, interaction is not necessarily the goal of every task. In fact, all sorts of tasks from the instructional domain focus on grammatical forms or meanings, and not on the co-construction of meaning in interaction. Finally, a real-life context in grammar assessment might be a desirable goal, but it is hardly a prerequisite for potential benefit.

Secondly, in task-based assessment, the emphasis is on the accomplishment of a task or **task fulfillment** (i.e., performance) rather than on the capacity to use grammatical knowledge in some context (grammatical ability). This is, as Bachman (2000) reminds us, similar to defining the construct according to what examinees can do in a *single* instance of communication rather than what they know, or have the capacity to do, in *any* instance of communication. For this reason, Bachman (2000) argues convincingly for an integrated approach to test development – one that involves a consideration of both the constructs being measured, the characteristics of the tasks being tested, and the integration of the two.

In my opinion, grammar tasks need to incorporate a broad range of procedures designed to elicit features of the TLU domain, no matter if that domain is instructional in nature, allowing for the assessment of discrete elements of a test-taker's grammatical knowledge, or if the domain revolves around real-life contexts that provide opportunities for the assessment of grammatical ability in interaction. In this regard, Bachman and Palmer's (1996) depiction of 'language use task' as 'an activity that involves individuals in using language for the purpose of achieving a particular goal or objective in a particular situation' (p. 44) is broad enough to encompass instances of language use, where the ability to use grammar in interaction is the sole object of observation, or where the goal of assessment is to provide more discrete information on a student's knowledge of grammar. As a result, **grammatical test task** in this book is defined as any activity designed to elicit scorable grammatical performance within a TLU domain, where without the requisite knowledge or ability the test-taker would not be able to complete the task successfully.

In an attempt to understand variation in test performance as a result of task, several testers have provided frameworks for characterizing tasks. The most comprehensive and generalizable of these to date is that proposed by Bachman and Palmer (1996). Building on Bachman's (1990b) characterization of test method facets, they relate performance on test tasks to instances of language use, and describe how test tasks can be drawn from TLU tasks as samples of the TLU domain. They describe two types of TLU domain: real-life and language-instruction. In **real-life domains**, language is used as a resource for transaction and negotiated interaction; in **language-instruction domains**, language is used in the context of language learning, whether that involves interaction or not. Let us now examine the individual characteristics of tasks.

What are the characteristics of grammatical test tasks?

As the goal of grammar assessment is to provide as useful a measurement as possible of our students' grammatical ability, we need to design test tasks in which the variability of our students' scores is attributed to the differences in their grammatical ability, and not to uncontrolled or irrelevant variability resulting from the types of tasks or the quality of the tasks that we have put on our tests. As all language teachers know, the kinds of tasks we use in tests and their quality can greatly influence how students will perform. Therefore, given the role that the effects of task characteristics play on performance, we need to strive to manage (or at least understand) the effects of task characteristics so that they will function the way we designed them to – as measures of the constructs we want to measure (Douglas, 2000). In other words, specifically designed tasks will work to produce the types of variability in test scores that can be attributed to the underlying constructs given the contexts in which they were measured (Tarone, 1998). To understand the characteristics of test tasks better, we turn to Bachman and Palmer's (1996) framework for analyzing target language use tasks and test tasks.

The Bachman and Palmer framework

Bachman and Palmer's (1996) framework of task characteristics represents the most recent thinking in language assessment of the potential relationships between task characteristics and test performance. In this framework, they outline five general aspects of tasks, each of which is characterized by a set of distinctive features. These five aspects describe characteristics of (1) the setting, (2) the test rubrics, (3) the input, (4) the expected response and (5) the relationship between the input and response. This framework can be used to (1) describe the TLU tasks as a basis for designing test tasks; (2) specify the test tasks; and (3) compare

Table 5.3 *Task characteristics for tests of grammatical ability*

Characteristics of the setting
Physical characteristics   Time of task
Participants

Characteristics of the test rubrics
Instructions   **Time allotment**
Language (native, target)
Channel (aural, visual)   **Scoring method**
Specification of procedures and tasks   Criteria for correctness
       Procedures for scoring the responses
Structure   Explicitness of criteria and procedures
Number, salience, and sequence of
    part/tasks
Number of tasks/items per part

Characteristics of the input
Format   **Language characteristics**
Channel (aural, visual)   • Grammatical knowledge (form,
Form (language, non-language, both)   meaning)
Language (native, target, both)   • Pragmatic knowledge (contextual,
Length (short, long)   sociolinguistic, sociocultural,
Type (item, prompt)   psychological and rhetorical)
Degree of speededness (speeded,
    non-speeded)   **Topical characteristics**
Vehicle ('live', 'reproduced', both)
       Strategic characteristics
       • Metacognitive and cognitive strategies

Characteristics of the expected response
Format   **Language characteristics**
Channel (aural, visual)   • Grammatical knowledge (form,
Form (language, non-language, both)   meaning)
Language (native, target, both)   • Pragmatic knowledge (contextual,
Length (short, long)   sociolinguistic, sociocultural,
Type (selected, limited production,   psychological and rhetorical)
    extended production)
Degree of speededness (speeded,   **Topical characteristics**
    non-speeded)
       Strategic characteristics
       • Metacognitive and cognitive strategies

Relationship between the input and response
Reactivity (reciprocal, non-reciprocal,   Directness of relationship (direct,
    adaptive)   indirect)
Scope of relationship (broad, narrow)

---

the characteristics of the TLU tasks with the test tasks (p. 47). Table 5.3 presents a slightly modified version of the framework as it might apply to the assessment of grammatical ability. I will describe only some of the more relevant characteristics. For further information, see Bachman and Palmer (1996).

Characteristics of the setting

The characteristics of the setting include the physical characteristics, the participants, and the time of the task. Obviously these characteristics can have a serious, unexpected effect on performance. For example, I once gave a speaking test to a group of ESL students in my discussion skills class at UCLA. I randomly placed students into groups of four, and each was given a problem to solve. Individuals then had to participate in a discussion in which they had to try to persuade their partners of their opinion. Each group's 20-minute discussion was videotaped. After the exam, I learned that a few students were so nervous being videotaped that they seriously questioned the quality of their performance. I also learned that, in one group, a participant became angry when the others did not agree with her and openly told them their ideas were 'stupid'. She also berated them for being quiet. The other students were so embarrassed they hardly said a word. In such a case, one participant had an undue effect on the others' ability to perform their best.

Characteristics of the test rubrics

The test rubrics include the instructions, the overall structure of the test, the time allotment and the method used to score the response. These characteristics can obviously influence test scores in unexpected ways (Madden, 1982; Cohen, 1984, 1993).

The **overall test instructions** (when included) introduce test-takers to the entire test. They make explicit the purpose of the overall test and the area(s) of language ability being measured. They also introduce examinees to the different parts of the test and their relative importance. The instructions make explicit the procedures for taking the entire test. Overall test instructions are common in all high-stakes tests.

The **test-task instructions** introduce test-takers to the task and make explicit the procedures for completing it. They often involve the purpose, an indication of the areas of grammatical ability being tested, the scoring method, and the recommended time allotment. Bachman and Palmer (1996) characterize test instructions by the degree to which the procedures and tasks are clearly and explicitly specified. In my opinion, this is determined by the degree to which test-takers readily understand what it is they are asked to do. If *anyone* has misunderstood or takes too long to understand, there may be a problem. In some cases, clarity is greatly enhanced by an example. Given the importance of understanding test instructions, they are sometimes given in the students' native language.

Although there is no single 'good' way of writing instructions, many textbooks on language testing (e.g., Bachman and Palmer, 1996; Hughes, 2003) have provided useful guidelines. For further ideas on how to write clear and concise instructions, novice test developers should also examine the instructions in already-published tests or in language textbooks as potential models.

A second characteristic of the test rubrics, the **structure**, makes explicit the number of parts or tasks, the salience and sequence of these parts or tasks, their relative importance in the overall test and the number of tasks or items per part. Each of these characteristics may in some way influence the test-taker's perception of the test and his or her performance.

Another important characteristic of the test rubric is the time allotted for the candidate to complete the task. A grammar test can be designed to be **speeded**, where tasks are all at about the same level of difficulty, and not all test-takers are expected to have the time to answer all the items. Speeded grammar-test tasks measure both grammatical knowledge and the ability to respond quickly; however, it is unclear what the addition of a time-pressure factor adds to the measurement of grammatical ability. In fact, it is likely that the addition of time pressure would confound the measurement of grammatical ability, even though Ellis (2001b) recommends the use of 'a time pressure factor as a practical way of measuring implicit knowledge' (p. 260).

Furthermore, in eliciting feedback on tests from test-takers, I have found it extremely difficult to gauge whether and for whom a test is speeded. The perception of speededness is individualistic, and I have found that, although examinees might have sufficient time to finish, many still perceive the test as speeded, which might, in turn, have significantly increased their anxiety and adversely influenced their performance, thereby further confounding the scores. According to Bachman (1990b), speeded test scores are partially derived from the examinees' ability and partially from their ability to complete the test quickly. They might also be derived from the test-takers' ability to cope with anxiety. If the goal of assessment is to measure an examinee's implicit (i.e., fully automatized) knowledge of grammar, we must set up tasks, as Blau (1990) suggests, that allow test-takers to engage in naturally paced, real-time interaction. This involves a complex system of continuous turn-taking that by its very nature constrains the processing. In this way, the likelihood is much greater that we will be tapping into an examinee's implicit knowledge of grammar. It still may also be the case that certain features of a test-taker's grammatical knowledge are still an artifact of declarative rather than proceduralized knowledge.

Finally, the test rubric includes the characteristics of the **scoring method**, or the ways in which responses are evaluated, and numbers assigned to responses. The scoring method includes the criteria used to judge the correctness of responses, the procedures for scoring the responses and the explicitness with which examinees are told how scores are determined.

An explicit description of the criteria used to judge test responses allows test-takers to understand what constitutes 'good' performance. For example, if students are told that their essays will be judged on grammatical accuracy, they are more likely to pay attention to accuracy. For greater alignment between assessment and instruction, the criteria used to judge performance should be an integral part of the learning space.

The scoring method specifies the procedures for scoring responses, a characteristic that can obviously have an enormous impact on test scores. There are essentially two ways in which test tasks are scored: adding up the scores for a task or providing a rating. Let us consider each. A multiple-choice grammar test might be designed to measure one feature of grammatical knowledge. It therefore contains one criterion for correctness. This item could be scored as either right or wrong according to an **answer key**. This **right/wrong scoring** method is clear and objective. Correct answers get one point; incorrect ones get none.

If we wanted to capture more precise information from test-taker responses, we could then assign some credit for partially correct answers. Adopting a **partial-credit scoring** method would provide test users with more precise information about the test-takers' specific strengths and weaknesses, and it would give credit for partial mastery of the feature. Imagine, for example, that we wished to measure the form and meaning of past tense verbs in English. We give students a dialogue with missing verbs and ask them to fill in the blanks. Since we have two criteria for correctness (form and meaning), we can assign two right/wrong scores for each item. For example, if an examinee put the correct answer *went (to . . .)*, he would get full credit (two points) or one point for the correct past tense form and one for the correct meaning. If he put **goed*, he would get partial credit (zero points for form and one for meaning). He would also get partial credit (one point for form and zero for meaning) if he wrote *left*. He would get no credit if he put *leave*.

Similarly, we could adopt another partial-credit scoring method in a situation in which we were interested in taking development into consideration in the way we defined the construct. We could give the full credit (1.0) for the selection of an interlanguage form that is completely 'target-like'. For example, if an item were designed to measure the past tense form and the test-taker chose *went*, he or she would get the **full credit** of one point. If, however, the test-taker chose **goed*, his or her response would show some development – overgeneralization of the past tense marker, and thus earn a score of 0.5. Finally, if the test-taker chose *go* or *going*, he or she would get no credit. We will discuss partial-credit scoring techniques in much more detail in Chapter 6.

The scoring process used to measure grammatical ability in larger pieces of spoken and written texts can potentially effect a change in performance to an even greater extent than with multiple-choice tasks. Will grammatical ability be scored by one or two raters? Will it be scored alongside other components of language ability as one global or holistic score? Or will grammatical ability be given as a separate score in addition to scores for the other components of language ability?

Essays or oral interviews are typically scored with reference to a **rating scale**. Rating scales provide a means for judging the quality of performance in terms of different levels of ability. They can be derived from theoretical definitions of the constructs to be measured or can be based empirically on data from samples of test performance (McNamara, 1996), or they can draw on both. Grammatical rating scales consist of a set of numbered categories, usually between three and ten, that represent distinct levels of grammatical ability. Each level is associated with a set of descriptors in terms of the areas of grammatical ability to be assessed. **Holistic rating scales** provide only one global rating of grammatical ability for the entire task. This is called **holistic scoring**.

Table 5.4 presents the 1991 version of the language rating scale of the *UCLA ESL Placement Exam* (ESLPE) composition rubric. This holistic rating scale is a measure of both grammatical knowledge (form and meaning) and pragmatic knowledge (sociolinguistic meanings conveyed through academic register).

Table 5.4 *UCLA ESLPE rating scale for language* (Revised version
September 1991)

	Descriptors for language (grammar, vocabulary, register, mechanics)
9–10	
a)	Except for rare minor errors (esp. articles), the grammar is native-like.
b)	There is an effective balance of simple and complex sentence patterns with co-ordination and subordination.
c)	Excellent, near-native academic vocabulary and register. Few problems with word choice.
7–8	
a)	Minor errors in articles, verb agreement, word form, verb form (tense, aspect) and no incomplete sentences. Meaning is never obscured and there is a clear grasp of English sentence structure.
b)	There is usually a good balance of simple and complex sentences, both appropriately constructed.
c)	Generally, there is appropriate use of academic vocabulary and register with some errors in word choice OR writing is fluent and native-like but lacks appropriate academic register and sophisticated vocabulary.
5–6	
a)	Errors in article use and verb agreement, and several errors in verb form and/or word form. May be some incomplete sentences. Errors almost never obscure meaning.
b)	Either too many simple sentences or complex ones that are too long to process.
c)	May be frequent errors with word choice; vocabulary is inaccurate or imprecise. Register lacks proper levels of sophistication.
3–4	
a)	Several errors in all areas of grammar, which often interfere with communication, although there is knowledge of basic sentence structure.
b)	No variation in sentence structure.
c)	Frequent errors in word choice (i.e., wrong word, not simply vague or informal word). Register is inappropriate for academic writing.
1–2	
a)	There are problems not only with verb formation, articles and incomplete sentences, but sentence construction is so poor that sentences are often incomprehensible.
b)	Sentences that are comprehensible are extremely simple constructions.
c)	Vocabulary too simple to express meaning and/or severe errors in word choice.
OR	Not enough material to evaluate.

Analytic rating scales provide separate ratings from each component of grammatical ability to be measured. This is called **analytic scoring.** We will discuss scoring method and rating scales in much more detail in Chapter 6. Table 5.5 presents an example of an analytic rating scale for grammatical knowledge (form and meaning).

Considerable research in language testing has examined the effects of scoring method on performance (see McNamara, 1996). For example, McNamara (1990) found that when highly skilled ESL teachers were trained to use a six-point analytic rubric to score speaking ability, control of linguistic features (i.e., grammar and cohesion) accounted for 60% of the shared variance, whereas comprehension of the input, appropriateness of the language, and mechanics (spelling and punctuation) accounted for much less. In other words, it appears that the raters' perception of morphosyntactic and lexical accuracy most influenced their judgment of overall communicative effectiveness. In short, one rater might judge one aspect of grammatical form (e.g., articles) more harshly than he or she does another; one rater might judge the grammar in one task type (e.g., essay) more harshly than he or she does in another; or nonnative speaker raters might judge the grammatical performance of examinees who come from their own language background more harshly than they do examinees from other language backgrounds. These systematic interactions between scoring method and test performance often produce biased and unreliable scores.

Several testers (e.g., Alderson, Clapham and Wall, 1995; Weigle, 2002), however, have cited ways of minimizing these sources of bias and unreliability. Some of these ways include (1) using a clear and detailed scoring rubric; (2) training the raters; (3) using samples of performance in the rater training session that exemplify the different points on the rubric; (4) scoring performance independently by two raters, with a third to adjudicate in the case of large discrepancies between raters; and (5) monitoring rater performance and providing raters with constructive feedback.

Characteristics of the input

According to Bachman and Palmer (1996), the characteristics of the input (sometimes called the stimulus) are critical features of performance in all test and TLU tasks. The input is the part of the task that test-takers must process in order to answer the question. It is characterized in terms of the format and language.

Table 5.5 *Analytic rating scale for grammatical ability*

Levels of control	Form	Meaning
Complete **(5)**	• Evidence of complete range of grammatical forms including lexical forms (noun + noun construction), morphosyntactic forms (past, past passive, *when*-clauses) and cohesive forms (chronology, result) for the task. • Evidence of complete accuracy in these forms; may have minor random errors, but never obscuring meaning.	• The message is completely and clearly conveyed. • Evidence of a wide range of and precise use of vocabulary for the task.
Extensive **(4)**	• Evidence of extensive range of grammatical forms including lexical, morphosyntactic and cohesive forms for the task. • Evidence of good accuracy in these forms; may have some errors, but meaning is never obscured.	• The message is generally well and clearly conveyed. • Evidence of a wide range of vocabulary for the task. May have some errors in word choice.
Moderate **(3)**	• Evidence of moderate range of grammatical forms including lexical, morphosyntactic and cohesive forms for the task. • Evidence of satisfactory accuracy in these forms; has some errors in form. Errors almost never obscure meaning.	• The message is adequately conveyed with some ambiguities. • Evidence of some problems with vocabulary choice for the task. May be incomplete or imprecise for the task.
Limited **(2)**	• Evidence of limited range of grammatical forms including lexical, morphosyntactic and cohesive forms for the task. • Evidence of errors in several target forms; has some errors in form. Errors sometimes obscure meaning.	• The message is sometimes confusing. • Evidence of frequent problems with vocabulary choice for the task. May be incomplete or imprecise for the task.
None **(1)**	• Evidence of very limited range of grammatical forms for the task. • Evidence of serious errors in form. Errors often obscure meaning. • Not enough material to evaluate.	• The message is barely conveyed or not at all. • Evidence of simple vocabulary; problems with vocabulary choice.

The format of the input involves several features. The input of a grammar task can be in the examinee's native language (e.g., a translation task) or in the target language; it can be linguistic or non-linguistic; it can be aural or visual; and it can be 'live', 'reproduced', or both. The input can also differ in length, ranging from a single word to extended discourse. For example, test input that contains complex sentences with several subordinate clauses would be expected to have a significant effect on performance, especially with low-ability students.

The type of test input used to elicit performance is also a critical feature of the task. This characteristic is directly responsible for eliciting samples of performance which display the types of grammar we want to observe and measure. The test input can be in the form of an item or a prompt. An **item** is a focused stimulus designed to elicit a response that requires examinees to select from two or more alternatives or a response that requires a limited amount of language production (e.g., a gap fill-in). A **prompt** is a stimulus designed to elicit an extended amount of language production (e.g., a dialogue). Test developers should be concerned both with the extent to which the test input actually elicits the performance samples they wish to observe, and with the degree to which these samples support the claims they wish to make about what test-takers know. In other words, to what degree do the tasks exhibit the qualities of naturalness, utility or essentialness with grammar produced by examinees?

In an effort to investigate the relationships between test input and the type of language functions elicited by the graph question in the *Test of Spoken English* (TSE Program Office, 1995), Lazaraton and Wagner (1996) found that the graph prompt elicited *only* a description of the graphic information at a 20–performance band (the lowest on a scale from 20 to 60), while at the 30 band it elicited a description and speculations, but the speculations were not performed accurately. At the 40 and 50 bands, the graph task elicited descriptions and, with some candidates, it elicited opinions. It also elicited speculations, but again they were not performed accurately. Finally, at the 60–band level, it elicited descriptions, speculations and sometimes opinions – all of which were performed accurately. This study clearly showed how the task input was effective in eliciting qualitatively different types of language at several ability levels. Questions remains, however, as to the degree to which the other questions also elicit a clear, specifiable hierarchy of ability.

Finally, the language used to deliver the input is critical and involves both language and topical characteristics. The language characteristics embody the grammatical and pragmatic components of the language.

The topical characteristics of the input refer to the range of topics that the input could encompass and the degree to which these topics tap into the examinees' topical knowledge. Both aspects of the input obviously influence performance.

Characteristics of the expected response

When we design a test task, we specify the rubric and input so that test-takers will respond in a way that will enable us to make inferences about the aspect of grammar ability we want to measure. The 'expected response' thus refers to the type of grammatical performance we want to elicit. The characteristics of the expected response are also considered in terms of the format and language. Similar to the input, the expected response of grammar tasks can vary according to channel (aural or visual), form (verbal, non-verbal), language (native or target) and vehicle (live or reproduced).

With regard to speededness, the expected response can also be designed to have a time pressure. As we have seen, this adds a confounding element to the measurement of grammatical ability. In other cases, time can be used for planning a response in order to elicit a more deliberate and planned response. In this case, the claim is that both explicit and implicit knowledge of grammar will be measured. According to Skehan (1998), when test-takers are given more planning time, they have more processing time to focus on fluency, complexity or accuracy. Skehan (1998) also speculates that 'planning, most of the time will predispose learners to try out "cutting edge" language, or to be pushed to express more complex ideas' (p. 74).

The type of expected response is a critical characteristic of test and language-use tasks in that it is directly responsible for displaying samples of the types of grammar we would like to observe and measure. Three types of expected responses can be specified. One type requires test-takers to *select* the response from two or more response alternatives. These are called **selected-response tasks**, and they are designed to measure an examinee's ability to recognize the correct, best or most appropriate answer.

A second type requires test-takers to *construct* a response by saying or writing anything from a word to an extended piece of discourse. Tasks that require a constructed response are referred to generally as **constructed-response tasks**. As these tasks can vary in length, it is useful to differentiate between two types of constructed responses. Constructed response requiring examinees to say or write anywhere from a word to a sentence are called **limited-production tasks** (e.g., sentence-completion task). Finally, constructed responses requiring test-takers to say or write more than two or three sentences are called **extended-production tasks** (e.g., an essay). The responses to test tasks provide evidence of the claims and constitute what will be scored and evaluated for correctness. They are thus the part of the task from which inferences about grammatical ability will be made.

The expected response can also be characterized in terms of its language and topical characteristics. The language characteristics are of most concern for grammatical assessment to the extent that they involve one or more areas of grammatical knowledge. The topical characteristics of the expected response refer to the topics, themes or subject matter that are communicated in grammar use. According to Bachman and Palmer (1996), 'the topical knowledge of language users is always involved in language use' and 'will always be a factor in test performance' (p. 120). Language testers must try to understand the role that the topical characteristics of the expected response play on grammatical performance.

Traditionally, language testers have argued that the effects of test-takers' topical knowledge on the test score variation should be minimized. In other words, the examinee's topical knowledge was seen as a potential source of test bias. This may be true in cases where we wish to make inferences about the grammatical ability *alone*, and not about topical knowledge. This is also true in cases where examinees are unable to display their grammatical ability because of a lack of topical knowledge. For example, if we wanted to measure the use of causatives in a group of ten-year-old ESL students, and we presented them with a task in which they had to discuss their plans for remodeling an apartment (e.g., *I'll get a plumber to put in a new sink*), we are likely to obtain poor performance samples due to the students' lack of topical information. From a measurement perspective, we would be unable to determine if the low test scores were due to their knowledge of the causatives or their knowledge of remodeling apartments. Obviously, test developers must be sensitive to the topical knowledge required to complete tasks; otherwise, we might inadvertently introduce topical bias into the assessment.

At other times, however, we wish to make inferences about both the test-takers' grammatical ability and their topical knowledge. For example, suppose we wanted to assess the ability of English-speaking engineering students in Quebec to use French to discuss the feasibility of constructing a parking garage. We could present them with a writing prompt in which the parameters of the garage were explained. Their job would be to write a feasibility report for the project. The engineers would need to use grammatically accurate and meaningful language (aspects of grammatical knowledge) to describe the advantages and disadvantages of building the garage (aspects of topical knowledge). We could then devise separate scoring rubrics for evaluating their grammatical ability and their topical knowledge. In this case, topical knowledge is not seen as a source of potential test bias, but as a fundamental part of the language-use domain.

Relationship between the input and response

A final category of task characteristics to consider in examining how test tasks impact performance is seen in how characteristics of the input can interact with characteristics of the response. One characteristic of this relationship involves 'the extent to which the input or the response affects subsequent input and responses' (Bachman and Palmer, 1996, p. 55). This is known as **reactivity. Reciprocal tasks**, which involve both interaction and feedback between two or more examinees, are examples of tasks that have a high degree of reactivity. However, **non-reciprocal tasks**, such as writing in a journal, have no reactivity since no interaction or feedback is required to complete the task. Finally, in **adaptive test tasks** there is no feedback, but there is interaction in the sense that the responses influence subsequent language use. For example, in computer adaptive tests such as the *BEST Plus* (Center for Applied Linguistics, 2002), students are presented with test questions tailored to their ability level. In other words, as the student responds to input, subsequent input is tailored to their proficiency level. In this respect, the input is adaptive since one response affects subsequent input, but no feedback is supplied to the examinee.

The relationship between the task input and the response can also be described in terms of the **scope** of the input that must be processed to supply the intended response. If the test-taker must respond to a great deal of input such as in a lecture or a reading passage, the scope between the input and response is **broad**. If the input involves only a sentence of processing, such as in a multiple-choice grammar task, the scope is **narrow**. Obviously, the degree of scope can have an effect on performance.

Finally, the relationship between the input and response can be direct or indirect. If the response is based primarily on information in the input, the relationship between the input and response is **direct**. If, however, the response cannot be based on the input, but rather needs other kinds of topical or pragmatic information, the relationship between the input and response is characterized as **indirect**.

Bachman and Palmer's (1996) framework of task characteristics provides a comprehensive means of describing language use and test tasks, thereby allowing us to consider individual characteristics of tasks in order to highlight the potential interactions between test method and test performance. In developing test tasks, we need to be sensitive to these interactions. Finally, this framework allows us to examine the degree to which language-use tasks correspond to test tasks and the degree to which we are justified in claiming that score-based inferences about grammatical ability can generalize to non-test-taking instances of language use.

In the next section, I will discuss specific grammar tasks in light of this framework.

Describing grammar test tasks

When language teachers consider tasks for grammar tests, they call to mind a large repertoire of task types that have been commonly used in teaching and testing contexts. We now know that these holistic task types constitute collections of task characteristics for eliciting performance and that these holistic task types can vary on a number of dimensions. We also need to remember that the tasks we include on tests should strive to match the types of language-use tasks found in real-life or language-instructional domains.

Traditionally, there have been many attempts at categorizing the types of tasks found on tests. Some have classified tasks according to scoring procedure. For example, **objective test tasks** (e.g., true–false tasks) are those in which no expert judgment is required to evaluate performance with regard to the criteria for correctness. **Subjective test tasks** (e.g., essays) are those that require expert judgment to interpret and evaluate performance with regard to the criteria for correctness.

Given that the main goal of a task is to elicit performance, I will discuss test tasks according to the type of response. I will refer to selected-response, limited-production and extended-production tasks. Table 5.6 presents a list of some of the more common testing activities categorized according to type of expected response.

Table 5.6 *Examples of task types*

Selected-response tasks	Limited-production tasks	Extended-production tasks
• Multiple-choice activities • True/false activities • Matching activities • Discrimination activities • Lexical list activities • Grammaticality judgment activities • Noticing activities	• Gap-filling activities • Cloze activities • Short-answer activities • Dictation activities • Information-transfer activities • Some information-gap activities • Dialogue (or discourse) completion activities	• Summaries, essays • Dialogues, interviews • Role-plays, simulations • Stories, reports • Some information-gap activities • Problem-solving activities • Decision-making activities

In designing grammar tests, we need to be familiar with a wide range of activities to elicit grammatical performance. In the rest of the chapter, I will describe several tasks in light of how they can be used to measure grammatical knowledge. I will use the Bachman and Palmer framework as a guide for task specification in this discussion. Task descriptions will revolve around the following critical task characteristics given in Table 5.7.

Selected-response task types

Selected-response tasks present input in the form of an item, and test-takers are expected to select the response. Other than that, all other task characteristics can vary. For example, the form of the input can be language, non-language or both, and the length of the input can vary from a word to larger pieces of discourse. In terms of the response, selected-response tasks are intended to measure recognition or recall of grammatical form and/or meaning. They are usually scored right/wrong, based on one criterion for correctness; however, in some instances, partial-credit scoring may be useful, depending on how the construct is defined. Finally, selected-response tasks can vary in terms of reactivity, scope and directness.

The multiple-choice (MC) task

This task presents input with gaps or underlined words or phrases. Examinees have to choose the correct answer from the response options

Table 5.7 *Critical characteristics of tasks*

Input

Type	Form	Length	Required topical info.
• Item • Prompt	• Language • Non-language • Both	Words, phrases and sentences Paragraphs and extended discourse	• General • Specific

Expected response

Type	Language of expected response	Required topical information	Typical scoring procedures

Selected-response
 	
Limited-production
	Grammatical knowledge
	
	Form
	• Phonological • Cohesive
	• Lexical • Info. management
	• Morphosyntactic • Interactional
	             scale
		• General
		• Specific
			• Right/
			   wrong
			• Partial
			   credit
			• Rating

Extended-production	**Meaning**
	• Phonological • Cohesive
	• Lexical • Info. management
	• Morphosyntactic • Interactional
	
	Pragmatic knowledge
	• Implied contextual • Sociocultural
	   meanings meanings
	• Sociolinguistic • Psychological
	   meanings meanings
	                 • Rhetorical meanings		

Relationship between the input and response

Reactivity	Scope	Directness

• Reciprocal
   + interaction + feedback
• Adaptive
   + interaction − feedback
• Non-reciprocal
   − interaction − feedback
	• Broad scope to be
	   processed
	• Narrow scope to be
	   processed
		• Direct from the input
		• Indirect from the input

given. The answer or **key** represents the best, correct or most appropriate, acceptable or natural choice; the other options are the **distractors.** MC items are well suited for testing many discrete features of grammatical knowledge. Administration and scoring of MC tasks are relatively easy. MC items are also easily pre-tested, so that their psychometric characteristics can be determined prior to operational testing. In this way, 'easy' or 'difficult' items can be selected and ordered as needed. MC tasks are scored objectively.

While the MC task has many advantages, the items can be difficult and time-consuming to develop. The format encourages guessing, and scores might be inflated due to test-wiseness, or the test-taker's knowledge about test taking. This can result in serious questions about the validity of inferences based on these items (Cohen, 1998). Finally, many educators argue that MC tasks are inauthentic language-use tasks.

Due to these potential shortcomings, many language educators are unduly critical of this task type. There is, however, nothing innately 'bad' about this or any test task, as long as it successfully elicits instances of performance from which valid inferences about grammatical ability can be made for the testing purpose.

Let us now consider some examples of MC tasks as measures of grammatical knowledge. Example 1 presents the input in the form of a two-part adjacency pair with a gap in the second-pair part.

Example 1: Multiple-choice task
Designed to test grammatical form (morphosyntax-word order)
Directions: Circle the correct answer.

A: Can't Tom drive us to the airport?
B: He has ____ to take us all.
    (a) such small a car   (c) a too small car
    (b) very small a car   (d) too small a car ✔   key = ✔

Although the first-pair part of this example provides context for the response, an understanding of this context is not essential to get the item correct. This item is designed to test grammatical form, or more specifically, syntactic accuracy. Semantically, all four answer choices would probably convey the meaning; however, syntactically, only one is correct. This item would be scored right or wrong.

A common variation of Example 1 is to change the form of input to a passage or to an extended dialogue with gaps to target the area(s) of grammatical knowledge to be measured. Response options are then provided. In these variations, the scope of the relationship between the input and response would be somewhat broader than what was previously seen.

Example 2 is a slightly different kind of multiple-choice task. The input is presented in the form of an adjacency pair, but in this example, person B needs to understand the previous utterance in order to respond as expected.

> **Example 2: Multiple-choice task**
> **Designed to test grammatical form and meaning (cohesive-ellipsis)**
> Directions: Circle the correct answer.
>
> A: Will you and Ann go away this summer?
> B: I imagine ____.
>
>   (a) it   (c) that
>   (b) so ✔   (d) we'll

This item is designed to test cohesive form and/or meaning. More specifically, it aims to measure ellipsis and referential meaning across the two turns. Although this item might appear reciprocal, the relationship between the input and response is non-reciprocal because the test-taker receives no feedback on the correctness of his or her response. This item would be scored right or wrong.

Example 3 presents the input in the form of a dialogue with three turns and two adjacency pairs.

> **Example 3: Multiple-choice task**
> **Designed to test grammatical form and meaning (multiple areas)**
> Directions: Circle the correct answer.
>
> A: Wow! You got a new hairdo. I love it!
> B: Thanks, but _____
> A: No, you don't. You look great!
>
>   (a) I liked it the other way.   (c) You look great.
>   (b) What happened to you?   (d) I look ridiculous! ✔

The first adjacency pair in this example involves a compliment about a new haircut (*You got a new hairdo. I love it!*). The second adjacency pair consists of an expression of gratitude (*Thanks*) and an assessment of the new hairdo (*I look ridiculous!*). This is the expected response. This response is followed by a disagreement (*No, you don't*) and a second compliment (*You look great!*). In this item, all the choices are grammatically correct, but as this item is designed to measure cohesive form and meaning, only option "d" fits the situation correctly. The cohesive link between *I look ridiculous* and *No, you don't* shows how the negative self-assessment is countered by a disagreement. In this task, the relationship between the input and response is reciprocal. Person B receives implicit feedback from person A on the relevance of her utterance (*No, you don't.*). This then affects subsequent input (*You look great!*). This item would most likely be scored right or wrong.

Multiple-choice error identification task

This task presents test-takers with an item that contains one incorrect, unacceptable, or inappropriate feature in the input. Examinees are required to identify the error. In the context of grammatical assessment, the errors in the input relate to grammatical accuracy and/or meaningfulness. These tasks are often used in editing to identify grammatical errors.

   Example 4 presents a multiple-choice error identification task designed to assess grammatical form, or more specifically the use of the preposition *on* with *foot*. We could *also* argue that this is designed to measure lexical form since *on foot* is a fixed or lexicalized expression. This item would be scored right or wrong.

> **Example 4: Multiple-choice error identification task**
> **Designed to measure grammatical form**
> Directions: Circle the letter corresponding to the error.
>
> <u>As</u> my car had broken <u>down</u>, I decided <u>to go</u> there <u>by</u> foot.
> A   B   C   D ✔

The matching task

This task presents input in the form of two lists of words, phrases or sentences. One list can also be in the form of visual cues. Examinees match one list with the other. To avoid guessing, one list has one or more extra distractors. Matching tasks are designed to test several discrete features of grammatical knowledge within the same task. They are also designed to encourage test-takers to cross-reference and examine the relationships between the two lists so that construct-related associations can be indicated. They are also easy to score.

Example 5 presents a matching task in which the input is presented in the form of a paragraph with underlined words. This is followed by a list of meanings.

Example 5: Matching task
Designed to measure grammatical meaning (denotation)
Directions: Match the letter of the underlined word(s) with its meaning. Write the letter on the line.

Last week while Tom and Jane were having dinner in a restaurant, thieves (a) <u>broke down</u> the front door of their pretty little house, went inside and (b) <u>broke into</u> their safe. Now they're (c) <u>broke</u>.

___ 1. poor	___ 3. enter to steal something
___ 2. make into two or more pieces	___ 4. enter by force

Test-takers are asked to match the words with their meanings. In some cases, examinees need to understand the context to be able to provide the intended response (e.g., broke into). This task is designed to test knowledge of lexical meaning. With regard to the relationship between the input and response, the scope is narrow for some items and broad for others. This task would be scored right or wrong.

The discrimination task

This task presents examinees with language and/or non-language input along with two response choices that are polar opposites or that contrast in some way. Some response possibilities include: true–false, right–wrong, same–different, agree–disagree, grammatical–ungrammatical and so forth. As seen in VanPatten's (1996) 'interpretation tasks', the input consists of two contrasting images and one utterance. The test-taker selects the image that is best expressed by the utterance. Similarly, the input could be varied to consist of one image and two related utterances. The test-takers would then select the utterance that best expresses the message in the image. Discrimination items are designed to measure the differences between two similar areas of grammatical knowledge.

Example 6 is a discrimination task in which the input is both non-language and language. The images represent contrasting messages. The test-takers must select which image is best represented by the utterance. Exercise 6 intends to test the grammatical meaning of pronouns, and would be scored dichotomously.

Example 6: Discrimination task
Designed to measure morphosyntactic meaning
Directions: Match the sentence with the picture by writing the number in the box on the line.

_____ Se la entregó a ella. [He delivered it to her.]

This task could be varied by changing the input to one image with two contrasting sentences. In this way, several pronoun meanings could be contrasted (*He delivered it to her, She delivered it to him*). One problem with discrimination tasks is that low-ability test-takers can significantly increase their scores above their ability level simply by guessing.

The noticing task

This task presents learners with a wide range of input in the form of language and/or non-language. Examinees are asked to indicate (e.g., by circling, highlighting) that they have identified some specific feature in the language. For example, examinees might be asked to underline the gerunds in a text or circle words that express possibility.

Example 7 presents the input in the form of a passage. Examinees need to indicate by circling and underlining when the modal *would* is used to refer to the past, the present or future. This item is designed to measure grammatical meaning. It would be scored right or wrong.

Example 7: Noticing task

Designed to measure grammatical meaning (morphosyntactic meaning)
Directions: Circle 'would' when it refers to the habitual past. Underline it when it refers to the present or future.

You know? You think you've got it bad. When I was a kid, we would have to walk up hill to and from school every day. We would even do it when it snowed – winter and summer. And we would never even think of complaining. We would smile and go about our business. I wouldn't change those days for anything. Would you now please 'shut up' and take out the garbage?

The noticing task, also referred to as a kind of consciousness-raising (CR) task, is intended to help students process input by getting them to construct a conscious form–meaning representation of the grammatical feature (Ellis, 1997), and for this reason, it seems to be particularly effective in promoting the acquisition of new grammar points (Tuz, 1993, cited in Ellis, 1997; VanPatten and Cadierno, 1993a, 1993b).

A final type of selected-response task is the **grammaticality-judgment task**. The grammaticality-judgment task presents learners with sentences that are either well or ill formed. Learners must then decide if these sentences are acceptable, or not. There is some debate as to whether grammaticality-judgment tasks tap into grammatical knowledge or whether they are simply a measure of the students' metagrammatical knowledge. For this reason, grammaticality-judgment tasks are almost exclusively used in SLA research, and not in other testing situations.

Limited-production task types

As seen in Table 5.7, limited-production tasks present input in the form of an item with language and/or non-language information that can vary in length or topic. Different from selected-response tasks, limited-production tasks elicit a response embodying a limited amount of language production. The length of this response can be anywhere from a word to a sentence. All task characteristics in limited-production tasks can vary with the exception of two: the type of input (always an 'item') and the type of expected response (always 'limited-production').

Limited-production tasks are intended to assess one or more areas of grammatical knowledge depending on the construct definition. Unlike selected-response items, which usually have only one possible answer, the range of possible answers for limited-production tasks can, at times, be large – even when the response involves a single word.

With regard to scoring, limited-production tasks can be scored in several ways. Items with a single criterion for correctness can be marked right/wrong, and those with multiple criteria can be scored right/wrong for each criterion. In the case of multiple criteria for correctness, the separate scores (e.g., grammatical form and meaning) can then be added up to form a separate composite score for each criterion (one for form and one for meaning). Alternatively, the separate scores for each item can be added up (e.g., form and meaning together), so that an item can receive full, partial or no credit. These aggregated scores can be added up to form a composite single score. In other situations, limited-production tasks can be scored with a holistic or analytic rating scale. This method is useful if we wish to judge distinct aspects of grammatical ability with different levels of ability or mastery. For more information on scoring, see Chapter 6, where this topic will be discussed at greater length.

The gap-filling task

This task presents input in the form of a sentence, passage or dialogue with a number of words deleted. The gaps are specifically selected to test one or more areas of grammatical knowledge. Examinees are required to fill the gap with an appropriate response for the context. Gap-filling tasks are designed to measure the learner's knowledge of grammatical forms and meanings.

Example 8 is a gap-filling task designed to measure grammatical form and lexical meaning. More specifically, it aims to measure morphosyntactic form of the simple and habitual past tense verb forms and lexical meaning.

> **Example 8: Gap-filling task**
> **Designed to measure grammatical form and meaning**
> Directions: Fill in the blank with an appropriate form of the verb.
>
> In about 20 AD Apicus was well known for the cookbooks he (1)
> _____ in his spare time. He was equally famous for the lavish
> meals he (2) _____ for his family and guests.
> (Adapted from Purpura and Pinkley, 2000)

The two intended criteria for correctness are grammatical form, measured in terms of morphosyntactic accuracy of the simple and habitual past tense verb forms, and lexical meaning, scored in terms of the lexical meaningfulness of words that fit the context. Given the limited amount of contextual control, the range of acceptable responses could be fairly large. This task would be scored right/wrong for both form and meaning.

A second type of gap-filling task is the **cued gap-filling task**. In these tasks, the gaps are preceded by one or more lexical items, or cues, which must be transformed in order to fill the gap correctly. For example, if we changed the input in Example 8 to include *write* and *prepare* before the gaps, we would eliminate the need to assess lexical meaning and could focus the measurement more specifically on morphosyntactic form. In this case, with one criterion for correctness, only morphosyntactic form would be scored.

A third type of gap-filling task is the **cloze**. This task presents the input as a passage or dialogue in which every fifth, sixth or seventh word is mechanically deleted and replaced by a gap. Examinees have to fill the gap with the best word for the context. From a grammatical perspective, the cloze is often a measure of grammatical form and meaning at both the sentential and discourse levels. However, given the broad scope of the input to be processed and the frequent indirectness of the relationship between the input and response, the gaps needing to be filled might also be a measure of pragmatic knowledge, especially when the meaning in the passage is derived from exophoric reference or other pragmatic meanings (Chihara et al., 1977). Over the years, the cloze task has been the object of an enormous amount of research in language testing – a discussion of this is beyond the purview of this book (for more information, see Oller and Jonz, 1994).

The short-answer task

This task presents input in the form of a question, incomplete sentence or some visual stimulus. Test-takers are expected to produce responses that range in length from a word to a sentence or two. The range of acceptable responses can vary considerably. Short-answer questions can be used to test several areas of grammatical ability, and are usually scored as right or wrong with one or more criteria for correctness or partial credit. Short-answer tasks can also be scored by means of a rating scale.

Example 9 presents examinees with input in the form of a job advertisement and an application form containing a set of implied questions. Examinees are expected to respond in short answers. This task aims to measure grammatical form and meaning. In order to fill out this application form, examinees also need to draw on personal or imagined information. The scoring of this item is slightly more complicated because some answers can be scored right/wrong with one criterion for correctness and others with multiple criteria for correctness (or by means of a rating scale).

Example 9: Short-answer task
Designed to measure grammatical form and meaning
Directions: Use the job ad to complete the application form.

WANTED

Intercultural Communications for International Corporation

A well-known, international corporation seeks applicants with expertise in cross-cultural communications to design cultural sensitivity training programs for employees bound for international employment. Applicants must have formal training in language, linguistics or cross-cultural studies. They must also have a successful record of international work experience. Must be willing to travel and remain abroad for extended periods of time. Must be fluent in several languages. Salary competitive with excellent benefits. Send letter along with resume to:
Sgarlatta@crossculturallights.com

Name: Job applied for:
Qualifications for job applied for:
Current job: Reason for leaving:

The dialogue (or discourse) completion task (DCT)

The DCT presents input in the form of a short exchange or dialogue with an entire turn or part of a turn deleted. Examinees are expected to complete the exchange with a response that is grammatically accurate and meaningful. DCTs are intended to measure the students' capacity to use grammatical forms to express a variety of literal or grammatical meanings (e.g., request), where the relationship between the form and the meaning is relatively direct. If, however, sufficient context is provided, DCTs can also be used as a measure of pragmatic knowledge, in which case they could also be scored for sociolinguistic or sociocultural appropriateness, contextual acceptability, or naturalness depending on the purpose of the test and the construct(s) being measured.

DCTs have been used extensively in applied linguistics research to investigate the use of semantic formulas and other linguistic devices to express a wide range of literal and implied contextual meanings (e.g., refusals, apologies, compliments). They have also been used to examine sociolinguistic and sociocultural meanings (social distance, power, register) associated with these contexts. This research has been performed with native and non-native speakers alike. Several researchers (e.g., Beebe and Cummins, 1996; Wolfson, Marmor and Jones, 1989) have found important differences in the actual wording, the semantic formulas and the response length between the data elicited from DCTs and those elicited in natural language use. Wolfson (1989) noted that DCTs can be an unreliable source of sociolinguistic performance by speakers. Nevertheless, several discourse analysts (e.g., Beebe and Takahashi, 1989) and language testers (e.g., Hudson, Detmer and Brown, 1995; Yamashita, 1996) have successfully used DCTs to measure grammatical forms and meanings as they encode certain sociolinguistic and sociocultural ascriptions. Korsko (2003) ingeniously used what she calls an interactive DCT to examine the narrative shape of two-party complaints with five different scenarios. In this study, a multi-turn dialogue in a written form was elicited back and forth between two speakers who negotiated a complaint from its inception to its conclusion. On average, this took six turns. DCTs are also widely used in instruction. Finally, although some have questioned the reliability and validity of DCTs for measuring pragmatic knowledge, no one has questioned their use to elicit samples of grammatical performance to communicate grammatical form and meaning. Minimally, DCTs can be scored for grammatical accuracy and meaningfulness, and in fact, with minimal context, this is all that can justifiably be scored.

Example 10 presents a DCT with three turns: an adjacency pair and a closing third. This task is designed to measure morphosyntactic form with second conditionals and grammatical meaning in the form of a suggestion.

Example 10: Discourse completion task
Designed to measure grammatical form and meaning on the discourse level
Directions: Complete the conversation the two friends are having.

A: I can't believe that disgusting little waiter told me 'to get a life' when I showed him the hair in my soup.
B: Well, if I were you, _____!
A: Nah, I don't want to be rude.

In this DCT the relationship between the input and response is recip-rocal since the response affects further turns. The closing third in this task is used to constrain the meaning of the expected response, thereby limiting the forms and the range of meanings that can be expressed in the response. For example, we could significantly change the nature of the expected response if we changed the closing third to: *No, I'm sick of being nice. I think he deserves a piece of my mind!* This task could be scored for grammatical accuracy and meaningfulness. If we wished to add a prag-matic component, we could explicitly ask students in the instructions to be polite or rude (sociolinguistic and sociocultural ascriptions) or take a condescending and arrogant stance (psychological ascriptions).

Extended-production tasks

Extended-production tasks present input in the form of a prompt instead of an item. The input can involve language and/or non-language infor-mation and can vary considerably in length. Extended-production tasks aim to elicit large amounts of data of which the quality and quantity can vary greatly for each test-taker. Given the real-time nature of some of these tasks, they are hypothesized to measure implicit grammatical knowledge. If planning time is given, they are also said to measure explicit knowledge. Extended-production tasks are particularly well suited for measuring the examinee's ability to use grammatical forms to convey meanings in instances of language use (i.e., speaking and writing). When assessing grammatical ability in the context of speaking, it is advisable, whenever possible, to audiotape or videotape the interaction. This will allow the performance samples to be scored more reliably and will provide time to record diagnostic feedback for students. The tapes can also be used for instructional purposes, as well as for teaching students to perform self and peer assessments.

The quality of the extended-production task responses is judged (1) with reference to the theoretical construct(s) being measured and (2) in terms of different levels of grammatical ability or mastery. For this reason, extended-production tasks are scored with the rating-scale method. To devise rating scales, we first need to define the **scales** in terms of the components of grammatical ability being assessed, and then we need to determine different levels of grammatical ability for each scale along with the kinds of evidence we would need to observe to support claims of the ability at each level. For example, if we were going to assess our students' use of conditionals, we might operationalize grammatical knowledge in terms of the accuracy of the conditional forms and the range of knowledge displayed. Following this, we could devise a rubric similar to the one below. Consider, for now, three levels from a five-point scoring rubric.

4 = Complete evidence of morphosyntactic knowledge	The response is accurate (i.e., it contains no errors in conditional form or meaning); the response displays a range of first, second and third conditional sentences.
2 = Moderate evidence of morphosyntactic knowledge	The response is moderately accurate (i.e., it contains well-formed first and second conditionals, but several errors with the third conditional); the response displays a wide range of conditional sentences, but not all with the same degree of accuracy.
0 = No evidence of morphosyntactic knowledge	The response avoids the use of the conditional or there is not enough information to judge performance.

Once we have devised the scales, we can rate the responses with reference to the rubric and in accordance with established scoring procedures. I will address the topic of scoring in more detail in Chapter 6.

The information-gap task (info-gap)

This task presents input in the form of two or more sets of partially complete information. Test-takers are instructed to ask each other questions to obtain one complete set of information. Being reciprocal in nature, info-gap tasks are intended to elicit data involving negotiated interaction and feedback, which can be used to measure the test-takers' ability to use grammatical forms to convey a range of literal functional meanings. Depending on how the situation is set up, info-gap tasks can also be used to measure pragmatic knowledge.

Info-gap tasks are scored by means of the rating-scale method as described above (for further information, see Chapter 6). In addition to specific areas of grammatical ability, these tasks can be scored according to the degree to which the responses have fulfilled the requirements of the task (task fulfillment). In other words, have the students exchanged information in a reciprocal manner? Did the students get all the information? As these tasks are often performed orally, they should be audiotaped or videotaped when used in assessment to allow for more reliable scoring and more extensive feedback. Alternatively, teachers might want to 'unobtrusively' listen in on the interaction and rate certain features.

Example 11 presents an info-gap task designed to measure the examinees' ability to use areas of grammatical knowledge to exchange information. More specifically, it aims to measure the students' knowledge of morphosyntactic forms and meanings (question formation) and interactional forms and meanings (repair, backchannel devices). This task can also be scored for task fulfillment. The responses should be audiotaped and then scored using a rating-scale rubric specifically designed to assess these morphosyntactic and interactional forms and meanings.

Example 11: Information-gap task
Designed to measure grammatical form and meaning on the sentence and discourse levels
Directions: Work with a partner. Student A looks at the information on Mozart; Student B looks at the information on Debussy. Each of you needs the other person's information to prepare a report on famous composers. Ask each other questions from the cues and record your answers.

INFORMATION CARD
Name: Year and place of birth:
Characteristics of music: Date of death:

[To be given to separate students before the test.]

INFORMATION CARD – Student A	**INFORMATION CARD – Student B**
Name: Wolfgang Amadeus Mozart	Name: Claude Debussy
Year of birth: 1756; place: Salzburg, Austria	Year of birth: 1862; place: Laye (near Paris), France
Characteristics of music: always technically perfect	Characteristics of music: rhythm more important than melody
Date of death: 1791	Date of death: 1918

(Adapted from Purpura and Pinkley, 2000)

Story-telling and reporting tasks

These tasks present test-takers with prompts that require them to use information from their own experience or imagination to tell a story or report information. These tasks can be used to measure the test-takers' ability to use grammatical forms to convey several meanings – both literal and implied. Given the real-time nature of these tasks, whether in the context of speaking or writing, they are intended to measure an examinee's implicit grammatical knowledge. Sometimes the relationship between the input and response is indirect, requiring special topical knowledge to complete the task as intended. If these tasks are spoken, again audio- or videorecording is advisable. Performance is scored by means of rating scales that have been derived from the test construct(s) for this particular task (see Chapter 6).

Example 12 is a two-part reporting task. The input in the first part presents examinees with pieces of evidence from which examinees must make speculations about a crime. This part of the task measures the examinees' knowledge of grammatical form and meaning with respect to the present and past modals of logical probability (*must have, could have*) to express speculations. As it may be 'natural', but not 'essential' to use the intended verb forms to complete the task, test instructions could ask test-takers to use modals whenever possible. This part could be scored for grammatical form and meaning using a rating scale.

Example 12: Reporting task

Designed to measure grammatical form and meaning on the sentence and discourse levels

Directions – Part A: Last night there was a break-in at the Santellis'. You are the detective on the case. For each piece of evidence below, make a written speculation about the burglary. Use modals whenever possible.

1. The kitchen lock was forced open and a window was broken.
2. Traces of cookies and milk were found on the kitchen counter.
3. There was a wet towel in the shower.
4. All of Mrs. Santelli's diamonds are missing.

Directions – Part B: Based on the evidence, draw some tentative conclusions about the thief. Write a brief progress report on the situation for a new colleague on the case.

(Adapted from Purpura and Pinkley, 2000)

The prompt in part B asks examinees to use the clues in part A to write up a progress report. This task aims to measure grammatical form and meaning in terms of the present and past modals used to express speculations about the crime and the cohesive forms and meanings used in connecting sentences. Finally, this task measures pragmatic knowledge in terms to the examinees' ability to organize the sentences into a coherent report (rhetorical control).

The role-play and simulation tasks

These tasks present test-takers with a prompt in which two or more examinees are asked to assume a role in order to solve a problem collaboratively, make a decision or perform some transaction. The input can be language and/or non-language, and it can contain varying amounts of information. In terms of the expected response, role-plays and simulation tasks elicit large amounts of language, invoking the test-takers' grammatical and pragmatic knowledge, their topical knowledge, strategic competence and affective schemata. The purpose of the test and the construct definition will determine what will be scored. The relationship between the input and response is reciprocal and indirect. These tasks are scored with the rating-scale method in light of the constructs being measured.

Example 13 is a problem-solving simulation. The prompt contains a description of the situation and the test-taker's goal. It also provides suggestions for carrying out the discussion. Finally, it contains a description of three possible roles to assume in solving the problem. Examinees are randomly assigned to one of the roles and given five minutes' planning time before engaging in the discussion. Examinees are then assigned to groups of at least three people. Each group contains at least one representative from each role.

Example 13: Simulation task
Designed to measure grammatical form and meaning on the discourse level
Directions: Your local government has just received a large amount of money to solve one of its problems. You are on the committee to decide which one to solve. You will be given a problem to advocate for. Your job is to convince your group that the city should solve <u>your</u> problem first. You will have five minutes to plan your argument.

Once you are in your group, describe your problem to the others. When you hear all the problems, work together to decide which problem the city should solve first. Try to get your problem solved first.

(Each student is given only one role)

Person A The city is upset about pollution. There are more and more cars every year, and they are aggravating the pollution problem. The government does not want to make pollution laws because it is afraid factories will close. However, more and more people are having pollution-related health problems. The city needs money to help the factories install anti-pollution technology.

Person B The city is worried about crime. In some neighborhoods crime has increased dramatically within the last year, and people are afraid to walk in certain areas at night. More and more people are reporting street crimes. Recently thieves broke into a bank and stole millions. Violent crime is increasing too. The city needs money to hire more policemen and to install modern crime technology.

Person C The schools are in desperate need of help. Classrooms are overcrowded and buildings are falling apart from lack of maintenance. New teachers do not want to begin their careers in these conditions and veteran teachers are leaving the schools to accept jobs in the suburbs, where they are paid twice as much. The schools also need funds to support ESL instruction for growing numbers of immigrant students. Every child deserves to have the opportunity for a good education.

(Adapted from Purpura and Pinkley, 1999)

This task is intended to measure the test-takers' ability to understand the prompt, assume one of the roles and use their knowledge of grammatical forms and meanings to participate in the discussion. More specifically, this task aims to measure the examinees' knowledge of grammatical forms for arguing (*I think we should . . . because . . .*), counter-arguing (*Yes, but if we did that, we would . . . and then we won't . . . therefore, I think we should . . . because . . .*), and conceding (*I see your point and agree . . ., but I think we somehow need to consider . . .*). Depending on how the construct is defined, this task could be scored for grammatical form and meaning by means of a rating scale. The rubric could include different levels of ability in terms of the examinees' ability to use a variety of grammatical forms to argue, counterargue and concede.

If we wanted to use this task to measure the examinees' pragmatic knowledge in terms of their ability to convey certain psychological meanings, we could assign roles like a concerned environmentalist, a scared citizen and an angry teacher, or if we wished to measure pragmatic knowledge in terms of the test-takers' ability to convey sociolinguistic meanings, we could assign roles like the mayor, a victims' rights activist and an elementary school teacher. In each case, we would probably want to modify the descriptions of the roles to some extent.

Summary

Given the central role of task in the development of grammar tests, this chapter has addressed the notion of task and task specification in the test development process. I discussed how task was originally conceptualized as a holistic method of eliciting performance and argued that the notion of task as a monolithic entity falls short of providing an adequate framework from which to specify tasks for the measurement of grammatical ability. I also argued that given the diversity of tasks that could emerge from real-life and instructional domains, a broad conceptualization of task is needed in grammatical assessment – one that could accommodate selected-response, limited-production and extended-production tasks.

For assessment, the process of operationalizing test constructs and the specification of test tasks are extremely important. They provide a means of controlling what is being measured, what evidence needs to be observed to support the measurement claims, what specific features can be manipulated to elicit the evidence of performance, and finally how the performance should be scored. This process is equally important for language teachers, materials writers and SLA researchers since any variation in the individual task characteristics can potentially influence what is practiced in classrooms or elicited on language tests. In this chapter, I argued that in developing grammar tasks, we needed to strive to control, or at least understand, the effects of these tasks in light of the inferences we make about examinees' grammatical ability.

Finally, I described Bachman and Palmer's (1996) framework for characterizing test tasks and showed how it could be used to characterize SL grammar tasks. This framework allows us to examine tasks that are currently in use, and more interestingly, it allows us to show how variations in task characteristics can be used to create new task types that might better serve our educational needs and goals.

In the next chapter, I will discuss the process of constructing a grammar test consisting of several tasks.

CHAPTER SIX

Developing tests to measure L2 grammatical ability

Introduction

In previous chapters, the contexts of grammar assessment were considered and the nature of grammatical ability defined for assessment purposes. Then, in Chapter 5, I discussed the notion of task and described how grammatical constructs could be operationalized to measure grammatical ability for different purposes. Building on the procedures for designing grammar-test tasks, this chapter addresses the process of grammar-test construction, that is the principles underlying the design, development and scoring of grammatical assessments. To do this, I will first describe the characteristics of 'useful' tests so that these qualities may be used to drive the test development process. I will discuss these qualities both generally and in relation to grammatical assessments. After that, I will detail the process used to construct tests of grammatical ability from the initial design phase through operational use. I will address the process of test construction principally, but not exclusively, from the perspective of large-scale assessment. Large-scale grammar assessment refers to tests that reach beyond the confines of the individual classroom. These include the grammar sections in placement or proficiency exams, the grammar sections of final exams given to several class sections in a school, or the grammar sections of measurement instruments used in research projects. The procedures for constructing large-scale assessments are somewhat different from those typically encountered in small-scale or classroom assessments, since they each have different goals and priorities. I will devote all of Chapter 8 to a discussion of the principles of grammar assessment as applied to small-scale or classroom assessment. Let us now begin the discussion with an examination of test usefulness.

What makes a grammar test 'useful'?

We concluded in the last chapter that the goal of every grammar test was to obtain (and provide) information on how well a student knows or can use grammar to convey meaning in some situation where the target language is used. The responses to the test items can then be used as a basis for assigning scores and for making inferences about the student's underlying grammatical ability. We discussed these responses in terms of inferences because it is not possible to observe a person's grammatical ability directly; rather, we must infer the underlying ability from responses to questions or from samples of actual performance. Since responses to test items are ultimately converted into scores, we say we can make **score-based inferences** about an examinee's grammatical ability. These inferences provide information to test-takers and other test-users (e.g., language teachers).

Score-based inferences from grammar tests can be used to make a variety of decisions. For example, classroom teachers use these scores as a basis for making inferences about learning or achievement. These inferences can then serve to provide feedback for learning and instruction, assign grades, promote students to the next level, or even award a certificate. They can also be used to help teachers or administrators make decisions about instruction or the curriculum.

The information derived from language tests, of which grammar tests are a subset, can be used to provide test-takers and other test-users with **formative** and **summative evaluations**. Formative evaluation relating to grammar assessment supplies information during a course of instruction or learning on how test-takers might increase their knowledge of grammar, or how they might improve their ability to use grammar in communicative contexts. It also provides teachers with information on how they might modify future instruction or fine-tune the curriculum. For example, feedback on an essay telling a student to review the passive voice would be formative in nature. Summative evaluation provides test stakeholders with an overall assessment of test-taker performance related to grammatical ability, typically at the end of a program of instruction. This is usually presented as a profile of one or more scores or as a single grade.

Score-based inferences from grammar tests can also be used to make, or contribute to, decisions about program placement. This information provides a basis for deciding how students might be placed into a level of a language program that best matches their knowledge base, or it might determine whether or not a student is eligible to be exempted from further L2 study. Finally, inferences about grammatical ability can make or contribute to other high-stakes decisions about an individual's readiness for learning or promotion, their admission to a program of study, or their selection for a job.

Given the goals and uses of tests in general, and grammar tests in particular, it is fitting to ask how we might actually know if a test is, indeed, able to elicit scorable behaviors from which to make trustworthy and meaningful inferences about an individual's ability. In other words, how do we know if a grammar test is 'good' or 'useful' for our particular context?

Many language testers (e.g., Harris, 1969; Lado, 1961) have addressed this question over the years. Most recently, Bachman and Palmer (1996) have proposed a framework of **test usefulness** by which all tests and test tasks can be judged, and which can inform test design, development and analysis. They consider a test 'useful' for any particular testing situation to the extent that it possesses a balance of the following six complementary qualities: reliability, construct validity, authenticity, interactiveness, impact and practicality. They further maintain that for a test to be 'useful', it needs to be developed with a specific purpose in mind, for a specific audience, and with reference to a specific target language use (TLU) domain. Given the importance of these qualities for grammar assessment, I will describe them in some detail.

The quality of reliability

When we talk about 'reliability' in reference to a car, we all know what that means. A car is said to be reliable if it readily starts up every time we want to use it regardless of the weather, the time of day or the user. It is also considered reliable if the brakes never fail, and the steering is consistently responsive. These mechanical functions, working together, make the car's performance anywhere from zero to one hundred percent reliable.

Similarly, the scores from tests or components of tests can also be characterized as being reliable when the tests provide the same results every time we administer them, regardless of the conditions under which they are administered. In other words, test scores should not fluctuate drastically as a result of the time of the test administration, the form of the test used (provided there exists more than one form), or the raters who might have scored the responses. This consistency of measurement is referred to as **test reliability**, and it ranges on a scale from zero (no consistency) to one (perfect consistency).

For example, if we gave a grammar placement test to students on Monday and gave them the same test again on Friday, the scores obtained from each occasion should not vary, assuming that test-takers' grammar ability has not changed, and their placement decision should be approximately the same. Similarly, if we constructed two equivalent forms of a grammar test – Form A and Form B – we would expect a student to receive approximately the same score, no matter which test form he took. Finally, if two teachers had been given training on how to score speech samples obtained from interviews for grammatical ability according to a rating scale, and then each was given the same set of tapes to score independently for grammatical accuracy or precision, the scores assigned by each independent rater should be relatively consistent. If so, we have evidence of reliability. In sum, reliability refers to the precision and consistency with which we are able to measure performance.

So how can we enhance test score reliability? One way is to use systematic procedures for designing and developing grammar tests. We will discuss these procedures later in this chapter. Another way is to adopt objective scoring procedures. **Objective scoring** techniques involve no expert decision-making in the scoring process such as in the scoring of selected-response items. In cases where right/wrong scoring is not appropriate, the scoring process can be 'objectified' by training raters to score consistently according to an agreed-upon scoring rubric, and by having more than one independent rater judging performance. Finally, reliability can be raised by increasing the number of tasks on a test, the number of test-takers or the number of judges. While we may have strong evidence of test reliability, it is important to remember that this still provides no guarantee that we are actually measuring what we *want* to be measuring – grammatical ability. To determine *what* the test is measuring, we need to look for evidence of construct validity.

The quality of construct validity

The second quality that all 'useful' tests possess is **construct validity.** Bachman and Palmer (1996) define construct validity as 'the extent to which we can interpret a given test score as an indicator of the ability(ies), or construct(s), we want to measure. Construct validity also has to do with the domain of generalization to which our score interpretations generalize' (p. 21). In other words, construct validity not only refers to the meaningfulness and appropriateness of the interpretations we make based on test scores, but it also pertains to the degree to which the score-based interpretations can be extrapolated beyond the testing situation to a particular TLU domain (Messick 1993). Construct validity of score-based interpretations needs to be supported through the collection and analysis of data grounded in research and theory.

To illustrate, suppose that in the context of preparing EFL students to write chemistry lab reports, we decided to measure their ability (1) to describe the steps in a lab procedure (e.g., *small pieces of litmus paper were dipped . . .*), (2) to report observed results (e.g., *the paper turned red*) and (3) to draw conclusions about the results (e.g., *the solutions were therefore the two acids . . .*). And suppose we did this by giving them a gap-filling task of grammatical form. Then, to measure their ability to produce these forms accurately and meaningfully, we decided to give them the lab report task. Based on the results of this test, we might decide to allow the high scorers to go on to the next lesson, to require the low scorers to get tutoring and to allow the middle scorers to decide for themselves. In examining the construct validity of our score-based inferences, we ask the following questions: To what extent are we justified in interpreting these test scores as indicators of grammatical ability, and not of some other ability, in the context of writing lab reports?

To collect evidence of validity, we could ask language and/or content teachers to comment on the degree to which the language produced on the test corresponded to the language needed to write up a lab report. If they corresponded, then we would have some support for validity. Another way of investigating validity would be to examine if the factors determining score variability can be attributed primarily to the degree to which the test-takers have mastered the grammar related to the past active and passive verb forms, and not to some test-method effect, such as the clarity of the instructions or the scoring by the judges. Or, for example, suppose that, after having given the lab report test, teachers reported that, based on subsequent classroom activities involving the active and passive verb forms, students who received high scores on all parts of the test really did know how to write grammatically accurate and meaningful lab reports, while those who scored low did not, and those in the middle showed lots of variation. The comparative results from the two assessment procedures (lab report test and classroom observation) would constitute evidence in support of the validity of our inferences. All of these results combined provide support for the score-based inferences we want to make about test-takers.

In sum, construct validity is clearly one of the most important qualities a test can possess. It tells us if we are measuring what we had intended to measure. Nonetheless, this information provides no information on how these assessment tasks resemble those that the learners might encounter in some non-testing situation or on what impact, if any, these assessments are having on the test-takers.

The quality of authenticity

A third quality of test usefulness is **authenticity**, a notion much discussed in language testing since the late 1970s, when communicative approaches to language teaching were first taking root. Building on these discussions, Bachman and Palmer (1996) refer to 'authenticity' as the degree of correspondence between the test-task characteristics and the TLU task characteristics. Given the framework for test-task characteristics discussed in Chapter 5, they provide a systematic way of matching test tasks with TLU tasks in terms of the features of the test setting, rubrics, input, expected response and the relationship between the input and response. Bachman and Palmer's framework provides an empirical basis for further research and, from the point of view of test development, an intuitively appealing scheme for defining authenticity and for providing authenticity evidence.

If discrete-point grammar tests (e.g., multiple-choice) are unpopular among language teachers, it is perhaps because they are perceived as lacking in authenticity. In fact, it is for this single characteristic of test usefulness that discrete-point grammar tasks, like those found in many high-stakes, standardized tests, have received the harshest criticism. If the purpose of a test is to measure grammatical ability and the TLU domain to which we wish to generalize is real life, then it might be difficult to match a selected-response task of grammatical form with a real-life TLU task. In short, we have little evidence of **authenticity of task**. However, if the purpose of the test is to measure knowledge of grammatical forms so that we can check on the students' understanding of these forms, and the TLU domain to which we wish to generalize is instructional, then selected-response tasks of grammatical form should not be perceived as lacking in authenticity. Given the purpose of the test and the TLU domain, the task selection would be justifiable.

So what are the characteristics of grammar tasks that most enhance authenticity, and how might we address this in the test-development process? Unfortunately, no empirical research to date has attempted to identify those task attributes that most influence the perception of authenticity. Nor do we know if the perceptions of authenticity among test stakeholders differ. Nonetheless, based on my own personal classroom experience, authenticity seems to be enhanced in a number of ways. First, it appears heightened when the content characteristics of both the test input and the expected response are rich in topic, theme or context. For example, instead of devising a discrete-point, multiple-choice task of passive voice form, where each item is independent of the other, we can present the same activity in the context of a cohesive theme such as a process description (e.g., How do we get the stripe in the toothpaste? How do you get drinking water out of salt water?). In other words, each multiple-choice item revolves around the different steps in the process description. This task may not have authenticity of task (a multiple-choice task), but it does have **authenticity of content**. I define **authenticity of content** as the degree to which the topical, thematic or contextual characteristics of the test tasks match those of the TLU tasks.

Finally, authenticity, in my view, is also enhanced when the linguistic characteristics of the test input appear 'natural'. In other words, to the greatest extent possible, the written or spoken input should resemble naturalistic discourse, conforming to the norms, preferences and expectations of naturally occurring talk or text. Similarly, tasks should be devised to elicit natural-sounding responses. I refer to this as **authenticity of response**, and define it as the degree to which the response of the test task corresponds to that which one would expect in a TLU task.

In sum, test authenticity resides in the relationship between the characteristics of the TLU domain and characteristics of the test tasks, and although a test task may be highly authentic, this does not necessarily mean it will engage the test-taker's grammatical ability. For this we turn to the quality of interactiveness.

The quality of interactiveness

A fourth quality of test usefulness outlined by Bachman and Palmer (1996) is **interactiveness**. This quality refers to the degree to which the aspects of the test-taker's language ability we want to measure (e.g., grammatical knowledge, language knowledge) are engaged by the test-task characteristics (e.g, the input response, and relationship between the input and response) based on the test constructs. In other words, the task should engage the characteristics we want to measure (e.g., grammatical knowledge) given the test purpose, and nothing else (e.g., topical knowledge, affective schemata); otherwise, this may mask the very constructs we are trying to measure. In the case of grammar assessment, test tasks can be characterized as 'interactive' to the extent that they require individuals to draw on and manage their cognitive and metacognitive strategies (i.e., their strategic competence) in order to use grammatical knowledge accurately and meaningfully. Consider, for example, the chemistry lab report task whose input requires examinees to invoke strategies to use their grammatical knowledge, the focus of measurement, to express their ideas about the lab procedure (topical knowledge). This task is likely to be more interactive than a task that is unsuccessful in engaging aspects of the test-taker's language ability to such a degree. The engagement of these construct-relevant characteristics with task characteristics is the essence of actual language use. Note again that for grammar assessment, what is important is that the task succeeds in engaging the examinee's grammatical ability as intended by the test design. A task may be interactive because it engages the examinee's topical knowledge and positive affective schemata; however, if the purpose of the test is to measure grammatical ability and the task does not engage the ability of interest, this is all construct irrelevant. If the construct is defined in such a way that it includes both grammatical knowledge and topical knowledge (i.e., language for specific purposes), then the task should be designed to engage these two constructs and little else.

The quality of impact

Testing plays an important role in society. Tests serve as gate-keeping devices or doors to opportunity. They can be used to punish and to praise. It is, therefore, important to recognize that tests reflect and represent the social, cultural and political values of any given society, and in the evaluation of test usefulness, we must take into consideration the possible consequences that may ensue from the decision to use test results for decision-making. Bachman and Palmer (1996) refer to the degree to which testing and test score decisions influence all aspects of society and the individuals within that society as test **impact.** Therefore, impact refers to the link between the inferences we make from scores and the decisions we make based on these interpretations. In terms of impact, most educators would agree that tests should promote positive test-taker experiences leading to positive attitudes (e.g., a feeling of accomplishment) and actions (e.g., studying hard).

A special case of test impact is **washback**, which is the degree to which testing has an influence on learning and instruction. Washback can be observed in grammar assessment through the actions and attitudes that test-takers display as a result of their perceptions of the test and its influence over them. For example, examinees who are able to use corrective feedback from assessments to clarify or extend their knowledge of grammar, or improve their ability to write lab reports, would most likely perceive these tests as being 'useful'. Positive actions constitute a commitment from students to do something they might not otherwise do, such as relearn a grammar point they were confused about. Tests are also said to be 'useful' when they promote positive attitudes on the part of test-takers and other test constituents to be more engaged in the testing–learning process.

Let us now consider test usefulness in terms of practicality.

The quality of practicality

Scores from a grammar test could be highly reliable and provide a basis for making valid inferences, but at the same time completely lacking in practicality. It may be completely beyond our means with respect to the available human, material or time resources. Test **practicality** is not a quality of a test itself, but is a function of the extent to which we are able to balance the costs associated with designing, developing, administering, and scoring a test in light of the available resources (Bachman, personal communication, 2002). For example, we may want to include limited- and extended-production tasks in a grammar test to measure students' explicit as well as their implicit knowledge of grammar, so in the test design stage we need to decide how important this is in relation to the other qualities of the test. If we decide, for example, that reliability is very important, we need to consider the costs (time and people) of scoring both the limited- and the extended-production tasks. If the scoring costs, however, outweigh the available resources, we must then reconsider the goals of the test and our priorities and, if needed, reallocate the resources by changing our design.

In sum, the characteristics of test usefulness, proposed by Bachman and Palmer (1996), are critical qualities to keep in mind in the development of a grammar test. While each testing situation may not emphasize the same characteristics to the same degree, it is important to consider these qualities and to determine an appropriate balance.

In the rest of the chapter, I will discuss the principles underlying test development as they apply to grammar-test construction.

Overview of grammar-test construction

Each testing situation is specific unto itself, with a specific purpose, a specific audience and a specific set of parameters that will affect the test design and development process. As a result, there is no one 'right' way to develop a test; nor are there any recipes for 'good' tests that could generalize to all situations. There are, however, several frameworks of test development that have been proposed (e.g., Alderson, Clapham and Wall, 1995; Bachman and Palmer, 1996; Brown, 1996; Davidson and Lynch, 2002) which serve to guide the test-development process so that the qualities of test usefulness will not be ignored. These frameworks detail the process of creating and using a test from its initial conceptualization to an archived product. I will draw on these frameworks to describe the process of grammar-test development in this chapter.

Test development is often presented as a linear process consisting of a number of stages and steps. In reality, the process is anything but linear. Instead, it should be viewed as iterative and recursive, where knowledge and experience gained at one stage of the process will require the reassessment of a previous stage, followed by a series of readjustments. In other words, the development of a test is in a constant state of improvement based on new information and reassessment.

Bachman and Palmer (1996) organize test development into three stages: design, operationalization and administration. I will discuss each of these stages in the process of describing grammar-test development.

Stage 1: Design

The design stage of test development involves the accumulation of information and making initial decisions about the entire test process. In tests involving one class, this may be a relatively informal process; however, in tests involving wider audiences, such as a joint final exam or a placement test, the decisions about test development must be discussed and negotiated with several stakeholders. The outcome of the design stage is a design statement. According to Bachman and Palmer (1996, p. 88), this document should contain the following components:

1. a description of the purpose(s) of the test,
2. a description of the TLU domains and task types,
3. a description of the test-takers,
4. a definition of the construct(s) to be measured,
5. a plan for evaluating test usefulness, and
6. a plan for dealing with resources.

Purpose

Test development begins with what Davidson and Lynch (2002) call a **mandate**. The test mandate grows out of a perceived need for a test by one or more stakeholders. This embodies the **test purpose(s)**, which, in the case of grammar assessment, makes explicit the inferences we wish to make about grammatical knowledge or the ability to use this knowledge and the uses we intend to make of these inferences. For example, the purpose statement might state: *The purpose of the test is to measure grammatical ability with regard to the comparative forms and meanings.* The purpose also articulates the decisions that the score-based inferences will be used for. These decisions could relate to student **progress** or **achievement** so that a grade can be assigned, or to **selection** of students for a program of study. We can also make decisions about **placement** into a language program, language **proficiency** for hiring purposes, or **diagnosis** of a student's grammatical strengths or weaknesses so tutoring can be recommended. The purpose statement could also include who is impacted by the decisions and whether the stakes are high or low. It could also specify how the results of the test are intended to be used. For example, in most classroom tests the results of assessment will be used to promote further learning or to inform instruction.

TLU domains and tasks

After describing the purpose, the TLU domain is identified (e.g., real-life and/or language-instructional) and the TLU task types are selected. To identify language-use tasks and the type of language needed to perform these tasks, a **needs analysis** must be performed. This involves the collection and analysis of information related to the students' target-language needs. Depending on the testing situation, a needs analysis can be relatively informal or very complex.

In some situations, however, the identification and selection of TLU tasks are not so easy to discern. These are cases where the real-life domain may be difficult to identify and where the language-instructional tasks are distant from the real-life tasks. This is seen, for example, in situations where students are enrolled in a grammar-oriented language course, which has no specific TLU domain in mind and which is not communicatively oriented. In other words, the language tasks are not necessarily intended to correspond to situations outside the classroom where interaction is emphasized. In this case, the TLU domain would be language-instructional, and the tasks would derive from the classroom.

In more and more language teaching situations, however, the focus is on communicative language teaching. Instruction in this approach is designed to correspond to real-life communication outside the classroom; therefore the intended TLU domain of communicative language tests is likely to be real-life. In this situation tasks should be designed to correspond to those found in communicative situations outside the classroom. While this is the ideal, many instructional tasks in communicative classrooms are still motivated by a need to focus on discrete features of language, and instruction often involves explicit grammar teaching of forms. As the TLU domain is not entirely independent of instructional considerations, the TLU domain for a test in this situation is obviously both language-instructional and real-life. Test tasks would then need to be drawn from instructional and real-life domains, depending, of course, on the domain to which inferences about the students' abilities are intended to generalize.

In some situations, the determination of a concrete TLU domain is difficult to ascertain. This was the situation encountered by the testing committee at Teachers College, Columbia University, as we attempted to identify the TLU domain for the Community English Program's (CEP) English language placement exam. Given the fact that the CEP welcomes students whose language proficiency ranges from absolute beginner to advanced and whose motivations for learning English extend from every-day language skills in the surrounding Harlem community to full integra-tion into the academic life of Columbia University, the testing committee felt unable to identify an appropriate real-life domain that would suit all test-takers. In the end, we created a test that matched the type of instruc-tion students would encounter in the CEP – a theme-based, integrated-skills and grammar approach. Therefore a unifying theme was chosen for the test and sections of the test, including grammar, were designed to measure the students' ability to communicate in everyday interactional contexts. Cummins (1980, 1983) refers to this as basic interpersonal com-munication skills (BICS). We also decided to measure the students' ability to function linguistically in an academic or professional setting (e.g., reading a map or graph), where knowledge of a wider range of complex grammatical forms is required. Cummins (1980, 1983) refers to this as cognitive and academic language proficiency (CALP). The TLU domain of this exam was clearly instructional. Although simplistic, the distinction between BICS and CALP provided a useful means of categorizing the TLU domain and of developing tasks for a population that had a wide range of learning goals.

Once the TLU domain has been determined and TLU tasks identified, these tasks must be specified so that test tasks can be drawn from them. The description of the TLU tasks involves the specification of the setting, the input, the response, and the relationships between the input and response, as we saw in Chapter 5.

Characteristics of test-takers

The design statement contains a detailed description of the characteris-tics of the test-takers, so that the population of test-takers for whom the test is intended and to whom the test scores might generalize can be made explicit. The personal attributes of test-takers which can poten-tially influence test results include age, native language, gender, level of language ability and so forth.

Construct(s) to be measured

The design statement also provides a theoretical definition of the con-struct(s) to be measured in the test. Construct definition can be based on a set of instructional objectives in a syllabus, a set of standards, a theoretical definition of the construct or some combination of them all. In grammar tests, construct definition based on a syllabus (or a textbook) is useful when we want to determine to what degree students have mastered the grammar points that have been taught during a certain period. For example, we might want to know how well students have learned to ask and answer questions about their family in a beginning language class. Construct definitions of grammatical ability based on a syllabus are more common in programs that have an objectives-based curriculum or that use a textbook as the default curriculum. Finally construct definitions for grammar tests can be theory-based. These can be derived from a model of grammatical knowledge such as the one discussed in Chapter 4. Construct definition is clearly a crucial part of the test design since it is the basis for test construction, score interpretation and test validation.

In addition to defining grammatical knowledge, the test designer must specify the role of topical knowledge in the construct definition of grammar tests. Bachman and Palmer (1996) provide three options for defining topical knowledge. The first is to exclude topical knowledge from the test construct(s). This is appropriate in situations where specific topics and themes are not a consideration in instruction, and where test-takers are not expected to have any special background knowledge to complete the task. Topic in these assessment tasks is not treated systematically, and score-based inferences are limited to grammatical knowledge. For example, a gap-filling task to test cohesive form and meaning would require no specific topical knowledge on the test-takers' part.

The second option is to include topical knowledge in the construct. This is appropriate in situations where specific topics or themes are an integral part of the curriculum and where topics or themes contextualize language, provide a social–cognitive context for the tasks, and serve to raise the students' interest level. Topic may be treated systematically, but the development of topical knowledge is seen as incidental. The focus of assessment is on contextualized language development, and not necessarily on topical development. An example of this is seen in theme-based language programs, where topic serves as a context for language learning. Topic in theme-based programs includes survival themes (e.g., shopping, travel), universal themes based on personal experience (e.g., people-watching, record-breaking), and, in the higher-proficiency levels, factual themes (e.g., global warming). For example, in a theme-based foreign-language program, the passive voice might be taught and tested in the context of processes (e.g., the decaffeination process), where every aspect of the lesson is presented in the context of a different process. However, students are tested on their ability to use the passive voice accurately and meaningfully in the context of describing processes. They would most likely not get a separate score for topical mastery, even though some development of topical knowledge would probably occur.

The third and most interesting option is to define topical knowledge separately from the language construct(s). This is appropriate in situations where the development of topical knowledge is as important as, if not more important than, the development of language knowledge in the curriculum. This is exemplified in content-based language programs (the adjuncted or sheltered models – see Brinton, Snow and Wesche, 1989) or language-for-specific-purposes programs (see Douglas, 2000), where language-for-specific-purposes ability is defined as topical knowledge and language knowledge. Topic in these cases involves a discipline-specific component of learning points and is usually determined in conjunction with a subject-matter specialist. The development of topical knowledge is seen as explicit, where both language ability and topical knowledge are assessed with separate scores. For example, in a content-based communication studies class, we might want to know to what degree students have learned the topical content as well as the grammar used to read and discuss that content. In this case, both constructs need to be defined and students receive a score for both grammatical expression and mastery of the content.

Finally, the test developer needs to decide if strategic competence needs to be specified in the construct definition of grammar tests. Strategic competence involves the use of metacognitive strategies (e.g., evaluating), cognitive strategies (e.g., associating), social strategies (e.g., cooperating) or affective strategies (e.g., managing anxiety) to process input and produce output in the context of a test (Bachman and Palmer, 1996; O'Malley and Chamot, 1990; Purpura, 1999). Although strategic competence is always assumed to be invoked in grammar tests, we are generally not interested in measuring it separately from grammar ability. However, there are instances in which we might want to make separate inferences to strategic competence, in which case it would need to be specified. For example, if we wanted to test the students' ability to use grammar to summarize and interpret a line graph as opposed to a bar graph, we might then need to specify one or more components of strategic competence and then develop scoring procedures from which to make score-based inferences about both strategic competence and language knowledge. Given our present understanding of the relationship between strategic competence and performance, we might, at this point, collect information on strategy use, so that the relationships between cognitive processing and performance can be investigated.

Plan for evaluating usefulness

The test design statement also provides a description of a plan for assessing the qualities of test usefulness. From the beginning of grammar-test development, it is important to consider all six qualities of test usefulness and to determine minimum acceptable levels for each quality. Bachman and Palmer (1996) suggest that a list of questions be provided to guide test developers to evaluate test usefulness throughout the process so that feedback can be provided. In addition, test developers should consider ways of providing empirical evidence of test usefulness (see Bachman and Palmer, 1996, Chapter 7, for a detailed list of questions to elicit information on the qualities of test usefulness).

Plan for managing resources

Finally, the test design makes explicit the human, material and time resources needed and available to develop the test. In cases of limited resources, priorities should be made in light of the qualities of test usefulness.

To summarize, Table 6.1 presents an example of a design statement for a grammar mid-semester exam revolving around a university chemistry lab class. This example is based on Bachman and Palmer (1996).

Table 6.1 *Design statement for the chemistry lab test*

Introduction:

This describes the development of a test designed to measure the students' ability to communicate accurately and meaningfully in a chemistry lab at a university. It is designed for students in a theme-based EFL program. One of the three themes covered in the course is 'the chemistry lab'. The test results will be used to determine to what degree students have mastered specific grammatical features needed to communicate in a chemistry lab. They will also be used to provide students with formative feedback on their grammatical development so that further learning can occur.

1. **Test purposes**
   A. **Inferences**
      To be made about test-takers' knowledge of selected grammatical points and their ability to use this knowledge to write a chemistry lab report.
   B. **Decisions**
      Moderate stakes; results to be used to assign one of three grades in a course (progress decision); students receiving low scores will have to seek tutoring (diagnostic decision).
   C. **Impact**
      Information will be used to promote further learning and to inform more focused instruction.

2. **Description of TLU domains and task types**
   A. **Identification of tasks**
      Real-life and language-instructional, based on the results of a needs analysis. Students in university chemistry classes have to acquire the skills to write a lab report. From a grammatical perspective, this involves a description of the lab procedures (past passive verb forms – *was added*; sequential connectors – *then*) along with the observed results (past verb forms – *turned*; causatives – *cause it to*) and an interpretation of the results (past verb forms – *was;* past logical conclusion modals – *must have been*; causal connectors – *hence*).
   B. **Description of TLU task types (for each task)**
      The TLU domain is instructional and real-life.

	TLU Task 1 Checking knowledge of verb forms	TLU Task 2 Checking knowledge of of logical connectors	TLU Task 3 Writing up a lab report
SETTING			
Participants	Teachers and test-takers	Same	Same
Time of task	Class time	Same	Same
INPUT			
Channel	Audio or visual	Same	Same
Form	Language	Same	Same

Table 6.1 *(cont.)*

Length	Short: 10 items	Short: 10 items	Short
Type	Items	Items	Prompt
Speededness	Unspeeded	Unspeeded	Moderate
Language characteristics			
Grammatical knowledge	Variable	Same	Same
Pragmatic knowledge	Variable	Same	Same
Topical knowledge	Restricted chemistry lab	Same	Same
EXPECTED RESPONSE			
Channel	Visual	Same	Same
Form	Non-language	Language	Language
Length	Short: 10 items	Short: 10 items	Medium: 1–2 pages
Type	Item: selected-response	Item: limited-production	Prompt: extended-production
Speededness	Moderately speeded	Same	Same
Language characteristics			
Grammatical knowledge	Grammatical form • Morphosyntactic forms (active and passive verb forms; causatives)	Grammatical meaning • Cohesive meanings (logical connectors)	Grammatical form • Morphosyntactic forms on the sentence and discourse levels (active and passive verbs; causatives) • Cohesive meaning (logical connectors) Grammatical meaning (conveyance of literal and intended meanings)
Pragmatic knowledge	Variable	Variable	Rhetorical meaning (display of lab report genre: actions, observed results, inferences)
Topical knowledge	Restricted chemistry lab	Same	Restricted knowledge of how to write up procedures for a lab report

Table 6.1 *(cont.)*

RELATIONSHIP BETWEEN INPUT and EXPECTED RESPONSE

Reactivity	Non-reciprocal	Same	Same
Scope of relationship	Extremely narrow	Narrow	Broad
Directness of relationship	Direct	Direct	Direct and indirect

3. **Description of characteristics of test-takers**
   A. **Personal characteristics**
      Age: 18 and above; mostly first year of college.
      Population: five intact classes taking a university EFL course.
      Native languages: mostly Turkish but also some Farsi, Arabic and Urdu.
   B. **Topical knowledge of test takers**
      Mostly science and technology.
   C. **Levels and profiles of language knowledge of test-takers**
      Levels: intermediate to advanced. Grammatical knowledge can vary widely.
   D. **Possible affective responses to taking the test**
      Given the treatment of the topic in class, most are likely to feel positive about the test.

4. **Definition of construct(s)**
   The test construct(s) are based on the theoretical definition of grammatical knowledge in Chapter 4. The test is being used to measure the control of grammatical form and meaning with a few structures on both the sentential and suprasentential levels. These structures were taught in the course. Topical knowledge is considered a part of the construct, but separate scores for topical knowledge will not be provided.
   A. **Knowledge of grammatical forms and meanings**
      Accuracy with regard to a range and complexity of morphosyntactic and cohesive forms Meaningfulness with regard to a range of lexical, morphosyntactic and cohesive meanings, and with regard to overall grammatical meaning.
   B. **Topical knowledge**
      Included in the construct definition as a lab report context.
   C. **Strategic competence**
      Not explicitly included in the construct.

5. **Plans for evaluating the qualities of usefulness**
   A. **Reliability**
      • Provide clear rubrics and scoring procedures.
      • Provide appropriate estimates of reliability.
   B. **Construct validity**
      • Examine the degree to which Tasks 1 and 2 relate to Task 3.
      • Ask test-takers or content teachers about how the results of this test generalize to the intended domain.
      • Ask test-takers to comment on the degree to which the decisions made based on the test scores are appropriate.

Table 6.1 *(cont.)*

C. **Authenticity**
   • Gather opinions on the degree to which the TLU tasks match the test tasks.
D. **Interactiveness**
   • Ask test-takers to report on the degree to which they feel their language knowledge, topical knowledge and strategic competence have been invoked by the test tasks.
E. **Impact**
   • Ask test-takers to report on the adequacy and fairness of the test, and on the usefulness of the information for further learning and instruction.
F. **Practicality**
   • Make a list of the required and available resources.
   • Prioritize the resources with reference to the qualities of test usefulness.

6. **Plans for allocation of resources**
   A. **Human resources**
      • Specify the human resources in number of hours.

	Design	Operationali- zation	Administration	Scoring	Analysis
Test coordinator	30	20		3	10
Test writers	15	15			
Reviewers	3	3			
Raters				30	
Administrators	1	1	1.5		
Secretary	2	2	2	2	2

   B. **Space resources**
      • 5 classrooms; assorted offices.
   C. **Equipment**
      • Computers, photocopiers, paper.
   D. **Costs**
      • Specify costs for the human, space and equipment resources.
   E. **Test development timeline**
      • Specify key dates for the development process.

Stage 2: Operationalization

The operationalization stage of grammar-test development describes how an entire test involving several grammar tasks is assembled, and how the individual tasks are specified, written and scored. The outcome of the operationalization phase is both a **blueprint** for the entire test including scoring materials and a draft version of the actual test. According to Bachman and Palmer (1996), the blueprint contains two parts: a description of the overall

structure of the test and a set of **test-task specifications** for each task. The blueprint serves as the basis for item writing and scoring.

The first part of the blueprint provides a description of the test structure. This involves an overview of the entire test. Minimally the test structure describes the number of test parts or tasks used to measure grammatical ability, the salience of these parts, their sequence, the importance of the parts, and the number of tasks per part. Other information can also be included in this overview, as seen in Table 6.2.

Test construction begins with the descriptions of tasks in the TLU domain. In examining students' grammatical knowledge base for writing lab reports, several potential tasks can be identified and selected from the TLU domain as a basis for assessment, as seen in the design statement. Those descriptions can be modified to produce test-task specifications. The **test-task specifications** consist of a detailed list of task characteristics, which form the basis for writing the test tasks. Test-task specifications are an important part of the operationalization phase because they provide a means of creating parallel forms of the same test – that is, alternate test forms containing the same task types and approximately the same test content and measurement characteristics. Specifications also establish a means of evaluating the congruence between what was supposed to be on a test and what is actually included in a test. Finally, according to Davidson and Lynch (2002), test specifications provide a focal point around which test developers can debate, explore, negotiate and reach a consensus for the final shape of the test.

According to Bachman and Palmer (1996), test-task specifications provide, for each task, a description of the following: the purpose, the construct definition, the characteristics of the setting, the time allotment, the instructions, the characteristics of the input and expected response, a description of the relationship between the input and response, and finally the scoring method. Many of these specifications are identical to those stipulated in the design statement, and should be repeated in the blueprint to guide the writing of the test. Since I have already explained many of these specifications in discussing the design statement, I will not repeat the explanation. (For further discussion and examples, see Bachman and Palmer, 1996.)

Once the blueprint is prepared, test writing begins. Instructions are written for each section. The operationalization phase of test development should end with a draft of the test that is ready to be tried out with test-takers.

In the next section, I will discuss the third phase of grammar-test development, the test administration. However, before doing that, I will describe

Table 6.2 *Overall structure of the chemistry lab test*

Task component and purpose	Topic	Type of input and expected response	Weight (%)	Length (items)	Time (mins.)	Scoring
Part 1: Verb forms task Grammatical form • morphosyntactic forms (past active and passive verb forms; causatives)	Chem. lab report	Item Sentences with 4 MC options Selected-response task type	25	10	8	Right/wrong scoring (0/1) • 1 correctness criterion 'form' • 1 scorer Total: 10 points
Part 2: Logical connector task Grammatical meaning • cohesive meanings (logical connectors)	Chem. lab report	Item Sentences with gaps Limited-production task type	25	10	8	Right/wrong scoring (0/1) • 1 correctness criterion 'meaning' • 1 scorer Total: 10 points
Part 3: Lab report task Grammatical form • Morphosyntactic forms (active and passive verbs; causatives) • Cohesive forms (logical connectors) Grammatical meaning (conveyance of literal and intended meanings) Rhetorical meaning (display of lab report genre: actions, observed results, inferences)	Chem. lab report	Prompt Extended-production task type	50	1	45	Rating scales (all 1 to 5) • Task fulfillment • Communicative meaningfulness • Communicative precision (accuracy) • Organization effectiveness Total: 20 points • 2 scorers • 2 point discrepancy gets third read • norming packet, 'blind ratings'

the different methods that can be used to score grammar tests. Given the importance and complexity of test scoring, I will describe these procedures in detail so that they can be specified properly in the blueprint.

Specifying the scoring method

As discussed in Chapter 5, the scoring method provides an explicit description of the criteria for correctness and the exact procedures for scoring the response. Generally speaking, tasks can be scored **objectively**, where the scorer does not need to make any expert judgments in determining if the answers are correct, or **subjectively**, where expert judgment is needed to judge performance.

Scoring selected-response tasks

The first task in the example chemistry lab test discussed above is a selected-response task (i.e., multiple-choice) of grammatical form. Scorers are provided with an answer key to determine if the answers are right or wrong – no further adjudication is necessary. In this task, each item is designed to measure a single area of explicit grammatical knowledge. As a result, there is a **single criterion for correctness**. This scoring method is called **dichotomous** or **right/wrong scoring** (Bachman and Palmer, 1996). In these instances, one point is given for a correct answer and zero for an incorrect one. The following is an example of an item that aims to measure morphosyntactic form – with one criterion for correctness.

> **Example 1. Designed to measure grammatical form (morphosyntactic form)**
> Directions: Check the correct answer.
>
> Water is then _____ to the solution.
>   ___ 1. add   ✔ 3. added   (✔ = key)
>   ___ 2. adds   ___ 4. adding

With selected-response items, however, there are times when we might wish to obtain information on more than one area of grammatical knowledge in light of our construct definition. In these cases, we can identify **multiple criteria for correctness**. As a result, we might give one point for each criterion in order to capture information on each area of grammatical knowledge. In such cases, we can score the different answer options based on the criteria. For example, suppose our goal was to measure morphosyntactic accuracy and lexical meaningfulness, and we gave the following selected-response question.

Example 2. Designed to measure grammatical form and meaning
Directions: Check the correct answer.

This _____ the litmus paper blue.

✔ 1. turned   ___ 3. changed

___ 2. makes   ___ 4. produces

We could then score responses as follows.

Table 6.3 *Right/wrong scoring with multiple criteria for correctness*

Response	Morphosyntactic accuracy	Lexical meaningfulness
turned	1	1
makes	0	1
changed	1	0
produces	0	0

In this case, *turned* is the only response that gets full credit as the response meets both criteria for correctness. The multiple right/wrong scoring method assigns two scores for each response, and if not machine-scored, would severely impact the practicality of the scoring process.

Another way of scoring this selected-response item is to score the responses using the multiple criteria but, instead of giving two scores, we give a *single* score for each response. In this case, a response that satisfies all criteria gets full credit, one that satisfies no criteria gets no credit and one that satisfies some criteria gets partial credit. This is called the **partial-credit scoring method**, as seen below.

Table 6.4 *Partial-credit scoring*

Response	Morphosyntactic accuracy	Lexical meaningfulness	Both
turned	1	1	2
makes	0	1	1
changed	1	0	1
produces	0	0	0

The basis for partial credit can be determined in many ways. Each criterion can receive equal emphasis, as seen above, or one criterion can be given greater priority than the others. For example, if we included 'spelling' as part of our construct, we might want to give a correctly spelled word a maximum of 0.5 points and 0 for incorrect spelling.

Aside from scoring selected-response grammar tasks, we can use the domain of response choices in selected-response tasks to measure different levels of grammatical knowledge. Some selected-response items have one and only one 'correct' answer, measuring seemingly only one area of grammatical ability. These items may be easier than items which are intended to measure more than one area of grammatical knowledge and which present several acceptable response options of which only one is the clear 'best'. When test-takers need to make subtle distinctions between the answer choices, the items could conceivably be more difficult. For example, the passive voice response *water is then added* might be preferable in some situations to active voice response *we then added water*. Tasks that require students to make finer distinctions should be described in the specifications, and procedures for scoring these tasks should also be clearly articulated.

In sum, the multiple right/wrong and partial-credit approaches to scoring are useful when we wish to measure multiple dimensions of our construct because they provide more information and better reflect the underlying constructs. First, they allow for different items within a selected-response grammar task to be scored differently, depending on the areas of grammatical knowledge that each item aims to measure. In other words, one item might be scored dichotomously and another item in the same part of the test might be scored partial credit. Secondly, by giving credit for partially correct responses, we can provide a more precise estimate of the test-takers' grammatical knowledge, and I believe we can better account for the fact that some areas of language ability develop at different rates. For example, the passive voice verb forms in English are relatively easy to learn, but their meanings present a much greater challenge, and are fully acquired later. On the other hand, the meaning of the definite article in German is relatively easy to acquire for English speakers, but the correct use of the forms is more challenging and develops much later. Multiple right/wrong and partial-credit scoring allow teachers to acknowledge with scores what they have always known – that some wrong answers reflect a greater degree of understanding than others. Finally, these scoring approaches allow us to provide potentially better diagnostic information to test-takers by reporting separate scores for the different areas of grammatical ability (e.g., morphosyntactic and cohesive accuracy and literal meaningfulness) in addition to a composite score. An obvious disadvantage to using more complicated scoring schemes, however, is the time it takes to determine a scoring scheme, to mark each item and to train the scorers, some of which could be mitigated by machine scoring.

Scoring limited-production tasks

The second task in the lab report test is a limited-production task. Limited-production tasks are designed to elicit a range of possible answers and can be used to measure one or more areas of grammatical knowledge. Task 2 in the lab test is designed to measure only cohesive meaningfulness. Consider the following item.

> **Example 3. Designed to measure grammatical meaningfulness**
> Directions: Complete the paragraph with the best answer for the context. Write the answer on the line.
>
> A gram of salt was first poured into the solution. __(1)__, the solution was shaken vigorously __(2)__ it turned green. This took about five seconds.

Items 1 and 2 are designed to measure cohesive meaning with logical connectors. Item 1 allows for a wide range of possible answers (e.g., *Then, Next, After that*) to be included on the scoring key. Item 2, on the other hand, has a much more restricted range of possible answers (e.g., *until, after which*). In each case, there is only one criterion for correctness – cohesive meaning, and the response is scored right/wrong. If we wished, we could include other criteria such as cohesive form or spelling as considerations for correctness, in which case, we would have multiple correctness criteria.

With most limited-production tasks, a range of possible answers is acceptable. The domain of answers extends from a word to a sentence, and from a relatively fixed set of answers to a very open one. As these tasks can measure more than one area of grammatical knowledge, they are usually scored with the multiple right/wrong or partial-credit scoring methods. Regardless of the method, test developers need to use an answer key in order to minimize the inconsistencies in scoring.

In some cases, limited-response tasks can elicit responses that require test-takers to produce multi-unit responses. This may encompass one or more clauses and may involve a variety of acceptable responses. They may also include a wide range of grammar points. For example, the following task is designed to measure two criteria for correctness – grammatical form and meaning – in the context of providing 'good' service.

Example 4. Designed to measure grammatical form and meaning on the discourse level

Directions: Complete the conversation the two people are having.

Customer: Excuse me, waiter, but I found a hair in my soup!
Waiter: _____
Customer: Thank you very much. I'd appreciate that.

Table 6.5 *Template for a grammatical knowledge and topical knowledge rating scale*

Level of control	Grammatical precision – descriptors
2 Complete	**Demonstrates complete control of grammatical forms for the task**; the forms are grammatically accurate; wide and sophisticated range of forms for the task.
1 Limited	**Demonstrates limited control of grammatical forms for the task**; the forms are mostly accurate; most errors do not inhibit communication; moderate range of forms for the task.
0 None	**Demonstrates little or no control of grammatical forms for the task;** too many errors in grammatical form; errors inhibit communication; narrow range of forms for the task.

Level of control	Communicative meaningfulness – descriptors
2 Complete	**Demonstrates full ability to get message across meaningfully for the task**; the grammatical meaning of the utterance(s) is conveyed; the message is relevant and valid.
1 Limited	**Demonstrates limited ability to get message across meaningfully for the task**; the grammatical meaning is partially conveyed; the message may lack some relevance or validity.
0 None	**Demonstrates little or no ability to get message across meaningfully for the task**; the grammatical meaning is not successfully conveyed; the message may lack relevance and/or validity.

Level of control	Control of topic – descriptors
2 Complete	**Demonstrates complete topical control for the task**; shows a wide range of relevant and valid information for the task.
1 Limited	**Demonstrates limited topical control for the task**; shows a moderate range of information for the task; some information may be irrelevant and/or inaccurate.
0 None	**Demonstrates little or no topical control for the task;** information is irrelevant and/or inaccurate; not enough material to evaluate.

Given the nature of the response, we could use a right/wrong scoring method or a partial-credit scoring method with multiple criteria for correctness as we did with the selected-response tasks. We could also decide to judge the extent to which each response is grammatically precise and communicatively meaningful by means of a **rating scale** method of scoring, which will be discussed in more detail below.

Table 6.5 presents an example of a rating scale that could be adapted to score grammatical accuracy or precision, communicative meaningfulness, and control of topic in limited-production tasks. Obviously, this is only a template and the descriptors would need adjusting in light of the specific areas of grammatical knowledge being measured.

If a student in example 4 above fills in the blank with *Sorry about that. Let me get you another bowl*, he or she would get 2 points for grammatical precision and 2 points for communicative meaningfulness. If the student answers, **I sorry. I get you different one*, he or she would get 0 points for grammatical precision (too many errors) and 2 points for communicative meaningfulness (since the student was fully successful in getting his or her message across and it was relevant and valid). As this discourse completion task does not really require much topical information beyond the grammatical meaning of the utterance, topical control would probably not be scored.

DCTs can also be used to measure pragmatic appropriateness, acceptability or naturalness. For example, if the waiter answered *OK lady, let me take it out for you, and just get over it*, the student would get a 2 for grammatical precision, a 2 for meaningfulness and a 0 for appropriateness – that is, if test-takers were instructed to respond politely. To assess pragmatic knowledge in terms of sociolinguistic or sociocultural appropriateness, we could use the following rating scale (or one similar to it), or we could devise separate scales for appropriateness, acceptability and naturalness.

Table 6.6 *Pragmatic appropriateness, acceptability and naturalness*

Level of control	Pragmatic effectiveness – descriptors
2 Complete	**Demonstrates full pragmatic control for the task**; pragmatic meaning(s) is communicated in a completely appropriate or acceptable way; grammar is natural sounding.
1 Limited	**Demonstrates partial pragmatic control for the task**; pragmatic meaning(s) is communicated in a marginally appropriate or acceptable way; grammar is relatively natural sounding.
0 None	**Demonstrates limited or no pragmatic control for the task**; pragmatic meaning(s) is communicated in an inappropriate or unacceptable way; grammar may sound unnatural and awkward.

Scoring extended-production tasks

The third task in the chemistry lab test asks test-takers to write an abbreviated version of a lab report based on topical cues in the input. This task is designed to elicit an array of grammatical features characteristic of chemical lab reports (e.g., past active and passive sentences). These features are specified in the design statement. However, given the nature of the task, there is no guarantee the test-takers will write the report using the passive. In addition to the target features, the task will elicit a variety of other features (e.g., articles). Instead of trying to evaluate every individual area of grammatical knowledge in such instances, we might specify which components of grammatical knowledge we wish to focus on based on the purpose of the assessment and the definition of the construct. Alternatively, we can assess the quality of the response by judging the students' overall level of grammatical ability, all the while keeping in mind those features the task aims to measure. According to Bachman and Palmer (1996), extended-production responses such as an essay or oral interview can be scored with reference to a rating scale that is specifically designed for its measurement purpose.

A rating scale provides a means of judging the quality of performance in terms of different levels of ability explicitly described in a scoring rubric. Grammatical rating scales consist of a set of numbered categories (e.g., 0, .5, 1 or 0 to 2 for limited-production tasks; 0–5 or 0–10 for extended-productions tasks) that represent different levels of grammatical performance or mastery. The scales are typically derived from a theoretical definition of grammatical ability according to what the test is generally held to be measuring. They can also come from syllabus-based, objectives-based or standard-based notions of grammatical mastery or from acquisitional notions of interlanguage development (e.g., Chang, 2002, 2004). Scales can also be obtained empirically from an analysis of the data produced while test-takers are taking the test (McNamara, 1996), or from a combination of methods mentioned. The levels in rating scales usually range from no evidence of ability or mastery to full target-like ability or mastery of the construct. It is important that we know how to develop and use rating scales to meet our test purposes since rating scales are the theoretical embodiment of the constructs being measured in our test (McNamara, 1996).

As with limited-production tasks, raters can use either a holistic or an analytic rating scale to judge grammatical performance. In dealing with large amounts of oral or written data from students, the holistic rating method treats grammatical ability as a single, unitary, underlying trait, which, according to White (1984), reflects an overall personal reaction to the performance sample. In addition to task fulfillment, raters doing holistic scoring are almost always asked to consider several components of grammatical ability simultaneously in order to supply one single holistic rating. One advantage of this method is practicality and convenience; however, in providing a single score, valuable diagnostic information is lost for test-takers who might have benefited from a more detailed portrait of their abilities. Another disadvantage is that the scores from holistic rubrics often present an interpretation problem since raters do not always focus on the same features of performance in determining their score (Weigle, 2002). The following is a holistic rating scale of grammatical form designed around the range of forms and their communicative accuracy.

Table 6.7 *A holistic rating scale of grammatical accuracy*

	Descriptors
9–10 Complete	Demonstrates **complete grammatical control** for the task; full range of grammatical forms; may have a few random minor errors; wide and sophisticated range of vocabulary
7–8 Extensive	Demonstrates **extensive grammatical control** for the task; large range of grammatical forms; may have some error types (e.g., articles) that do not impede communication; wide range of vocabulary
5–6 Moderate	Demonstrates **moderate to good grammatical control** for the task; limited range of grammatical forms; may have a few errors which impede communication; a moderate range of vocabulary
3–4 Limited	Demonstrates **limited grammatical control** for the task; small range of grammatical forms; may have several error types which impede communication; a limited range of vocabulary
1–2 None	Demonstrates **poor grammatical control** for the task; extremely limited range of grammatical forms; may have several error types which often impede communication; a limited range of vocabulary

Unlike holistic rating scales, **analytic rating scales** provide *separate* ratings for each defined component of grammatical ability. These scores may be presented to test-takers separately, or may be totaled to provide an overall assessment as well. Again, analytic scales allow us to account for differential development of grammatical ability by assessing several components of grammatical knowledge separately. In other words, a test-taker may have learned the subjunctive verb forms in Portuguese, and may even know the rules for using them, but he may not know how the meaning of the verb actually changes when the verb is put in the subjunctive. As we discussed with limited-production tasks, analytic rating scales should be designed with reference to both a theoretical definition of grammatical knowledge and an examination of the performance samples. The different levels of performance also range from no evidence of mastery to full target-like mastery of the construct(s).

Regardless of the type of rating scales used, the rubric accompanying these scales should not only be clear and explicit, but should also be usable by raters (and possibly students) and interpretable by all stakeholders (Weigle, 2002). Following Weigle (2002), factors to include in designing a scoring rubric include: Who is going to use the rubric?; What aspects of grammatical ability are the most important and how will they be divided up?; How many points or what scoring levels will be used?; and How will the scores be reported? For an informative discussion of rating scales, the research driving their use and procedures for creating and using rating scales, see Weigle (2002).

Again, following Weigle (2002), descriptors at the various levels of a grammatical scale can be determined in several ways. Scales can be defined in relation to the areas of grammatical ability being measured and then levels of attainment can be determined, usually from zero level of control to complete control. The advantage of defining scales in this way according to Bachman and Palmer (1996) is that inferences about the test-takers' abilities can be determined on an absolute scale; however, this 'mastery approach' requires training for raters to differentiate the different levels. Another method of deriving scale descriptors is to administer the test and, from the responses, select examples of items that display complete control, limited control and no control. Teachers can then characterize the different levels from which scale descriptions can be derived. This 'descriptive approach' is useful in determining how learners vary in their performance on this one task. The results, however, are not generalizable to how they might perform on other tasks. Nonetheless, there are times in grammar assessment where mastery, defined in terms of zero to complete accuracy, meaningfulness, appropriateness, acceptability or naturalness, is insufficient to capture the performance. In these cases, we might also consider the range, scope or even the developmental level (based on information from the interlanguage studies) of the grammar as evidence of mastery. In sum, descriptors in a rubric need to consider both the theoretical construct(s) that an item is designed to measure, as well as the characteristics of the item performance if we hope to provide useful and interpretable descriptions of correctness.

Using scoring rubrics

Once the scoring rubric has been constructed, the scoring process can be determined. In an attempt to avoid unreliability due to the scoring process, certain basic procedures should be followed. First of all, raters should be normed. To do this, raters are given a norming packet containing the scoring rubric and samples of tasks typifying the different levels. These **benchmark** samples serve to familiarize raters with the rubric and how performance might be leveled. Words such as 'accurate' and 'meaningful' should be explained and operationalized. In oral assessment, raters are provided with a norming video or audiotape. Raters are then convened to discuss the ratings and, if necessary, fine-tune the rubric. In training raters, it should be noted that some degree of rater variability is unavoidable and expected. However, raters who consistently rate higher or lower than the others should be given feedback and perhaps more detailed training. Once questions about scoring have been answered, live rating can begin. It is important to make sure that items or prompts be scored by at least two raters. If two scores are discrepant beyond some criterion score, a third rater should adjudicate the rating. Rating should be 'blind' (without knowing whose paper it is) and independent (without knowing how the other raters scored the sample). Rating sheets, such as the one below can be created to score the tasks efficiently.

Table 6.8 *Grammatical knowledge and topical control rating sheet*

		Rating
Grammatical control	5 Points: Demonstrates complete grammatical control for the task	
	4 Points: Demonstrates extensive grammatical control	
	3 Points: Demonstrates moderate to good grammatical control	
	2 Points: Demonstrates limited grammatical control	
	1 Point: Demonstrates poor grammatical control	_____
Topical control	2 Points: Demonstrates complete topical control for the task	
	1 Point: Demonstrates limited topical control	
	0 Points: Demonstrates little or no topical control	_____
	Total points	_____

Grading

The blueprint should describe the relative importance of the test sections. This can be used to determine a final score on the test. In the chemistry lab test blueprint, the selected-response and the limited-production tasks together account for fifty percent of the points (20 points), while the extended-production task accounts for the other fifty percent (20 points). To determine the score for the entire test, we could add up the total number of points for each test section and then calculate a percentage-correct score for the entire test by dividing the number of correct items by the total number of points on the test. This percentage-correct score can then be converted into a grade based on some grading policy.

Stage 3: Test administration and analysis

The final stage in the process of developing grammar tests involves the administration of the test to individual students or small groups, and then to a large group of examinees on a trial basis. **Piloting** the entire test or individual test tasks allows for the collection of response data and other sorts of information to support and/or improve the usefulness of the test. This information can then be analyzed and the test revised before being put to operational use. In short, before a test, especially a high-stakes test, can be used with larger groups of test-takers, it must go through a series of analyses and revisions. In classroom situations, however, extensive piloting is not always feasible. In such cases, care should be taken in the interpretation of results and the decisions made about test-takers. Nonetheless, if the same tests are used in subsequent administrations, the tasks should be reviewed, and the test revised before the next administration.

The actual administration of the test should transpire in a setting that is physically comfortable and free from distraction, and a supportive testing environment should be established. Instructions should be clear and the administration orderly. Test administration provides an excellent opportunity for collecting information about the test-takers' initial reaction to the test tasks and information about certain test procedures such as the allotment of time. When possible, empirical information in the form of a questionnaire or interview should be elicited from the examinees after the test. Test-takers are often happy to report on issues such as the clarity of the instructions or the test items, the occurrence of items with double or no keys, the time allotment and other characteristics of the test procedures that elicit strong, initial reactions.

Once the pre-test responses have been collected and scored, a number of statistical analyses should be performed in order to examine the psychometric properties of the test. Although the implementation of statistical procedures is beyond the purview of this book, it is important for language educators to be aware of the types of procedures available and how they can provide information for test improvement. For detailed information on test analysis, see Hatch and Lazaraton (1991), Alderson, Clapham and Wall (1995), Brown (1996), and Bachman (2004).

Test analyses provide different types of information to evaluate the characteristics of test usefulness. This information serves as a basis for revising the test before it goes operational, at which time further data are collected and analyses performed in an iterative and recursive manner. In the end, we will have a bank of test tasks that will be **archived** and from which we can draw upon in further test administrations.

Summary

In this chapter, I used Bachman and Palmer's framework to discuss the qualities of grammar tests that make them 'useful'. I discussed how the qualities of reliability, construct validity, authenticity, interactiveness, impact, and practicality work in a complementary fashion, and how the decision to emphasize one characteristic over another depends on the test mandate and the usefulness qualities that are most relevant for the particular situation. For example, if the mandate calls for large numbers of students to be placed into a language program with a quick turnaround and with limited human resources, we might select test tasks and scoring procedures that maximize the quality of practicality. Teachers could then be asked to compensate for the qualities of construct validity and reliability by adjusting student placements within the first couple of class sessions. The use of these scores, however, could create serious problems for novice teachers who are unfamiliar with the course levels and who might not know what level would be best for a student.

I also discussed the process of grammar-test construction and attempted to show how the concerns for test usefulness could serve as a springboard for the development of grammar tests. Grammar tests are prepared in three stages. The design stage describes the purpose(s) and intended uses of the test, and provides a detailed plan for creating test tasks that aim to elicit instances of language use that correspond to those observed in the target language use domain. The operationalization phase provides a blueprint for test writing. The blueprint outlines the test structure and provides a set of specifications for each test task. The writing of the actual test also takes place in the operationalization phase. The scoring procedures are also specified in this phase. The last stage of grammar-test development involves the administration and the analysis of the exam results. This stage specifies procedures for administering the exam and collecting data intended to improve the test or support the qualities of test usefulness. Although the test-development process outlined in this chapter provides a set of procedures for the creation of grammar tests, these procedures are meant to serve as a guide, rather than a precise recipe, for test development, with each part of the process being adapted as the situation calls for it.

CHAPTER SEVEN

Illustrative tests of grammatical ability

Introduction

In this chapter I will examine several examples of professionally developed language tests that measure grammatical ability. Some of these tests contain separate sections that are exclusively devoted to the assessment of grammatical ability, while others measure grammatical knowledge along with other components of language ability in the context of language use – that is while test-takers are listening, speaking, reading or writing. The purpose of examining these tests is to illustrate how a few large-scale grammar tests have been designed and operationalized in light of their purpose(s), intended use(s) and the construct(s) they are trying to measure. The framework of grammatical knowledge presented in Chapter 4 provides a backdrop for considerations of construct definition. A second goal of this chapter is to examine these grammar tests in view of the qualities of test usefulness discussed in the previous chapter. Given limitations of space, I will comment briefly on all the qualities except practicality. Since the tests I have chosen to review are all operational, practicality might be considered a bottom-line function of how the other qualities were prioritized and resources allocated (Bachman, personal communication, 2002); therefore, I will focus this discussion on how the priorities of test usefulness appear to be prioritized. Finally, this chapter makes no attempt at providing a comprehensive review of all grammar tests available; nor does it attempt to provide model examples of how grammatical ability should be conceived and operationalized in language tests.

I will begin the analysis of each test by describing the context of the test, its purpose and its intended use(s). After that, I will turn to how the construct of grammatical ability was defined and operationalized. I will then describe the grammar task(s) taking into account the areas of grammatical knowledge being measured and will summarize the critical features of the test tasks. Finally, I will discuss these tests in terms of their purpose and the qualities of test usefulness. In so doing, I will highlight the priorities and compromises made in the process of balancing the qualities of test usefulness.

The First Certificate in English Language Test (FCE)

Purpose

The *First Certificate in English* (*FCE*) exam was first developed by the University of Cambridge Local Examinations Syndicate (UCLES, now Cambridge ESOL) in 1939 and has been revised periodically ever since. This exam is the most widely taken Cambridge ESOL examination with an annual candidature of over 270,000 (see http://www.cambridgeesol.org/exam/index.cfm). The purpose of the *FCE* (Cambridge ESOL, 2001a) is to assess the general English language proficiency of learners as measured by their abilities in reading, writing, speaking, listening, and knowledge of the lexical and grammatical systems of English (Cambridge ESOL, 1995, p. 4). More specifically, the *FCE* is a level-three exam in the Cambridge main suite of exams, and consists of five compulsory subtests or 'papers': reading, writing, use of English, listening and speaking (Cambridge ESOL, 1996, p. 8). Students who pass the *FCE* are assumed to have sufficient proficiency to handle routine office jobs (clerical, managerial) and to take courses given in English (Cambridge ESOL, 2001a, p. 6). Given that the *FCE* can be used as certification of English language proficiency for certain types of jobs, it is considered a high-stakes test.

In this review, I will focus on how grammatical ability is measured in the Use of English or grammar section of the *FCE*. I will then examine how grammatical ability is measured in the writing and speaking sections.

Construct definition and operationalization

According to the *FCE Handbook* (Cambridge ESOL, 2001a), the Use of English paper is designed to measure the test-takers' ability to 'demonstrate their knowledge and control of the language system by completing a number of tasks, some of which are based on specially written texts' (p. 7). The handbook further states 'learners at this level are expected to be able to handle the main structures of the language with some confidence, demonstrate knowledge of a wide range of vocabulary and use appropriate communicative strategies in a variety of social situations' (p. 6). In terms of the model of grammatical knowledge presented in Figure 4.2 (p. 91), the use of English section of the *FCE* (based on the example presented in the *FCE Handbook*, Cambridge ESOL, 1996) appears to measure grammatical knowledge in terms of lexical, morphosyntactic and cohesive form and meaning, as depicted in Figure 7.1.

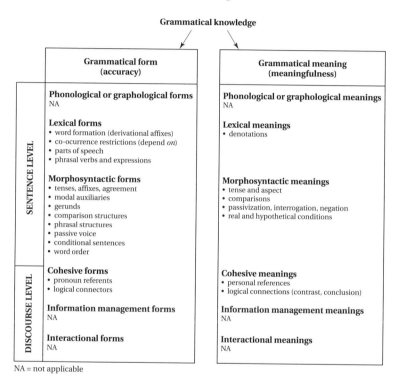

NA = not applicable

Figure 7.1 Components of grammatical knowledge measured in the *FCE* Use of English paper

This Use of English paper consists of five tasks with 65 items, as summarized in Table 7.1. The area(s) of grammatical knowledge depicted below are expressed in terms of the model of grammatical knowledge presented in Figure 4.2. This paper is administered in one hour and 15 minutes. Separate results for the Use of English paper are not provided. The results for the whole *FCE* are reported as one mark with a special indication for papers that are either outstanding or weak. The minimum pass score is a 'C', which corresponds to sixty percent for the whole *FCE* (Cambridge ESOL, 2001a, p. 8).

Excerpts from these test sections are presented in Figure 7.2.

Table 7.1 *An overview of the FCE Use of English paper*

Part	Area(s) of grammatical knowledge	Task type	Task input and expected response	No. of items	Scoring
1.	• Lexical meaning	Multiple-choice cloze (selected-response)	One passage with 15 selected gaps followed by 4-option MC questions. All options have different lexical choices.	15	Right/wrong; 1 criterion for correctness
2.	• Morphosyntactic form and meaning • Lexical meaning	Open cloze (limited-production)	One passage with 15 selected gaps, needing one word.	15	Right/wrong; 1 criterion for correctness
3.	• Morphosyntactic form and meaning; • Lexical form	'Key' word transformation (limited-production)	Using a key word, test-takers complete a sentence gap to have the same meaning as a lead-in sentence. Gaps have 2–5 words.	10	Partial credit ranging from 0 to 2 points. Possibly 2 criteria for correctness
4.	• Morphosyntactic form and meaning	Error identification and correction (selected-response)	Test-takers identify the error in a sentence and correct it, or they note the absence of any error.	15	Right/wrong; 1 criterion for correctness
5.	• Lexical form	Word formation (limited-production)	A passage with 10 gaps and 10 key words. The form of each key word is changed to fit the gap.	10	Right/wrong; 1 criterion for correctness

Measuring grammatical ability through language use

In addition to measuring grammatical ability in the Use of English paper of the test, the *FCE* measures grammatical ability in the writing and speaking sections. The writing paper consists of two tasks: one compulsory and one to be chosen by the candidate. The compulsory task involves writing a transactional letter and the second task asks test-takers to choose from a number of writing options (e.g., an article, descriptive narrative, report). An example of the *FCE* compulsory writing task is presented in Figure 7.3.

Language use in the writing paper is measured in the contexts of writing letters, articles, reports and compositions (Cambridge ESOL, 2001a, p. 7). Scores are derived from a six-point (0–5), holistic rating scale based on 'the control, organization and cohesion, range of structures and vocabulary, register and format, and [the effect made on] the target reader indicated in the task' (Cambridge ESOL, 2001a, p. 19). More specifically, grammatical ability is rated according to the range of structures and vocabulary within the task set and the accuracy of structures based on the number of errors. Grammatical ability is also measured at the discourse level in terms of cohesive forms and meanings. Although not explicitly stated, grammatical meaning appears to be measured alongside grammatical form by the degree to which the language achieves or impedes communication by realizing the task. Finally, pragmatic meanings are considered as they relate to the appropriacy of the register and format in view of the purpose and audience (i.e., sociolinguistic/sociocultural meanings) and the effectiveness of the organization (i.e., rhetorical meanings – coherence and genre) (Cambridge ESOL, 2001a, p. 19). Figure 7.4 presents the scoring descriptors from bands 1, 3 and 5 of the *FCE* writing rubric.

The published literature for the writing paper contains sample answers for each performance level along with rater comments. The rater comments address the stated criteria and help illustrate the role of grammatical performance in writing. For example, one rater who gave an overall score of 'very good' to a response described the grammar as follows:

> The language is virtually error-free and there is a wide range of vocabulary and structure (*has found the strength in herself to resist him, she chooses to take the difficult path*).
>
> (Cambridge ESOL, 1995, p. 44)

Part 1 – Excerpt

For questions 1–15, read the text below and decide which answer (**A, B, C** or **D**) best fits each space. There is an example at the beginning (0). Mark your answers **on the separate answer sheet.**

Example:

0	**A** bank	**B** border	**C** shore	**D** coast

0	**A**	**B**	**C**	**D**
	■	☐	☐	☐

THE LONDON TEA TRADE

The London Tea Trade Centre is on the north (0) . . . of the River Thames. It is the centre of industry of (1) . . . importance in the (2) . . . lives of the British. Tea is without (3) . . . the British national drink: every man woman and child over ten years of ages has (4) . . . average over four cups a day or some 1500 cups annually.

1	**A** high	**B** wide	**C** great	**D** large
2	**A** common	**B** typical	**C** everyday	**D** usual
3	**A** doubt	**B** dispute	**C** disbelief	**D** uncertainly
4	**A** for	**B** by	**C** at	**D** on

Part 2 – Excerpt

For questions 16–30, read the text below and think of the word which best fits each space. Use only one word in each space. There is an example at the beginning (0). Write your answers **on the separate answer sheet.**

Example:

0	*doing*

DEPARTMENT STORES

In 1846 an Irish immigrant in New York named Alexander Stewart opened a business called the Marble Dry-Goods Palace. By (0) . . . so, he gave the world something completely new – the department store. Before this, no-one (16) . . . tried to bring together such a wide range of goods (17) . . . a single roof.

Figure 7.2 (*continued on next page*)

Part 3 – Excerpt

For questions 31–40, complete the second sentence so that it has a similar meaning to the first sentence, using the word given. **Do not change the word given.** You must use between **two** and **five** words, including the word given. There is an example at the beginning (0). Write **only** the missing words **on the separate answer sheet.**

Example:

0	My brother is too young to drive a car.
NOT	
My brother is _____ drive a car.	

The gap can be filled by:

0	*not old enough to*

31	Why are you interested in taking up a new hobby?
	want
	Why .... up a new hobby?

Part 4 – Excerpt

For questions 41–55, read the text below and look carefully at each line. Some of the lines are correct, and some have a word which should not be there. If a line is correct, put a tick (✔) by the number **on the separate answer sheet.** If the line has a word which should **not** be there, write the word **on the separate answer sheet.** There are two examples at the beginning (0 and 00).

Example:

0	*over*

00	✔

A HOLIDAY JOB

0	Congratulations on getting over your teaching diploma. Your
00	parents must be really proud of you. I've got some great news.
41	One of my father's friends who has a small travel agency, and
41	she has been very kindly given me a holiday job.

Figure 7.2 (*continued on next page*)

Part 5 – Excerpt

For questions 56–65, read the text below. Use the word given in capitals at the end of each line to form a word that fits in the space in the same line. There is an example at the beginning (0). Write your answers **on the separate answer sheet.**

Example:

0	*ability*

COMPUTERS THAT PLAY GAMES

Computers have had the (0) *ability* to play chess for many years   **ABLE**

now, and their (56) . . . in games against the best players in the   **PERFORM**

world has shown steady (57) . . .   **IMPROVE**

Figure 7.2 FCE Paper 3 (Cambridge ESOL, 2001a, *FCE Handbook*, Use of English Section)

You *must* answer the question. You have just retuned from a Johnson's Activity Holiday, which was very disappointing. You decide to write to the company to complain about your holiday and ask for some money back.

    Read the advertisement below carefully, on which you have made some notes. Then, using the information, write a letter to the company. You may add other relevant points of your own.

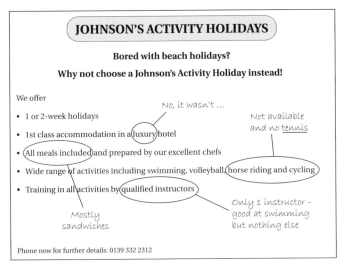

Write a letter of **120** to **180** words in an appropriate style on the opposite page. Don't write any addresses.

Figure 7.3 *FCE* Paper 2: A compulsory writing task (Cambridge ESOL, 1996, *FCE Handbook*, p. 32)

Band 5	Full realization of the task set.
	All content points included with appropriate expansion.
	Wide range of structure and vocabulary within the task set.
	Minimal errors, perhaps due to ambition; well-developed control of language.
	Ideas effectively organized, with a variety of linking devices.
	Register and format consistently appropriate to purpose and audience.
	Fully achieves the desired effect on the target reader.
Band 3	Reasonable achievement of the task set.
	All major content points included; some minor omissions.
	Adequate range of structure and vocabulary, which fulfils the requirements of the task.
	A number of errors may be present, but do not impede communication.
	Ideas adequately organized, with simple linking devices.
	Reasonable, if not always successful attempt at register and format appropriate to purpose and audience.
	Achieves, on the whole, the desired effect on the target reader.
Band 1	Poor attempt at the task set.
	Notable content omissions and/or considerable irrelevance, possibly due to misinterpretation of the task set.
	Narrow range of structure and vocabulary.
	Frequent errors which obscure communication; little evidence of language control.
	Lack of organization or linking devices.
	Little or no awareness of appropriate register and format.
	Very negative effect on the target reader.

Figure 7.4 Part of the *FCE* scoring rubric for writing (Cambridge ESOL, 2001a, p. 19)

Another rater who assigned a score of 'less than satisfactory' wrote:

> There are a few good examples of vocabulary and structure (*she could be considered as a competitor; the competitors*). However communication breaks down in the second paragraph and there are other basic errors (*being teached, was an artistic nature, entral exam, too[very?] hard*) which could have a negative effect on the reader.
>
> (Cambridge ESOL, 1995, p. 40)

Raters are normed before beginning the rating process. To maximize consistency, the *FCE Handbook* (Cambridge ESOL, 2001a) states that 'a rigorous process of co-ordination and checking is carried out before and throughout the marking process' (p. 20). However, the majority of writing papers are scored by only one rater to maximize practicality. This compromise may be emphasized at the expense of reliability.

The *FCE* speaking paper consists of four tasks: an interview (three minutes), an 'individual long turn' or monologue (four minutes), a two-way collaborative task between two candidates (three minutes) and a collaborative task between three candidates (four minutes). Language use is measured in the contexts of 'exchanging personal and factual information, expressing and finding out about attitudes and opinions' (Cambridge ESOL, 2001a, p. 45). This might involve functions such as agreeing and disagreeing, and suggesting and speculating. Although there are four tasks, assessment is based on the overall performance of the candidate, and not on the individual part of the test (Cambridge ESOL, 2001a, p. 48). Speaking performance is based on the ratings of two independent judges: one who uses an analytic rating scale and one who, serving as an examiner/interlocutor, uses a global rating scale.

The analytic rubric for the speaking paper contains four scales: grammar and vocabulary, discourse management, pronunciation, and interactive communication. The grammar and vocabulary scale operationalizes grammatical form in terms of the accuracy, range and appropriateness of the lexical and morphosyntactic forms for the task. The discourse management scale operationalizes the rhetorical component of pragmatic ability by measuring the coherence, relevance and extent of the candidate's contribution. The pronunciation scale operationalizes phonological forms and meanings in terms of the comprehensibility with which the candidates can produce individual sounds and prosodic features to convey meanings. This scale also considers the impact that the candidate's pronunciation has on the listener, as well as the effort needed to understand the candidate. Finally, the interactive communication scale operationalizes interactional forms and meanings by measuring the candidate's ability to use interactional forms appropriately to maintain and repair communication in accordance with the norms of turn-taking and interaction.

The global scale operationalizes communicative effectiveness (i.e., grammatical meaning) by considering the candidate's ability to use grammatical forms to achieve meaningful communication in accomplishing the tasks effectively. Topical knowledge (i.e., content control) is not defined as part of the construct being measured.

Unfortunately, the actual analytic scales used by Cambridge ESOL are not available for public dissemination. Also, rater comments on speaking performance are not included in the published literature, as they were with the writing paper.

The FCE and the qualities of test usefulness

In terms of the qualities of test usefulness, the *FCE* clearly gives priority to construct validity, especially as this relates to the measurement of grammatical ability as one component of English language proficiency. The published *FCE* literature provides clear, albeit very general, information on the aspects of grammatical knowledge being measured in the Use of English paper. Also, the *FCE* literature makes explicit the importance of grammatical ability when describing the criteria for rating the writing and speaking papers of the test. This is made even more salient by the inclusion of rater comments on the quality of writing samples, where explicit rater judgments about grammatical performance are expressed. It is also seen in the speaking-test videos, which show examples of different performance levels. With respect to the construct of grammatical knowledge depicted in Chapter 4, the *FCE* appears to measure knowledge of a wide range of grammatical forms and meanings at both the sentence and discourse levels. Also, with grammatical ability being measured by two selected-response tasks, three limited-production tasks and six extended-production tasks (two in the writing and four in the speaking sections), it is safe to say that the *FCE* provides a broad sampling of the domain of grammatical ability, thereby increasing the generalizability of its score-based interpretations.

In terms of validation, UCLES has undertaken itself or commissioned a modest number of studies investigating the validity of the *FCE*. These reports can be found on the Research Notes Archive page of the Cambridge ESOL website. Regrettably, research evidence on the validity of the *FCE* has not been made available in the *FCE Handbook* (Cambridge ESOL, 1996) or in the manual of *FCE Specifications and Sample Papers for the REVISED FCE Examination* (Cambridge ESOL, 1995). Given the high stakes of this exam, it is puzzling why this information is not included, so that test users can have a research basis for interpreting the scores and the precision with which the test is measuring proficiency.

With regard to the quality of reliability, the *FCE* highlights the importance of consistent measurement by describing a set of rigorous test development procedures that includes pre-testing, trialing, and item analysis (Cambridge ESOL, 1995). Reliability concerns in the test design have motivated the Use of English paper to utilize selected-response and limited-production tasks, where task characteristics can be highly controlled so as to avoid, to the extent possible, construct-irrelevant variability in the responses. Reliability with the *FCE* is also promoted by the use of objective scoring procedures for the Use of English paper. While reliability estimates are not included in the *FCE Handbook*, Saville (2003) reports that the reliability for the *FCE*, estimated as a composite score following Feldt and Brennen (1989), is 0.94. Also, the internal consistency reliability estimates for successive administrations of the Use of English paper from 1999 to 2003 have ranged from 0.88 to 0.93 (Cambridge ESOL, 2003), thereby providing strong evidence of score consistency in the Use of English paper.

With regard to the ratings of writing and speaking sections, the *FCE* reports using highly trained raters along with a detailed set of rating procedures to score performance as indicated above. For the writing papers, some are scored by two raters and some are marked by only one, leaving the possibility of scoring inconsistencies. For the speaking paper, however, performance is double rated by two independent judges, and adjudicated by a third rater in cases of discrepancies. According to Saville (e-mail communication, 2003), 'the inter-rater correlations for first and second raters in speaking are 0.80 to 0.85', providing an acceptable level of inter-rater reliability.

Given the purpose and uses of the *FCE*, the establishment of a discrete, empirical relationship between the target language use tasks and the test tasks in the Use of English paper of the test is difficult to determine from the published literature. However, Cambridge ESOL appears to have dedicated a considerable amount of effort to the authenticity of its assessments, a quality that distinguishes it from many other tests. To assess target language use needs for the *FCE* candidature, information sheets and market survey questionnaires were administered to test-takers, teachers and oral examiners, and needs were determined (Cambridge ESOL, 1995, pp. 6–7). The results generated a comprehensive list of test contexts (e.g., travel and tourism) and topics (e.g., the media) for use in test design (for more information, consult Cambridge ESOL, 1995). Although the tasks in the Use of English paper are more reflective of an instructional than of a real-life target language use domain, they are all contextualized, which, in my opinion, significantly increases the perception of authenticity.

With regard to interactiveness, the Use of English paper aims to present examinees with contextualized tasks that are likely to engage their language knowledge. Although the input is contextualized, it seems that no specialized topical knowledge is engaged by this test paper, as topical knowledge is not a part of the test construct. The grammar section also provides a good mix of selected-response and limited-production tasks, thereby increasing somewhat the test-takers' involvement with the construct being measured. Interactiveness is highly increased when grammatical ability is measured in the context of extended-production tasks of writing and speaking. Given the range of tasks and the likelihood of their engaging the test-takers' grammatical knowledge, the *FCE* seems to have a high degree of interactiveness.

Considering the high stakes of the *FCE*, the decisions made as a result of score-based interpretations are likely to have an enormous impact on individuals, as well as on other test constituents (e.g., teachers). As a result, Cambridge ESOL is concerned with the impact this test is having on its constituents. As for the individual test-takers, Cambridge ESOL (2001a) reports that most candidates are students (under 25 years) and eighty percent of the candidature prepares for the *FCE* through prior language instruction ranging from eight to twenty-four weeks (p. 7). Around thirty-seven percent of the candidates hope to use the results to gain employment. Also, thirty percent of the candidates hope to pursue further study usually in their own country. The consequences of not passing could be devastating. Around thirty-three percent have other personal reasons for taking the test. Similarly, the consequences of passing could be professionally enriching. Finally, given that in some countries (e.g., Greece), the *FCE* is used for licensure or certification, the consequences of false positives (those who pass, but shouldn't) and false negatives (those who fail, but shouldn't) could be serious. Therefore, the degree to which the test scores are consistent, appropriate and relevant to the decisions made is important. Cambridge ESOL has engaged in large-scale impact studies relating to the *FCE* Revision Project (Saville, 2003). This study surveyed over 25,000 students, 5,000 teachers and 1,200 oral examiners, as well as 120 institutions by means of questionnaires and interviews for their perspective on the revised *FCE*. The results of this study are still pending. Cambridge ESOL has also gone to great lengths to provide the public with information about the *FCE* as seen in the numerous sample papers, answer keys and examination reports available on the website. Finally, the candidates taking the *FCE* receive one summative score along with a 'graphical profile' of their performance across the

various components of the exam. This information provides some opportunity for test-takers to receive feedback for improvement.

Summary

Given the assessment purposes and the intended uses of the *FCE*, the *FCE*
grammar assessments privilege construct validity, authenticity, interactiveness and impact. This is done by the way the construct of grammatical ability is defined. This is also done by the ways in which these abilities
are tapped into, and the ways in which the task characteristics are likely
to engage the examinee in using grammatical knowledge and other components of language ability in processing input to formulate responses.
Finally, this is done by the way in which Cambridge ESOL has promoted
public understanding of the *FCE*, its purpose and procedures, and has
made available certain kinds of information on the test. These qualities
may, however, have been stressed at the expense of reliability.

The Comprehensive English Language Test (CELT)

Purpose

The *Comprehensive English Language Test (CELT)* (Harris and Palmer,
1970a, 1986) was designed to measure the English language ability of non-
native speakers of English. The authors claim in the technical manual
(Harris and Palmer, 1970b) that this test is most appropriate for students
at the intermediate or advanced levels of proficiency. English language
proficiency is measured by means of a structure subtest, a vocabulary
subtest and a listening subtest. According to the authors, these subtests
can be used alone or in combination (p. 1). Scores from the *CELT* have
been used to make decisions related to placement in a language program,
acceptance into a university and achievement in a language course
(Harris and Palmer, 1970b, p. 1), and for this reason, it may be considered
a high-stakes test. One or more subtests of the *CELT* have also been used
as a measure of English language proficiency in SLA research.

In this review, I will concentrate on how grammatical ability is measured in the structure subtest of the *CELT*. Following that, the listening
subtest will be discussed in terms of how it provides a context for measuring grammatical ability.

Construct definition and operationalization

According to the *CELT Technical Manual* (Harris and Palmer, 1970b), the structure subtest is intended to measure the students' 'ability to manipulate the grammatical structures occurring in spoken English' (p. 1). It targets five types of grammatical structures, as seen in Table 7.2.

Table 7.2 *Structures measured on the structure subtest of the CELT*

Structural categories	Percent of test items
Choice of verb forms and modals	44
Form and choice of nouns, pronouns, adjectives and adverbs	27
Word order	11
Choice of prepositions	9
Formation of tag questions and elliptical responses	9
	100

Source: Harris and Palmer, 1970b, p. 4.

In terms of the model of grammatical knowledge presented in Figure 4.2, the structure subtest is designed to measure grammatical knowledge in terms of lexical, morphosyntactic, and cohesive form and meaning. As seen in Figure 7.5, the structure subtest measures knowledge of lexical forms with items testing co-occurrence restrictions (e.g., interested *in*); morphosyntactic form with items testing several structures including word order and tenses; and cohesive form with items testing ellipsis. Although morphosyntactic form is measured by a wide range of structures, it is surprising, given the intended use of the test scores for academic decision-making (e.g., placement), that so few forms are measured on the discourse level. For example, we might have expected this test to cover more types of cohesion (e.g., logical connectors), complex sentences with lots of embedding and participials, and a range of forms for ordering information (e.g., cleft sentences, parallelism).

Administered in one hour and 15 minutes, the structure subtest contains only one task type with 75 four-option, multiple-choice items, as summarized in Table 7.3. Items are scored dichotomously; however, in the final score calculation, points were taken off for wrong or missing answers. The *CELT* provides a conversion table to convert the total number of errors to a test score. Conversion tables are also provided to convert test scores to percentile ranks.

Each item is non-specific in terms of topic despite the fact that the

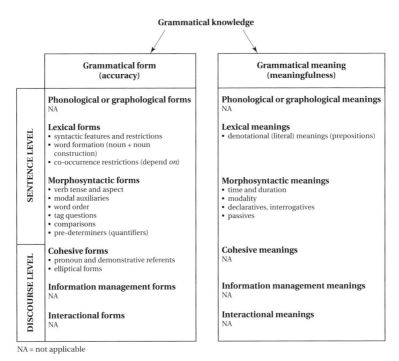

Figure 7.5 Components of grammatical knowledge measured in the structure subtest of the *CELT*

CELT claims to be appropriate for making decisions in academic settings. Of the 75 items in Form A, 11 deal with superficial classroom topics. These items require little or no specialized topical knowledge to perform the task. The *CELT* was specifically intended to be non-speeded (Harris and Palmer 1970b, p. 8). Evidence of this is supported in the *CELT Technical Manual* by the fact that all five pilot-test groups finished the test within the prescribed time limit.

The *CELT* was grounded in Lado's (1961) 'skills-and-elements' model of language proficiency, discussed in Chapter 3. In this model, language proficiency is defined in terms of how independent dimensions of language knowledge (e.g., structure and vocabulary) occur in the different language skills. The underlying assumption is that 'proficient' second language learners are able to use the structural and lexical dimensions of language knowledge to communicate by performing a language skill (i.e., while speaking or reading). The emphasis in this view is on the language components and on linguistic accuracy; language skills are used primarily as contexts in which to measure grammatical knowledge. The

Table 7.3 *An overview of the CELT structure test*

Part	Area(s) of grammatical knowledge	Task type	Task input and expected response	No. of items	Scoring
1.	• Lexical forms and meanings • Morphosyntactic forms and meanings • Cohesive forms and meanings	Selected-response (multiple-choice with 4 options)	A two-turn exchange with the second pair part containing one gap followed by 4-option MC questions. Each item is independent from the others.	75	Right/wrong; 1 criterion for correctness depending on construct; points taken off for errors

inclusion of a separate structure and vocabulary section in the *CELT*, and the fact that each item was considered to be independent from the others, reflected the discrete-point approach to language testing that prevailed when the test was created.

Measuring grammatical ability through language use

In addition to measuring grammatical knowledge in the structure subtest, grammatical knowledge is also measured in the listening subtest. According to the *Technical Manual*, the listening subtest is designed to measure the test-takers' 'ability to understand short statements, questions, and dialogues as spoken by a native speaker' (p. 1). The listening section has three tasks. In the first task, candidates hear a *wh-* or a yes/no question (*When are you going to New York?*) and are asked to select one correct response to this question (e.g., *Next Friday*) from four options. To get this item right, examinees need to understand the lexical item *when* and associate it with a time expression in the response. This item is obviously designed to measure the student's ability to understand lexical meaning.

A second listening task presents test-takers with a sentence involving conditions, comparisons, and time and number expressions (Harris and Palmer, 1970b, p. 2). The candidates then choose from among four options to select 'the one accurate paraphrase' for the sentence they heard. For example:

> Student hears: 'George has just returned from vacation.'
> (A) George is spending his vacation at home
> (B) George has just finished his vacation.
> (C) George is just about to begin his vacation.
> (D) George has decided not to take a vacation.
>
> (Harris and Palmer, 1970a, p. 2)

This item type seems to be designed to measure the examinees' ability to understand grammatical meaning, or the literal and intended meaning of the utterance in the input. Given the slightly indirect association that examinees need to make between 'finishing a vacation' (i.e., travel may or may not be involved in the response) and 'returning from vacation' (i.e., travel is presumed in the input), it could be argued that this item is measuring knowledge of grammatical meaning, where the relationship between form and meaning is relatively, but not entirely, direct.

The third task in the *CELT* presents students with a more elaborated, two-turn exchange in the input. A third voice then asks a comprehension question, and test-takers select from one of four responses to the question. In this case, the scope of the input is broader than in the first two tasks, since test-takers need to understand both an elaborated exchange and the question. For example:

> (man): 'Are you still planning to leave for New York next Monday?'
>
> (woman): 'I'm afraid not. My husband just found out that he'll be in a meeting until late that afternoon, so we won't be able to get started until the following morning.'
>
> (3rd voice): 'On what day does the woman expect to leave for New York?'
>
> (A) Sunday   (C) Tuesday
> (B) Monday   (D) Wednesday
>
> (Harris and Palmer, 1970a, p. 3)

To get this item right, examinees need to understand the exchange paying close attention to 'Monday' and 'the following morning', and need to make an association between these time-referenced lexical items and the time-referenced lexical expression 'on what day' in the question. This item appears to be a measure of grammatical meaning with special emphasis on time referencing.

The CELT and the qualities of test usefulness

In terms of the qualities of test usefulness, the intended purpose of the *CELT* structure subtest is to measure 'the students' ability to manipulate the grammatical structures in spoken English' (Harris and Palmer, 1970b, p. 1). This claim leads us to believe that the *CELT* structure subtest is designed to measure grammatical ability in the context of speaking. It also suggests that the test tasks will elicit limited or extended production of student performance. As the *CELT* structure subtest does not require speaking, and is limited to the selected-response task type, we would hardly be justified to make inferences from the scores on this subtest to 'the students' ability to manipulate the grammatical structures in spoken English'.

Grammatical ability on the structure subtest appears to involve the capacity to recognize several grammatical forms and meanings on the sentence level, as well as some forms and meanings on the discourse level. As seen in Table 7.3, a wide range of structures have been sampled from the domain of grammar; however, sampling might have inadvertently underrepresented the types of grammatical forms required of students intending to study at the university level in an English-medium university (e.g., complex sentences, logical connectors, parallel structures), especially for students at the advanced level of proficiency.

Evidence supporting validity interpretation was provided by comparing the structure subtest with other measures of grammatical ability. This is referred to as **criterion-related evidence of validity.** Harris and Palmer (1970b) reported that when candidate scores on the *CELT* structure subtests were compared with the structure sections of the *TOEFL*, the *University of Michigan Achievement Series A*, and the *University of Michigan Test of English Language Proficiency*, correlations of .83, .84, and .70 respectively were observed, suggesting that the three tests, although not identical, appeared to be measuring the same underlying construct – presumably that of grammatical knowledge. Harris and Palmer (1970b) provided further criterion-related evidence in support of the *CELT* score interpretations by examining the correspondence between students who scored low, medium and high on the *CELT* and those who were placed into low-, medium- and high-level classes based on the results of an objective test and an interview. In all cases, the *CELT* results corresponded to the placement results based on the other assessment results, thereby providing some evidence of validity for score interpretation and use for placement.

The *CELT*, as stated in its purpose, gave highest priority to reliability. As a result, the entire grammar test was based on selected-response questions, where characteristics of the task would not vary in unmotivated ways from one occasion to another, from one setting to another, or from one test-taker to another. The *CELT* structure subtest is scored objectively. Also, according to the *Technical Manual*, items were pretested on large samples of students and improved by means of item analysis and teacher feedback. The *Technical Manual* provides a clear description of evidence in support of the reliability of test scores, stating that KR20 reliability estimates across four administrations ranged from a high .88 (with a standard error of measurement of 4.96) to a very high .96 (with a standard error of measurement of 3.85). These results suggest a high degree of consistency in the measurement.

Given the multiple purposes and uses of the *CELT*, it is difficult to establish a close relationship between the target language use tasks that the *CELT* candidature might encounter and the test tasks on the structure subtest. Since the TLU domain of the *CELT* is presumed to be English for academic purposes, we would not expect to encounter many multiple-choice tasks in the language-use domains, except, for example, in instances where content knowledge was being assessed or in some language classrooms. In an academic setting, we are more likely to encounter tasks such as reading texts, writing papers or interacting with teachers and peers. Since the *CELT* is solely dependent upon the multiple-choice question type, we can say that it falls at the lower end of the authenticity continuum, thereby seriously jeopardizing the generalizability of the results to situations beyond the language test.

In terms of interactiveness, the tasks on the *CELT* are presented in decontextualized, discrete-point MC format. The test-takers need to invoke a very narrow range of grammatical knowledge in order to process the task. Also, it is highly unlikely that the characteristics of the input would engage an examinee's topical knowledge.

Given that the scores from the *CELT* were used to make a number of high-stakes decisions (e.g., admissions, placement, research), the *CELT* is likely to have a strong impact on individuals and other users of the test scores. The authors report that the placement decisions based on score-based inferences from this test have been accurate. Unfortunately, test-takers are not given feedback for improvement.

Finally, while the *CELT* is still used today, this test has not been revised in many years. Also, the two forms that exist are available for purchase, and the items fully disclosed, making these tests inappropriate for high-stakes decisions. In short, if test-takers were to obtain copies of the test, this would severely limit its usefulness as a measure of proficiency.

Summary

In terms of the purposes and intended uses of the *CELT*, the authors explicitly stated, 'the CELT is designed to provide a series of reliable and easy-to-administer tests for measuring English language ability of non-native speakers' (Harris and Palmer, 1970b, p. 1). As a result, concerns for high reliability and ease of administration led the authors to make choices privileging reliability and practicality over other qualities of test usefulness. To maximize consistency of measurement, the authors used only selected-response task types throughout the test, allowing for minimal fluctuations in the scores due to characteristics of the test method. This allowed them to adopt 'easy-to-administer' and 'easy-to-score' procedures for maximum practicality and reliability. Reliability was also enhanced by pre-testing items with the goal of improving their psychometric characteristics.

In my opinion, reliability might have been emphasized at the expense of other important test qualities, such as construct validity, authenticity, interactiveness and impact. For example, construct validity was severely compromised by the mismatch among the purpose of the test, the way the construct was defined and the types of tasks used to operationalize the constructs. In short, scores from discrete-point grammar tasks were used to make inferences about speaking ability rather than make interpretations about the test-takers' explicit grammatical knowledge.

Finally, authenticity in the *CELT* was low due to the exclusive use of multiple-choice tasks and the lack of correspondence between these tasks and those one might encounter in the target language use domain. Interactiveness was also low due to the test's inability to fully involve the test-takers' grammatical ability in performing the tests. The impact of the *CELT* on stakeholders is not documented in the published manual.

In all fairness, the *CELT* was a product of its time, when emphasis was on discrete-point testing and reliability, and when language testers were not yet discussing qualities of test usefulness in terms of authenticity, interactiveness and impact.

The Community English Program (CEP) Placement Test

Purpose

The *Community English Program (CEP) Placement Test* was first developed by students and faculty in the TESOL and Applied Linguistics Programs at Teachers College, Columbia University, in 2002, and is revised regularly. Unlike the previous tests reviewed, the *CEP Placement Test* is a theme-based assessment designed to measure the communicative language ability of learners entering the Community English Program, a low-cost, adult ESL program servicing Columbia University staff and people in the neighboring community. The *CEP Placement Test* consists of five sections: listening, grammar, reading, writing and speaking. The first four sections take one hour and 35 minutes to complete; the speaking test involves a ten-minute interview. Inferences from the test scores are used to place students in the program course that best matches their level of communicative English language ability. Like all placement tests, the *CEP Placement Test* aims to measure a wide band of abilities so that students can be grouped with others at their ability level (Brown, 1996). Given that CEP teachers can change misplaced students to another level, this test is relatively low-stakes.

In this review, I will focus on the grammar section, but will also discuss how grammatical ability is measured in the writing section.

Construct definition and operationalization

Given that the CEP is a theme-based ESL program, where language instruction is contextualized within a number of different themes throughout the different levels, the *CEP Placement Test* is also theme-based. The theme for the *CEP Placement Test* under review is 'Cooperation and Competition'. This is not one of the themes students encounter in the program. In this test, all five test sections assess different aspects of language ability while exposing examinees to different aspects of the theme. To illustrate, the reading subtest presents students with a passage on ants that explains how ants both cooperate and compete; the listening subtest presents a passage on how students cooperate and compete in US schools; and the grammar subtest presents a gapped passage that revolves around competition in advertisements. Excerpts from these test sections are presented in Figure 7.6.

More specifically, the grammar section of the *CEP Placement Test* is intended to measure the students' grammatical knowledge in terms of a wide range of grammatical forms and meanings at both the sentence and the discourse levels. Items on the test are designed to measure the students' knowledge of lexical, morphosyntactic and cohesive forms and meanings. The model of grammatical knowledge underlying the grammar section is presented in Figure 7.7.

In order to maximize scoring efficiency given the short turnaround time for the exam results, it was decided (after experimenting with limited-production items) that the grammar section of the test should contain four multiple-choice tasks with 40 items, as summarized in Table 7.4. The tasks vary with regard to the type of input (dialogue, passage, sentences). Scoring is dichotomous. Placement decisions (not scores) are reported to students.

Measuring grammatical ability through language use

In addition to measuring grammatical ability in the grammar section, grammatical ability is also measured in the writing and speaking sections of the test. The writing section consists of one 30-minute essay to be

---

Part 1

For questions 1–15, read the text below and decide which answer (**A, B, C** or **D**) best fits each space.

Grammar Task 1

Directions: Mark the best answer on your answer sheet.

1. One area of human activity in which competition
   _____ fierce is business.
   - a. can be
   - c. ought to
   - b. had better
   - d. would rather

2. Companies _____ products are similar compete intensely
   to sell their products.
   - a. what
   - c. which
   - b. whom
   - d. whose

Grammar Task 2

Directions: What does each sentence mean? Mark the best answer on your answer sheet.

1. Jane cannot type as fast as Susan.
   - a. Susan cannot type very fast.
   - b. Jane types slower than Susan.
   - c. Neither Jane nor Susan types fast.
   - d. Jane and Susan type at the same speed.

Figure 7.6 *CEP Placement Test:* Grammar section (excerpt)

written on the theme of 'cooperation and competition'. Scores are derived from a four-point analytic scoring rubric in which overall task fulfillment, content, organization, vocabulary and language control are scored. The rubric constitutes an adapted version of a rubric devised by Jacobs et al. (1981). Language use (i.e., grammatical ability) is implicitly defined in terms of the complexity of grammatical forms, the number of errors and the range of vocabulary. For example, the highest level descriptors (4) describe performance as 'effective complex constructions; few errors of grammar, and sophisticated range of vocabulary'. The lowest level (1) states: 'virtually no mastery of sentence construction rules; dominated by errors; does not communicate; OR not enough to evaluate' (Park, 2004, p.20). All essays are scored 'blind' by two trained raters, with a third adjudicating discrepancies greater than two points.

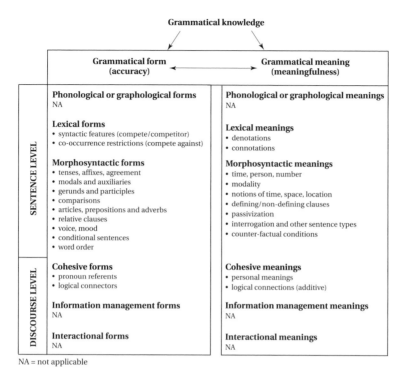

Figure 7.7 Components of grammatical knowledge measured in the *CEP Placement Test*

The CEP Placement Test and the qualities of test usefulness

In terms of the qualities of test usefulness, the developers of the grammar section of the *CEP Placement Test* prioritize construct validity, reliability and practicality. With regard to construct validity, the grammar section of this test was designed to measure both grammatical form and meaning on the sentential and discourse levels, sampling from a wide range of grammatical features. In this test, grammatical ability is measured by means of four tasks in the grammar section, one task in the writing section, and by several tasks in the speaking section. In short, the *CEP Placement Test* measures both explicit and implicit knowledge of grammar. Placement decisions based on interpretations of the *CEP Placement Test* scores seem to be appropriate as only a handful of mis-placements are reported each term.

As the goal of placement testing is to measure a wide band of ability levels, item analyses were performed on the grammar data from four

Table 7.4 *An overview of the CEP Placement Test: Grammar section*

Part	Area(s) of grammatical knowledge	Task type	Task input and expected response	No. of items	Scoring
1.	• Lexical meaning • Morphosyntactic form and meaning • Cohesive meaning	Multiple-choice gap-fill (selected-response)	One continuous dialogue with 12 selected gaps followed by 4-option MC questions	12	Right/wrong; 1 criterion for correctness
2.	• Lexical form and meaning • Morphosyntactic form and meaning	Multiple-choice gap-fill (selected-response)	Three related passages with 16 selected gaps followed by 4-option MC questions	16	Right/wrong; 1 criterion for correctness
3.	• Lexical form and meaning • Morphosyntactic form • Cohesive meaning	Multiple-choice gap-fill (selected-response)	One passage with 7 selected gaps followed by 4-option MC questions	7	Right/wrong; 1 criterion for correctness
4.	• Grammatical meaning	Synonymous sentences (selected-response)	Test-takers presented with 5 related sentences; they indicate the best paraphrase for each sentence from among 4 choices	5	Right/wrong; 1 criterion for correctness

administrations of the test. Item facilities (p-values) in each test were examined to ensure that the items measured different ability levels. According to Liao (2002), results showed a good mix of items at different ability levels. The hardest items across the four administrations ranged from having a 21% to a 30% chance of getting the item right, and the easiest items ranged from having an 81% to an 87% chance of getting the item right, as seen in Table 7.5.

Table 7.5 *A comparison of item facility ranges across four administrations of the CEP Placement Test*

Administration	Hardest item (p-value)	Easiest item (p-value)
Time 1	.27	.86
Time 2	.21	.87
Time 3	.24	.81
Time 4	.30	.83

The reliability of the grammar-test scores was also considered a priority from the design stage of test development as seen in the procedures for item development, test piloting and scoring. In an effort to promote consistency (and quick return of the results), the CEP Placement Test developers decided to use only multiple-choice tasks in the grammar section. This decision was based on the results of the pilot tests, where the use of limited-production grammar tasks showed inconsistent scoring results and put a strain on time resources. Although MC tasks were used to measure grammatical knowledge, the theme of the input was designed to be aligned with the test theme, and the type of input in each task varied (dialogue, advertisement, passage). Once the test design was established, the grammar tasks were developed, reviewed and piloted a number of times before the test became operational. Scoring is objective and machine-scored. To provide evidence of test-score consistency, Liao (2002) reported internal consistency reliability estimates across the first four administrations for the grammar section, to range from .91 to .93, as seen in Table 7.6.

Park (2004) reported an internal consistency reliability estimate of .938 for the writing section of the test. Inter-rater reliability estimates for the four scales were reported as follows: overall task fulfillment (.81), content control (.77), organization (.77) and language control (.78). In sum, the results for the grammar and writing sections of the test suggest a high degree of measurement consistency.

Table 7.6 *Reliability estimates for the CEP Placement Test across four administrations*

Administration	Reliability (alpha=)
Time 1	.9228
Time 2	.9254
Time 3	.9224
Time 4	.9121

Test authenticity was another major concern for the *CEP Placement Test* development team. Therefore, in the test design phase of test development, it was decided that test forms should contain one coherent theme across all test tasks in order to establish a close correspondence between the TLU tasks (i.e., ones that might be encountered in a theme-based curriculum) and the test tasks on the *CEP Placement Test*. It was also decided that grammatical ability would be measured by means of selected-response tasks in the grammar section and extended-production tasks in the writing and speaking sections, with both task types supporting the same overarching test theme.

It must be noted that the use of one overarching theme in a placement test can be controversial because of the potential for content bias. In other words, if one group of students (e.g., the science students) is familiar with the theme, they may be unfairly advantaged. In an attempt to minimize construct-irrelevant variance, several measures were taken. First, one goal of the test was to actually teach test-takers something about the theme in the process of taking the test so that they could develop an opinion about the theme by the time they got to the writing and speaking sections. To this end, terms and concepts relating to the theme were explained in the listening and grammar sections and reinforced throughout the test in an attempt to create, to the extent possible, a direct relationship between the input and expected responses. Second, the theme was approached from many angles – cooperation and competition in family relationships, in schools, in the animal kingdom and so forth. Third, each task was reviewed for its newsworthiness. In other words, if the test developers felt that the information in the task was 'common knowledge' for the test population, the text was changed. Finally, in piloting the test, test-takers were asked their opinions about the use of the theme. Results from this survey did not lead the testing committee to suspect bias due to the use of a common theme. Further empirical analyses obviously need to be undertaken, and this will be done when more test forms are created.

In terms of interactiveness, MC questions such as those found in the *CELT* mitigate against a high degree of involvement on the part of the test-takers. However, the MC tasks found in the *CEP Placement Test* support the theme of the test, and may have characteristics that may actually encourage involvement of the test-takers' topical knowledge while their grammatical knowledge is being measured. Although some may feel that the examinees' engagement in the topic introduces variance that may be irrelevant to the construct of grammatical knowledge, test developers felt that, given the purpose of this test for the CEP curriculum, the grammar used to express the test topic represented the content domain better than grammar that was decontextualized. Furthermore, the variance associated with the topic was likely to be construct-relevant for the test purpose. Finally, the characteristics of the writing and speaking tasks were highly interactive in that they required examinees to engage grammatical knowledge to communicate about the topic.

Given that the scores from the *CEP Placement Test* are used to make placement decisions, the test is likely to have a considerable impact on the examinees. Unfortunately, at this point, students are provided with no feedback other than their course placement. The results of this test have also had a strong impact on the CEP, since the program now has a much better system for grouping students according to ability levels than it previously had. Unfortunately, no research on impact is available.

Summary

Given the purposes and the intended uses of the *CEP Placement Test*, the grammar section privileges authenticity, construct validity, reliability and practicality. Similar to tasks in the instruction, the theme-based test tasks all support the same overarching theme presented from different perspectives. Then, the construct of grammatical knowledge is defined in terms of the grammar used to express the theme. Given the multiple-choice format and the piloting of items, reliability is an important concern. Finally, the multiple-choice format is used over a limited-production format to maximize practicality. This compromise is certainly emphasized at the expense of construct validity and authenticity (of task).

Nonetheless, grammatical ability is also measured in the writing and speaking parts of the *CEP Placement Test.* These sections privilege construct validity, reliability, authenticity and interactiveness. In these tasks, students are asked to use grammatical resources to write about and discuss the theme they have been learning about during the test. In both the writing and speaking sections, grammatical ability is a separately scored part of the scoring rubric, and definitions of grammatical knowledge are derived from theory and from an examination of benchmark samples. Reliability is addressed by scoring all writing and speaking performance samples 'blind' by two raters. In terms of authenticity and interactiveness, these test sections seek to establish a strong correspondence between the test tasks and the type of tasks encountered in theme-based language instruction – that is, examinees listen to texts in which the theme is presented, they learn new grammar and use it to express ideas related to the theme, they then read, write and speak about the theme. The writing and speaking sections require examinees to engage both language and topical knowledge to complete the tasks. In both cases, grammatical control and topical control are scored separately. Finally, while these test sections prioritize construct validity, reliability, authenticity and interactiveness, it is certainly at the expense of practicality and impact.

Summary

In this chapter I have examined the assessment of grammatical ability in three large-scale tests. I have also examined how grammatical ability was assessed in instances of language use. In terms of construct definition, all three tests define grammatical ability mostly in terms of grammatical form. In this respect, most tests measure knowledge of lexical forms, morphosyntactic forms and cohesive forms. The three tests also define grammatical ability in terms of grammatical meaning. This is sometimes measured globally in terms of the literal and intended meanings of one or more utterances (communicative effectiveness or communicative success), and sometimes examined more specifically in terms of lexical, morphosyntactic or cohesive meaning. In terms of operationalization, all three tests depended heavily on selected-response items to measure grammatical knowledge, mostly for their ease of administration and scoring. Only the *FCE* uses limited-production tasks. Both the *FCE* and the *CEP Placement Test* measure grammatical ability by means of extended-production tasks during language use (writing and speaking).

Finally, in terms of the qualities of test usefulness, each test has its priorities, and these priorities affect to some degree the other qualities of test usefulness. Tensions such as these are unavoidable. In the end, the way test developers prioritize the qualities of test usefulness will depend on their own beliefs and biases as to how that relates to the context of assessment and the test mandate.

In the next chapter I will focus on the issues related to the assessment of grammatical ability in language classroom contexts.

CHAPTER EIGHT

Learning-oriented assessments of grammatical ability

Introduction

The language tests reviewed in the previous chapter involved the grammar sections from large-scale tests designed to measure global language proficiency, typically for academic purposes. Like other large-scale and often high-stakes tests, they were designed to make institutional decisions related to placement into or exit from a language program, screening for language proficiency or reclassification of school status based on whether a student had achieved the language skills necessary to benefit from instruction in the target language. These tests provide assessments for several components of language ability including, among others, aspects of grammatical knowledge. In terms of the grammar sections of the tests reviewed, a wide range of grammar points were assessed and, except perhaps for the *CEP Placement Test*, the selection of test content was relatively removed from the local constraints of instruction in specific contexts. These large-scale tests were designed as one-shot, timed assessments for examinees who bring to the testing situation a variety of experiences and proficiency levels. The tests were different in the ways in which the qualities of usefulness were prioritized, and the compromises that ensued from these decisions.

Although large-scale, standardized tests have an important role to play in some school decisions and can have a positive impact on learning and instruction, the primary mandate of large-scale exams is different from that of classroom assessment. In the first place, large-scale language assessments are not necessarily designed to promote learning and influence teaching in local contexts. They rarely provide detailed feedback or diagnostic information to students and teachers, and they are primarily oriented toward the measurement of learner abilities at one point in time rather than continuously over a stretch of time. Finally, large-scale language assessments do not benefit from the knowledge that teachers bring to the assessment context regarding their students' instructional histories. As a result, score-based information provided by large-scale, standardized tests is often of little practical use to classroom teachers for pursuing a program designed to enhance learning and personalize instruction. Since the goals of classroom assessment are somewhat different from those of large-scale assessment, it follows then that the development of assessments for classroom purposes should reflect different assessment goals. That is, in addition to construct validity, authenticity and interactiveness, priority should be given to the impact that classroom assessments have in promoting learning and informing instruction.

In the context of learning grammar, **learning-oriented assessment of grammar** reflects a growing belief among educational assessment experts (e.g., Stiggins, 1987; Gipps, 1994; Pellegrinio, Baxter and Glaser, 1999; Rea-Dickins and Gardner, 2000) that if assessment, curriculum and instruction were more integrally connected, student learning would improve (National Research Council, 2001b). This approach attempts to provide teachers and learners with summative and/or formative information on the test-takers' grammatical ability. **Summative information** from assessment allows teachers to assign grades based on specific assessment criteria, report student progress at a single moment or over time, and reward and motivate student learning. **Formative information** from assessment provides teachers and learners with concrete information on what aspects of the grammar students have and have not mastered and involves them in the regulation and assessment of their own learning, so that further learning can take place independently or in collaboration with teachers and other students.

In pursuing a learning-oriented approach to grammar assessment, language instructors teaching students at different proficiency levels need to consider the degree to which grammar assessments: (1) are aligned with the learning goals of the course, the curriculum or some external performance standards; (2) provide accurate, appropriate and meaningful information about what grammar the learners know and can use, and what grammar they need to improve; (3) use tasks that resemble those that test-takers are likely to encounter in real-life or instructional situations; and (4) succeed in engaging test-takers in the constructs they are trying to measure. Outside the learning focus, teachers should naturally strive to be consistent and fair in their scoring and grading, and they should try to minimize the costs of constructing, administering, scoring and providing useful feedback.

A learning-oriented approach to grammar assessment addresses the following questions.

- How do I know if my students have learned and internalized the grammar points covered in the course?

- How do I know if my students can use these grammar points to communicate spontaneously in real-life situations?

- How do I know if the test tasks make it essential for my students to use the target grammar points?

- How can I use grammar assessment results to provide feedback for guiding learning?

- How will the results from this grammar test provide information to me on what to (re)teach?

- How can I design interesting and cognitively engaging grammar tasks so my students will enjoy learning grammar?

In this chapter, I will describe how classroom-based grammar assessments can be designed to promote grammar learning and inform instruction. I will first define learning-oriented assessment of grammar and contrast it with other forms of classroom assessment. I will then argue that to implement a learning-oriented approach to grammar assessment teachers need to design assessments taking into account considerations from both grammar-testing theory and L2 learning theory. Finally, I will illustrate how learning-oriented assessment of grammar can be applied to a sample achievement test of grammar.

What is learning-oriented assessment of grammar?

In reaction to conventional testing practices typified by large-scale, discrete-point, multiple-choice tests of language ability, several educators (e.g., Herman, Aschbacher and Winters, 1992; Short, 1993; Shohamy, 1995; Shepard, 2000) have advocated reforms so that assessment practices might better capture educational outcomes and might be more consistent with classroom goals, curricula and instruction. The terms

alternative assessment, authentic assessment and **performance assessment** have all been associated with calls for reform to both large-scale and classroom assessment contexts. While alternative, authentic and performance assessment are all viewed to be essentially the same, they emphasize slightly different aspects of a move away from conventional, discrete-point, standardized assessment. Let us take a brief look at these approaches and see how they differ from learning-oriented assessment.

Alternative assessment emphasizes an alternative to and rejection of selected-response, timed and one-shot approaches to assessment, whether they occur in large-scale or classroom assessment contexts. Alternative assessment encourages assessments in which students are asked to perform, create, produce or do meaningful tasks that both tap into higher-level thinking (e.g., problem-solving) and have real-world implications (Herman et al., 1992). Alternative assessments are scored by humans, not machines.

Similar to alternative assessment, **authentic assessment** stresses measurement practices which engage students' knowledge and skills in ways similar to those one can observe while performing some real-life or 'authentic' task (O'Malley and Valdez-Pierce, 1996). It also encourages tasks that require students to perform some complex, extended-production activity, and emphasizes the need for assessment to be strictly aligned with classroom goals, curricula and instruction. Self-assessment is considered a key component of this approach.

Performance assessment refers to the evaluation of outcomes relevant to a domain of interest (e.g., grammatical ability), which are derived from the observation of students performing complex tasks that invoke real-world applications (Norris et al., 1998). As with most performance data, assessments are scored by human judges (Stiggins, 1987; Herman et al., 1992; Brown, 1998) according to a scoring rubric that describes what test-takers need to do in order to demonstrate knowledge or ability at a given performance level. Bachman (2002) characterized language performance assessment as typically: (1) involving more complex constructs than those measured in selected-response tasks; (2) utilizing more complex and authentic tasks; and (3) fostering greater interactions between the characteristics of the test-takers and the characteristics of the assessment tasks than in other types of assessments. Performance assessment encourages self-assessment by making explicit the performance criteria in a scoring rubric. In this way, students can then use the criteria to evaluate their performance and contribute proactively to their own learning.

While these three approaches better reflect the types of academic competencies that most language educators value and wish to promote, a learning-oriented approach to assessment maintains a clear and unambiguous focus on assessment for the purpose of fostering further learning relevant to some domain of interest (e.g., grammatical ability). **Learning is defined here as the accumulation of knowledge and the ability to use this knowledge for some purpose** (i.e., skill). To highlight the learning mandate in the assessment of grammar in classroom contexts, I will use the term **learning-oriented assessment of grammar**. Unlike the other approaches, learning-oriented assessment of grammar draws on both a theory of grammar testing (as described in Chapters 3 and 4) and a theory of second language learning (i.e., grammar processing as described by VanPatten, 1996, and Lee and VanPatten, 2003, in Chapter 2). It is concerned not only with issues of grammar testing and measurement, but also with issues of instructed learning. For this reason, learning-oriented assessment of grammar aims to provide information about the grammar that students know, understand, or can use in certain contexts, and the implications that this information might have for grammar processing. Finally, moving beyond grammar performance per se, learning-oriented assessment can also provide teachers with information about what students feel or believe about learning grammar and about themselves as learners of grammar – other aspects of the instructional variable.

In terms of method, learning-oriented assessment of grammar reflects the belief that assessments must remain open to all task types if the mandate is to provide information about student performance on the one hand, and information about the processing of grammatical input and the production of grammatical output on the other. Therefore, unlike with other approaches, operationalization involves the use of selected-response, limited-production and complex, extended-production tasks that may or may not invoke real-life applications or interaction. Just as in large-scale assessments, though, the specification of test tasks varies according to the specific purpose of the assessment and the claims we would like to make about what learners know and can do, and in fact, in some instances, a multiple-choice task may be the most appropriate task type available.

Finally, learning-oriented assessment is designed to be an integral part of instruction, occurring formally or informally at any stage of the learning process. Learning-oriented assessment data can also be collected at one point in time or over a period of time. Unlike large-scale assessments, learning-oriented assessment is fundamentally iterative and recursive in that feedback from one assessment is intended to provide information for subsequent learning and assessment, until a criterion level of mastery has been achieved. Finally, these assessments are scored by machines or humans, depending on the nature of the task and the scoring procedures, as described in earlier chapters.

In sum, a learning-oriented approach to grammar assessment raises critical issues for classroom teachers when it comes to decisions for constructing assessments designed to fulfill a learning mandate. One set of decisions relates to test construction, especially as this pertains to test design and issues of purpose, construct definition, task selection and method of scoring. Another set of issues relates to the role that assessment can play in promoting learning in general and grammar processing in particular. Teachers must grapple with issues related to *what* exactly should be assessed *when* in the learning process, what kinds of assessments should be presented at different learning junctures, how assessment results should be presented to learners to promote further development, and how learners can collaborate with their teachers and peers in their own learning and assessment.

In the next section, I will discuss how the large-scale assessment procedures outlined in Chapter 6 can be modified to implement learning-oriented assessment designed for language classroom contexts.

Implementing learning-oriented assessment of grammar

Considerations from grammar-testing theory

The development procedures for constructing large-scale assessments of grammatical ability discussed in Chapter 6 are similar to those needed to develop learning-oriented assessments of grammar for classroom purposes with the exception that the decisions made from classroom assessments will be somewhat different due to the learning-oriented mandate of classroom assessment. Also, given the usual low-stakes nature of the decisions in classroom assessment, the amount of resources that needs to be expended is generally less than that required for large-scale assessment. In this section, without repeating what was discussed in Chapter 6, I will highlight some of the implications this mandate might have for test design and operationalization. I will also argue that in learning-oriented assessment of grammar, test developers need to plan for and specify how assessment will be used to promote further learning from the initial stages of test design.

Implications for test design

In designing classroom-based, learning-oriented assessments, we need to provide a much more explicit depiction of the assessment mandate than we might do for large-scale assessments. This is because classroom assessment, especially in school contexts, has many interested stakeholders (e.g., students, teachers, parents, tutors, principals, school districts), who are likely to be held accountable for learning and who will use the assessment information to evaluate instructional outcomes and plan for further instruction. Therefore, in the design stage of test construction, classroom teachers need to specify whom we are doing the assessment for, why assessment information is needed and what kind of information is needed. Once this information is clarified, we can specify the assessment purpose, including a description of the inferences and decisions, as described in Chapter 6. Figure 8.1 shows how assessment mandates can vary and how this can affect the types of information we use assessment for.

A second consideration in which the design stage of classroom-based, learning-oriented assessment may differ from that of large-scale assessment is construct definition. Learning-oriented assessment aims to measure simple and/or complex constructs depending on both the claims that the assessment is designed to make and the feedback that can result from an observation of performances. Applied to grammar learning, a 'simple' construct might involve the assessment of regular and irregular past tense verb forms presented in a passage with gaps about the disappearance of the dinosaurs. A complex construct might entail the use of multiple informational sources to construct an explanation for some event for which a single explanation is not readily accepted or available (e.g., Why did the dinosaurs disappear?). The former example can be characterized as simple since the assessment involves the grammatical knowledge of only one verb form, whereas the latter is 'complex' because, to complete this task, test-takers need to invoke the knowledge of several grammatical forms and meanings. It may also be the case that that task also engages topical knowledge (e.g., information from multiple sources) and strategic competence (i.e., the ability to use strategies to carry out a historical, investigative reasoning task by processing input, linking topical information from different sources and constructing a response with logical supports). Assessments involving face-to-face interaction might also tap into the students' personal characteristics (e.g., shyness) and their affective schemata (e.g. nervousness). Thus, in learning-oriented assessments of grammar, where complex constructs are used,

Context		
• Private language school in Thailand • Teens class (11 and 12 year olds) • Low Intermediate EFL	• Theme-based program • Lesson focus: past modals used to criticize	

Who the assessment is for	Why the assessment information is needed	What kind of information is needed
My students	• So students can learn if they have internalized the past modal forms to criticize themselves and others (e.g., I should have . . .) • So students can learn to soften criticism by using hedging devices (e.g., I think, maybe) • So students can learn if their criticisms make sense • So students can use the assessment process to learn to set further learning goals	• Students need feedback on the correctness of the forms • Students need feedback on the use of hedges • Students need feedback on the viability of their criticisms and suggestions • Students need feedback on their future learning goals
Teachers	• So I can learn if my students have mastered the past modal forms (with and without hedges) • So I can learn if my students can use the forms to offer meaningful criticisms and suggestions • So I can learn if my students should move on to more complicated tasks • So I can learn if my students can use assessments to set learning goals for themselves	• I need performance information on each student so I can help clear up misunderstandings • I need performance information on the entire class so I can decide how to proceed with instruction • I need grades from multiple assessments so I can give a course grade • I need to document each student's growth as an autonomous learner
Parents	• So parents can offer appropriate help • So parents can offer encouragement and foster motivation • So parents can be involved in their child's learning	• Parents need concrete information on students' strengths and weaknesses • Parents need conference time feedback on their child's academic progress and motivation

Figure 8.1 Assessment mandates

the central issue that this raises for the test developer is the extent to which components other than grammatical knowledge (e.g., topical knowledge) are defined as part of the construct. If they are part of the construct, then the construct being measured is much broader than grammatical ability. If not, these other factors may be sources of construct-irrelevant variance. In learning-oriented assessments, test developers, therefore, must recognize the tension between using simple and complex constructs and the effect that these decisions will have on the types of tasks they decide to use, the inferences they will make about grammatical ability, the generalizability of the score interpretations and the types of improvement feedback that can be derived from the assessment.

A third consideration for classroom-based, learning-oriented assessment is the need to measure the students' explicit as well as their implicit knowledge of grammar. Selected-response and limited-production tasks, or tasks that include planning time, will elicit the students' explicit knowledge of grammar. In addition, it is important to assess the students' implicit or internalized knowledge of the grammar. To do this, students should be asked to demonstrate their capacity to use grammatical knowledge to perform complex, real-time tasks that invoke the language performances one would expect to observe in instructional or real-life situations. Obviously, more complex tasks should be designed to take into account the critical characteristics of the learners, such as their age, cognitive development or proficiency level. The systematic and principled inclusion of *both* simple and complex tasks enables teachers to provide a more comprehensive assessment of the test-taker's grammatical ability – that is, both their explicit and their implicit knowledge of grammar, as described in earlier chapters.

Implications for operationalization

The operationalization stage of classroom-based, learning-oriented assessment is also similar to that of large-scale assessments. That is, the outcome should be a blueprint for the assessment, as described in Chapter 6. The learning mandate, however, will obviously affect the specification of test tasks so that characteristics such as the setting, the rubrics or the expected response can be better aligned with instructional goals. For example, in classroom-based assessment, we may wish to collect information about grammar ability during the course of instruction, and we may decide to evaluate performance by means of teacher observation reports, or we may wish to assess grammatical ability by means of informal oral interviews conducted over several days. Whichever way we choose to assess grammatical ability, it is important to plan for assessment by specifying task characteristics and by adapting the process of large-scale test development to the classroom context. In other words, we need to develop test specifications, as described in Chapter 6, even if they are less detailed than they might be for large-scale assessments. In this way, we are more likely to obtain assessment information that meets the standards of reliability and validity, thereby increasing the chances that our assessment goal will be met.

Learning-oriented assessment of grammar may be achieved by means of a wide array of data-gathering methods in classroom contexts. These obviously include conventional quizzes and tests containing selected-response, limited-production and all sorts of extended-production tasks, as discussed earlier. These conventional methods provide achievement or diagnostic information to test-users, and can occur before, during or after instruction, depending on the assessment goals. They are often viewed as 'separate' from instruction in terms of their administration. These assessments are what most teachers typically call to mind when they think of classroom tests.

In addition to using stand-alone tests, learning-oriented assessment promotes the collection of data on students' grammatical ability as an integral part of instruction. While teachers have always evaluated student performance incidentally in class with no other apparent purpose than to make instructional choices, classroom assessment activities can be made more systematic by means of learning-oriented assessment. Typical methods of assessing grammatical ability as a regular part of teaching and curricular activities include the use of the following extended-production tasks: **chats** involving conversations, free and structured interviews and conferences; **recasts** or the re-creation of some activity in a slightly different form such as retellings, rewrites, narrations and eyewitness reports; **simulations** such as role-plays, dramatizations and improvisations; and many different types of **project work** such as portfolios and poster sessions. (For examples of classroom assessment tasks, see O'Malley and Valdez-Pierce, 1996; Brown, 1998; Trussell-Cullen, 1998; Lee and VanPatten, 2003.) Other methods used commonly in classroom assessment include **observation** and **reflection**. An overview of classroom methods is given in Table 8.1.

Many of the assessment tasks in Table 8.1 involve complex, extended-production tasks in which students are given the opportunity to express

Table 8.1 *Examples of classroom-based assessment tasks*

| | | Constructed-response | | |
| | | Extended-production (performance-based assessment) | | |
Selected-response	Limited-production	Product-focused	Performance-focused	Process-focused
• multiple-choice • matching • true-false • same/different • grammatical/ ungrammatical	• gap-fill • cloze • sentence completion • DCT • Short answer	*Project work* • essays • reports • science projects • presentations • debates • poster sessions • portfolios	*Simulation* • role-plays • dramatizations • improvisations *Recasts* • retellings • rewrites • narrations *Chats* • information gaps • interviews • conferences • recorded on-line chats	*Observation* • checklists • rubrics • anecdotal reports *Reflection* • journals • think-alouds • learning logs

Source: Adapted from McTighe and Ferrara, 1998, cited in National Research Council, 2001b, p. 63

themselves on a wide range of possible topics. They also provide teachers with rich samples of grammatical performance taken at one point in time or accumulated over a period of time. Some of these methods, in particular observation and reflection, may be designed to provide information on grammar processing or on other variables influencing grammar learning. As I have already described the use of extended-production tasks to elicit grammar performance in detail in Chapter 5, I will not repeat that discussion. Instead, I will discuss how decisions about operationalization could vary to accommodate a learning mandate. After that, I will describe a few of the assessment methods in Table 8.1 that have not been discussed previously (i.e., observation and reflection).

In order to situate how a grammar-learning mandate in classroom contexts can impact operationalization decisions, consider the following situation. Imagine you are teaching an intermediate foreign-language course in a theme-based program. The overarching unit theme is crime investigation or the 'whodunit' (i.e., 'who done it', short for a detective story or mystery à la Agatha Christie or Detective Trudeau). This theme is used to teach and assess modal auxiliary forms for the purpose of expressing degrees of certainty (e.g., It may/might/could/can't/must/has to be the butler who stole the jewelry). Students are taught to speculate about possible crime suspects by providing motives and drawing logical conclusions. They are also taught to question their partner's suspicions and describe why they agree or disagree with their conclusions. Finally, in order to assess how well they have mastered the modal forms to express meanings in whodunit contexts, they are instructed to work in pairs to complete the task presented in Figure 8.2.

Depending on the learning mandate and the purpose of assessment, this task could be used as a stand-alone achievement test, similar to those discussed in large-scale assessments. Students could be paired off, given some time to prepare their responses, and their performance would be audio- or videotaped. The interactions would then be judged by one or more raters using holistic or analytic rating scales. Finally, students would be presented their scores based on the scoring rubric.

Operationalization in classroom-based assessment, however, need not be limited to this conventional approach to assessment. Teachers can obviously specify the characteristics of the test setting, the characteristics of the test rubrics and other task characteristics for that matter, in many other ways depending on the learning mandate and the goals of assessment. Let us examine how the setting and test rubrics, for example, can be modified to assess grammar for different learning goals.

Instructions

Read the police report. Work with a partner to figure out which suspect most likely robbed the safe and why you think so. Make sure you discuss each suspect in light of your suspicions and the suspect's motives. You and your partner may reach different conclusions, but these must be justified.

Police report

Crime:	Stolen: diamond tiara, black pearl earrings, cash, family sauce recipe (secret)
Victim:	Lucretia Scarlatta, 74 years old
Time of crime:	Between 11 pm and 8 am, 31 October 2004
Place of crime:	Hillside villa in Caccomo, Sicily

Possible suspects	Possible motives
Joe Scarlatta, son	• recent court battle with mother over land deal
Gina Scarlatta, daughter	• dropped from will if wedded to Tony; loves diamonds and gold
Tony Giordano, daughter's fiancé	• unemployed; madly in love with Gina; wants Gina happy
Maria Caduta, housekeeper, cook	• never forgave Lucretia for treatment of mother; hates her job
Victor Fiore, gardener	• recently fired for stealing vegetables; family desperate
Marc Ladro, lawyer	• owes thousands in unpaid legal bills
Paola Conti, accountant	• had full access to accounts and safe; new business failing

Figure 8.2 The whodunit task

In specifying the test setting, teachers may have some reason to decide to vary the participants or the time of the task. For example, they may decide to assess their students' ability to use the modals as an organic part of classroom instruction. In this case, they could have students perform the task in Figure 8.2 in groups, while moving from group to group and evaluating performance by means of some established rating scale or by means of written notes recorded in an observation log. Teachers might also decide to have two or more students audiotape the task in Figure 8.2 outside of class or, varying the participants, they could ask students to videotape the task with a fluent speaker of the target language. Finally, considering assessment from a grammar-processing perspective, teachers might wish to incorporate this type of assessment task at a point in the lesson when they feel that their students have begun to incorporate the new grammatical features into their developing interlanguage, as described by the work of Swain (1985), VanPatten (1996, 2003) and Doughty and Williams (1998). In short, varying the characteristics of the test setting offers alternative ways of implementing classroom assessment, but these variations should, of course, be principled and consistent with the goals of assessment in light of the learning mandate.

In specifying the characteristics of the test rubrics, teachers might decide to vary the scoring method to accommodate different learning-oriented assessment goals. For example, after giving the task in Figure 8.2, they might choose to score the recorded performance samples themselves, by means of an analytic rating scale that measures modal usage in terms of accuracy, range, complexity and meaningfulness. They might also have students listen to the tapes to score their own and their peers' performances. In some instances, teachers might decide not to provide a score at all, but rather provide students with written comments about their use of modals based on focused observations during group work. Ultimately, the language produced in these tasks could be incorporated into a learner corpus, and the types of errors students typically make could be identified, tagged, examined and used to provide tailored feedback to the students and classes (Granger, 2002).

In classroom assessments designed to promote learning, the scoring process, whether implemented by teachers, the students themselves or their peers, results in a written or oral evaluation of candidate responses. This, in turn, provides learners with summative and/or formative information (i.e., **feedback**) so that they can compare or 'notice' the differences between their interlanguage utterances and the target-language utterances. According to Schmidt (1990, 1993), Sharwood Smith (1993) and Skehan (1998), this information makes the learners more ready to accommodate the differences between their interlanguage and the target language, thereby contributing to the ultimate internalization of the learning point. Therefore, a crucial feature of learning-oriented assessment is the scoring process and how it provides, or allows test-takers to discover for themselves, positive and negative evidence on their grammatical ability. **Positive evidence** refers to information about the forms one can use in the target language to convey the intended meanings, while **negative evidence** references information about the forms one cannot use in a correct, meaningful or appropriate manner. (For an informative review of the research on the role of feedback and grammar learning, see Doughty and Williams, 1998; and for information on the role of feedback and grammar learning in Computer-Assisted Language Learning, see Granger, 2003a, 2003b.)

Given the critical role that feedback on grammatical performance plays in learning, teachers should consider carefully what assessment-based information is presented to students and how best to focus and report it. In other words, while a single grammar score and grade on a chapter achievement test can inform students about their level of mastery of the material, individual scores for each task, linked to construct-related criteria for correctness and expressed in the language of the rubric, would provide much more meaningful and constructive guidance on what to notice and how to improve, especially if this feedback were followed by a plan for further learning. Thus, for classroom assessment, the use of a holistic rubric is appropriate when practicality is an overriding priority or when there is no expectation of formative feedback. At other times, the use of an analytic rubric is preferred since it provides more focused information on each construct being measured. Also, analytic rubrics can be used flexibly to allow teachers to choose which scales to score for, based on the focus of assessment, and they can be adapted to suit individual assessment tasks and contexts.

In addition to teacher feedback, the scoring method in learning-oriented assessment can be specified to involve students. From a learning perspective, students need to develop the capacity for **self-assessment** so that they can learn to 'notice' for themselves how their language compares with the target-language norms. Learning to mark their own (or their peers') work can, in itself, trigger further reanalysis and restructuring of interlanguage forms, as discussed in Chapter 2. It can also foster the development of skills needed to regulate their own learning and it places more responsibility for learning on the students (Rief, 1990). While self-assessment can serve many learning goals, it basically relates to how assessments are scored and how the results of assessment are recorded and reported.

In learning-oriented assessment, self-assessments can vary considerably depending on the proficiency level and age of the test-takers. Most students at both high and low proficiency levels can be successfully trained to evaluate their own (or their peers') work with reference to rating scales and a set of guiding questions. Beginning learners can be asked questions about their performance while teachers record their comments and, according to Sperling (1993), even pre-school children can identify certain criteria for good work. Figure 8.3 presents a self-assessment task designed to measure students' use of modals while carrying out the whodunit task.

Self-assessment tasks can also be used to collect information on grammar processing and other variables that have an effect on grammar

Name:				
Check the box that shows what you can do. Add comments if you want to.				
	Ability level			
How well can you use the modals?	Not so well	Fairly well	Very well	**Comments**
1. I can speculate about possible suspects by using 'might'.				
2. I can justify my speculations by presenting motives.				
3. I can speculate about possible suspects by using 'may'.				
4. I can speculate about possible suspects by using 'could'.				
5. I can ask my partner for reasons about his/her speculations (e.g., Why do you think . . .?)				
6. I can state my best guess about the criminal by using 'must' followed by reasons for my choice.				
7. I can reject my partner's best guess by using 'can't' followed by reasons.				
8. I can ask my partner for his/her best guess by using 'must'.				
What I learned from this assessment and what I'll do next:				

Figure 8.3 Self-assessment: use of modals

learning such as student attitudes and their feelings toward learning and using grammar. For example, the self-assessment questionnaire in Figure 8.4 is designed to measure students' confidence with the new learning point (statements 1–8), their perception toward group work (9–10), their level of anxiety (11) and their attitudes toward the task (12–13).

In learner-oriented assessment, teachers might also wish to specify the scoring method to include the student peers in the marking process. **Peer assessment** provides a means by which trained students can evaluate each other's grammatical performance using established rating scales or guiding questions. While some students may feel reluctant or unable to assess their peers' work, this is usually overcome in time with lots of practice (O'Malley and Valdez-Pierce, 1996). The peer assessment in Figure 8.5 is designed to provide information on the participants' grammatical performance on the whodunit task.

As with large-scale assessment, student raters need to be trained before being asked to evaluate their own or their peers' work. Students will first need a scoring rubric or a set of evaluation questions that they understand and can easily use. Then, teachers need to engage learners in a discussion of how to evaluate their own or their partner's work using the rubric or set of questions. As discussed in Chapter 6, rater training should be done with examples of student work at the different performance levels, together with a discussion of how the samples have or have not met the stated criteria. Student raters then need practice scoring and they need to receive constructive feedback on their scoring ability. By engaging regularly in self- and peer assessment, students are more likely to learn to understand the criteria for correctness and to apply them to their own work. For further information on self-assessment, see Oskarasson (1978), Ekbatani and Pierson (2000) and North (2000).

Having shown how some task characteristics can be varied for learner-oriented assessment, I will discuss two common classroom assessment methods that have not been discussed previously and that could be used to collect information on grammatical ability. These are observation and reflection. **Observation** is a natural part of every classroom. It can be done either live or on tape, in class or in more informal settings, and it is a particularly useful assessment tool for examining the grammatical ability of young learners. To use observation in assessment, however, requires that the results of observation be documented. This can be done by means of a checklist, a scoring rubric, an anecdotal record or some combination of the three. A **checklist** is used to record the presence or absence of features in the construct under observation. The checklist in Figure 8.6 is designed

Name:		Date:				
Check the appropriate box. Add comments if you want to.						

How did you do and how do you feel about it?	Level of agreement					Comments
	Disagree ——————— Agree					
	1	2	3	4	5	
1. I was successful in getting my point across in this task.						
2. I was successful in expressing myself without grammar errors.						
3. My partner and I did a good job on this task.						
4. I could understand everything my partner said to me.						
5. My partner could understand me well.						
6. I feel confident about using modals (may, might, could) to make speculations.						
7. I feel confident about using modals to draw logical conclusions (must, can't).						
8. I could do this again with no problem.						
9. My partner and I worked well together.						
10. I helped my partner out as much as I could.						
11. I felt really nervous doing this task.						
12. I enjoyed doing this task.						
13. I found this task useful.						
14. What I learned about my grammar from doing the whodunit task:						
15. What I now plan to do to improve my grammar:						

Figure 8.4 Self-assessment: attitudes toward learning and using grammar

Name:				
Part 1: Check the appropriate box. Add comments where possible.				
	Yes	**Sometimes**	**No**	**Comments**
1. My partner's suspicions about the suspects were clearly expressed.				
2. My partner's descriptions of the suspects' motives were clearly expressed.				
3. My partner's final deduction about the thief was clearly expressed.				
4. My partner gave clearly expressed reasons for his/her final deduction.				
5. My partner's grammar made him/her easy to understand.				
Part 2: Finish the sentences.				
6. My partner was good at				
7. Maybe my partner could still work on				

Figure 8.5 Peer assessment: use of modals

to tally the number of times a student uses modals while performing the whodunit task. Comments, notes or examples of student performance can also be recorded. Teachers can use the results of this checklist to discuss performance and plan for further learning with individual students or they can use the results to plan instruction for the entire class.

Assessment by observation can also be carried out using a holistic or analytic scoring rubric. Such rubrics permit the observer not only to record the presence of a grammatical feature, but also to assess the degree to which the feature is used accurately or meaningfully. Again, the

Student name:		
Observer:		

Use of modals	✔ # of times	Comments on accuracy, range or meaningfulness
1. Uses modals to speculate about the possible suspect (e.g., he may, might, could be the thief)		
2. Uses modals to ask for reasons (Why do you think it might be here? Do you think it could be him?)		
3. Uses modals to make deduction (It must/has to be her because . . .)		
4. Uses modals to reject a possible suspect (It can't be her because . . .)		
5. Avoids modals with 'maybe'		

Figure 8.6 Whodunit checklist

results of these assessments can be used on an individual or class level to determine further learning plans.

Finally, teachers might observe and record students' strengths and weaknesses by means of **anecdotal records** such as an **anecdotal notebook**. Anecdotal records consist of brief notes taken about some aspect of student performance during or after the completion of a task (O'Malley and Valdez-Pierce, 1996). These notes provide a description of student performance supported by examples. Anecdotal records are also useful for keeping track of progress over time and for providing concrete examples of student growth. An example of an anecdotal record for the whodunit task appears in Figure 8.7.

Reflection is another method of collecting information on students' grammatical ability at one point in time or over a period of time. It can also be used to assess students' feelings and attitudes toward learning grammar, as well as any other variables influencing grammar learning. Reflection tasks allow learners to write about topics of their own choosing such as their thoughts and feelings about certain topics. They can also

Student: _Eliseu_	• _100% accurate use of 'might' to speculate and ask for speculation reasons_
Date: _9/23/04_	_ex. 'Why do you think he might be the thief?'_
Activity: _Whodunit_	• _Sometimes confuses: 'could' with 'should'_
	ex. 'I think it should be the mother'
Focus of Observation:	• _Sometimes conjugates verb form after modal_
Precise use of	_ex. 'She must thinks . . .'_
modals in	• _Avoids using modals_
communicating	_ex. 'Maybe Tony took the black pearl earrings'_
meaningfully	• _Usually able to get ideas across; use of modals sometimes inhibits communication._

Figure 8.7 Example of an anecdotal record

be seeded with questions that require learners to respond to specific probes. In this way, students can be directed to reflect upon several variables related to grammar learning and testing. The grammar produced by students is then assessed.

One common reflection task used to obtain information about grammar learning is the **student journal**. Like a diary, this contains regular entries from students on a topic of the students' choosing, or entries in response to questions. The journal allows teachers to examine grammatical ability over time and to provide students with grammatical feedback, especially if the message being conveyed is incomprehensible or ambiguous. Although journals are not typically intended to focus on accuracy or appropriateness per se, it is difficult to ignore what students can and cannot express meaningfully. In other words, when the communicative effectiveness is negatively impacted by the students' use of grammar, teachers can provide help. Journal data can also give teachers a rich empirical basis for discussing learning plans with students and for planning class instruction. Finally, journals can be used to assess the students' attitudes and motivation toward learning grammar as well as their strategies. Two examples of journal tasks appear in Figure 8.8. Task 1 allows students to work with the whodunit theme in a more creative and personal way, while Task 2 elicits student reactions to the whodunit theme.

Another common reflection task for obtaining information about grammar learning (and performance) is the **learning log**. While a journal can be on any topic, a learning log specifically documents student learning with relation to the new grammatical feature(s). Again, this can be

---

Journal Task 1

Respond to one question in your journals.

1. Have you ever read a mystery novel or seen a TV show or a movie about a mystery? Describe the background information of the crime. Then describe the suspects, their motives, your suspicions, the clues, their alibis and your logical conclusions.
2. Are you currently living a whodunit in your personal life? Describe the background information of the offense, the suspects, their motives, your suspicions, the clues and your logical conclusions.
3. Are there any current whodunits in the news now? (e.g., Where are the terrorists hiding and who are they getting help from?) Describe the background information, the suspects, their motives, your suspicions, the clues and your logical conclusions.
4. Write a fictional episode of a whodunit involving the people in your class. Describe the background information, the suspects, the motives, the investigator's suspicions, the clues, alibis and the logical conclusions. Make sure you include some dialogue in your story.

Journal Task 2

Respond to the question in your journals.

1. What is your opinion about the unit theme? Did you enjoy talking about crime investigation? Do you think this is a useful theme? Did it help you learn the grammar point? Did this theme motivate you to learn more about mysteries and crime investigation?

Figure 8.8 Journal tasks

open-ended or seeded with questions about what students have learned, what remains unclear to them, what their attitudes and motivations are, and what strategies they have used to remember the new feature. It can also document experiences in which they have noticed the target grammatical feature in real-life input or used it in communicative output. Teachers can then use the data from the learning logs for student feedback or for further instructional planning. The following learning log task might be used to engage students in a substantive conversation about a grammar point.

Learning log entry

Respond to one or more questions below.

1. Describe the extent to which you understand the form and meaning of the modals in this unit. What are you confused about? What are you confident about?
2. Describe the extent to which you feel able to use the modals in writing or in speaking. What are you having trouble with? What are you confident about?
3. Describe what you learned about your understanding of the modals from your test results. What are your plans for further learning?
4. Have you tried using the modals you studied in real life? How effective were you in conveying your meaning? How accurate were you?

Figure 8.9 Learning log

Planning for further learning

The usefulness of learning-oriented, classroom assessment is to a great extent predicated upon the quality and explicitness of information obtained and its relevance for further action. Research has shown, however, that the quality of feedback contributes more to further learning than the actual presence or absence of it (Bangert-Downs et al., 1991). Therefore, in learning-oriented classroom assessment, the test blueprint should, in my opinion, include explicit information on how the assessment plans to satisfy the learning mandate. In other words, how will the results of assessment be presented to learners, when will they be given to them and how might the results be used to set new learning goals?

Teachers have many options for presenting assessment results to students. They could present students with feedback in the form of a single overall test score, a score for each test component, scores referenced to a rubric, a narrative summary of teacher observations or a profile of scores showing development over time. Feedback can also be presented in a private conference with the individual student. In an effort to understand the effect of feedback on further learning, Butler (1987) presented test-takers with feedback from an assessment in one of three forms: (1) focused written comments that addressed criteria test-takers were aware of before the assessment; (2) grades derived from numerical scoring; and (3) grades and comments. Test-takers were then given two subsequent tasks, and significant gains were observed with those who received the detailed comments. Scores declined for those who received both comments and grades, and for those who received only grades, scores dropped and then rose between the second and third tasks. In short, Butler's study makes a case for the use of descriptive, criterion-referenced feedback in which learners are aware of the assessment criteria.

Furthermore, research has also demonstrated that feedback focusing on learning goals has led to greater learning gains than, for example, feedback emphasizing self-esteem (Butler, 1988). Therefore, feedback from assessments should provide information on not only the quality of the work at hand, but also the identification of student improvement goals. While feedback can be provided by teachers, students should be involved in identifying areas for improvement and for setting realistic improvement goals. In fact, considerable research (e.g., Darling-Hammond, Ancess and Falk, 1995) has shown the learning benefits of engaging students in self- and peer assessment. In a large-scale, controlled study, White and Frederiksen (2000) examined the impact of reflective inquiry by comparing the results of students who were continually engaged in self- and peer assessment with those who were asked to provide their opinions about the curriculum. Results showed that classes engaged in self- and peer assessment made higher gains (especially in the low-achieving groups). More importantly, gains from each component of the test were compared, and the effect for the group engaging in self- and peer assessment was greatest in the more difficult part of the assessment. While this study was carried out in the context of learning science, the results have resonance for assessment oriented toward learning a second or foreign language.

Goal-setting can be formalized by having students record their strengths and weaknesses along with their specific plans for addressing the weaknesses, as seen in Figure 8.10.

Name:

Date:

1. Consider the information you have received from assessment. What does this show you can do well?

2. Describe one thing that you still need to work on.

3. Describe what you are willing to do to improve. Be specific.

Figure 8.10 Planning for improvement

Finally, results from assessments should be given to students as soon as possible so that the feedback can be used to trigger reanalysis and restructuring of the learner's interlanguage, as discussed in Chapter 2.

In sum, the learning mandate in classroom assessment has several implications for grammar assessment. In terms of the design, I discussed the implications it had for the specification of test mandates and construct definition, and for the need to provide multiple opportunities for assessment in which both explicit and implicit knowledge of grammar are tapped into. In terms of test operationalization, I discussed how certain characteristics of test tasks could vary considerably in light of the learning mandate. In particular, I showed how the setting and the scoring method of test tasks could be modified to promote a learning agenda. Finally, I argued that test blueprints for learning-oriented assessments of grammar need to specify in the planning stage how the results of assessment will be used to promote improvement. In this respect, the teachers' and students' roles in this process should be specified so that students can ultimately develop a common understanding of what constitutes quality work and how to gauge the quality of their work. In this way, they may come to understand how assessment can serve as a vehicle for further learning.

Considerations from L2 learning theory

Given that learning-oriented assessment involves the collection and interpretation of evidence about performance so that judgments can be made about further language development, learning-oriented assessment of grammar needs to be rooted not only in a theory of grammar testing or language proficiency, but also in a theory of L2 learning. What is striking in the literature is that models of language ability rarely refer to models of language learning, and models of language learning rarely make reference to models of language ability. In learning-oriented assessment, the consideration of both perspectives is critical.

As we have seen, implementing grammar assessment with a learning mandate has implications for test construction. Some of these implications have already been discussed. However, implementing learning-oriented assessment of grammar is not only about task design and operationalization, teachers also need to consider how assessment relates to and can help promote grammar acquisition, as described by VanPatten (1996) in Chapter 2. This will affect not only what is assessed (e.g., meaning alone or form and meaning) and how it is assessed (e.g., simple and complex constructs and tasks), but also when in the lesson aspects of grammatical knowledge are best assessed, and what the results mean for learners to improve. As I have touched upon many of these topics before, I will focus this discussion on how assessment relates to the grammar acquisitional processes.

SLA processes – briefly revisited

As discussed in Chapter 2, research in SLA suggests that learning an L2 involves three simultaneously occurring processes: input processing (VanPatten, 1996), system change (Schmidt, 1990) and output processing (Swain, 1985; Lee and VanPatten, 2003). Input processing relates to how the learner understands the meaning of a new grammatical feature or how form–meaning connections are made (Ellis, 1993; VanPatten, 1996). A critical first stage of acquisition is the conversion of input to 'intake'. The second set of processes, system change, refers to how learners *accommodate* new grammatical forms into their interlanguage and how this change helps *restructure* their interlanguage so that it is more target-like (McLaughlin, 1987; DeKeyser, 1998). Finally, output processing relates to how learners *access* or make use of implicit grammatical knowledge to produce utterances spontaneously in real time (Swain, 1995). VanPatten (1996) depicts the SLA processes as follows:

	I		II		III	
Input	→	Intake	→	Developing system	→	Output

I = input processing; II = accommodation, restructuring; III = access

Figure 8.11 Three sets of processes in SLA and use (VanPatten, 1996, p. 154)

   As assessment occurs in one form or another throughout the learning process, I believe that language teachers should be aware of these processes so that appropriate assessments can be devised to target these processes during the course of instruction. Information obtained from these assessments can then provide more focused information about the development of grammatical knowledge and the types of instructional interventions that need to occur.

Assessing for intake

VanPatten and Cadierno (1993b) describe this critical first stage of acquisition as the process of converting input into 'intake'. In language classrooms, considerable time is spent on determining if students have
understood. As most teachers know, however, it is difficult to discern if
their students have mapped meaning onto the form. In fact, some students can fake their way through an entire lesson without having really
understood the meaning of the target forms. Given that communicative
language classrooms encourage the use of tasks in which learners must
use language meaningfully (Savignon, 1983; Nunan, 1989) and the use
of comprehensible input as an essential component of instruction
(Krashen, 1982; Krashen and Terrell, 1983), I believe that teachers should
explicitly assess for intake as a routine part of instruction.

Learning-oriented assessment can draw on several task types to assess
for intake. One of these is what Ellis (1997) refers to as the 'interpretation'
or the 'comprehension' task. These tasks (1) allow learners to identify the
meaning(s) encoded in a specific grammatical feature; (2) enhance input
so that the grammatical feature is more salient and therefore noticed by
the learner; and (3) enable learners to notice the gap between the actual
meaning of a grammatical feature and the meaning they have assigned to
that feature. In other words, they tap into the learner's explicit knowledge
of the form–meaning connection.

Assessing for intake requires that learners understand the target forms,
but do not produce them themselves. This can be achieved by selected-
response and limited-production tasks in which learners need to make
form–meaning connections. Three examples of interpretation tasks
designed to assess for intake are presented below. (For additional examples of interpretation tasks, see Ellis, 1997; Lee and VanPatten, 2003; and
VanPatten, 1996, 2003.)

To assess test-takers' understanding of *still* and *anymore*, they are shown
a drawing and presented two or more sentences in which the new grammatical feature is used. They are then asked to choose the sentence that
best describes the content of the picture. For example, students see a
drawing of a man fixing a car. They then have to choose between: *the
mechanic is still fixing the car* and *the mechanic isn't fixing the car anymore*.

Another way of assessing intake, according to Lee and VanPatten
(2003), is to present test-takers with sentences that test their ability to
attach meaning to grammar, and then ask them to do something with the

input (e.g., agree/disagree, accept/reject). The example in Figure 8.12 is designed to assess the learner's knowledge of present and past tense verb forms and their associated meanings. Meaning is kept in focus by requiring test-takers to identify the time frame of the utterance and then by asking them to respond personally to the utterance.

Indicate whether the speaker is talking about his or her childhood or about the present. Then, decide whether or not this applies to you.

Model: (*you hear*) We would always visit relatives over the holidays.
         (*you indicate*) childhood.
         (*you indicate*) This applies to me too.

1.	____	Present	____	This doesn't apply to me.
	____	Childhood	____	This applies to me too.
2.	____	Present	____	This doesn't apply to me.
	____	Childhood	____	This applies to me too.
3.	____	Present	____	This doesn't apply to me.
	____	Childhood	____	This applies to me.

[Test-takers hear: 1. We love spending the day at the beach. 2. We'd spend our summers searching for seashells. 3. We used to eat out pretty often.]
(adapted from Lee and VanPatten, 2003, p. 185)

Figure 8.12 Interpretation task

A final example of how to assess for intake is presented in Figure 8.13. Test-takers are given a conversation in which communication is inhibited by the confusion of three similar grammatical forms. Task-takers are asked to repair the meaning of the sentence by selecting the appropriate form for the gap. More specifically, in this example, test-takers have to distinguish between active and passive verb forms and meanings.

While it is important to assess for intake, the results from interpretation tasks, such as the one in Figure 8.13, must not be overgeneralized to assume mastery of the learner's implicit knowledge of the grammatical form. To make such claims, further assessment information is needed. Nonetheless, some research evidence, while not conclusive, has shown that from an instructional perspective the inclusion of comprehension-based approaches has enabled learners to better develop the kind of knowledge needed for both the comprehension and production of target grammatical

Read the dialogue. Select the response that correctly completes the sentence.

A: You know. I really don't like big cities. I get intimidated by them.

B: I'm the same. I intimidate big cities too.

A: What? Oh, I think you mean you _____ big cities.

         __ a. intimidate

         __ b. are intimidating

         __ c. are intimidated by

B: Yeah, and especially I confuse cities with lots of little streets like Venice or Istanbul.

A: What in the world are you talking about?

B: Oh, I mean I _____ cities with lots of little streets.

         __ a. confuse

         __ b. are confusing

         __ c. get confused by

A: I see. I do, too.

Figure 8.13 Repair task to recognize form–meaning mappings

features (Doughty, 1991; VanPatten and Cadierno, 1993a). How the assessment of intake might impact this development is yet to be seen.

Assessing to push restructuring

Once input has been converted into intake, the new grammatical feature is ready to be 'accommodated' into the learner's developing linguistic system, causing a restructuring of the entire system (VanPatten, 1996). To initiate this process, teachers provide students with tasks that enable them to use the new grammatical forms in decreasingly controlled situations so they can incorporate these forms into their existing system of implicit grammatical knowledge. By attending to grammatical input and by getting feedback, learners are able to accommodate the differences between their interlanguage and the target language. Assessment plays an important role in pushing this restructuring process forward since it contributes concrete information to learners on the differences between the grammatical forms they are using and those they should be using to communicate the intended meanings.

To assess for restructuring, we can again draw upon many tasks to measure the extent to which the new grammatical forms have been accommodated into the developing interlanguage system. As described in Chapter 5, limited-production tasks are particularly effective in tapping into a learner's explicit knowledge of grammar, as are those extended-production tasks that allow for planning time or that do not require real-time responses.

For example, the task in Figure 8.14 is designed to measure the test-takers' knowledge of the present and passive verb forms. This task presents test-takers with a dialogue in which they have to notice the difference between what was expressed and what should have been expressed. Then, unlike in Figure 8.13, they have to supply the grammatical forms that best express the meaning for the context.

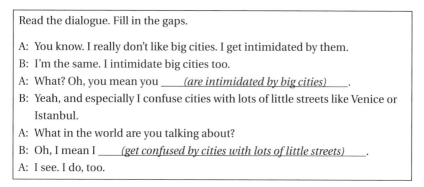

Read the dialogue. Fill in the gaps.

A: You know. I really don't like big cities. I get intimidated by them.
B: I'm the same. I intimidate big cities too.
A: What? Oh, you mean you _____ *(are intimidated by big cities)* _____.
B: Yeah, and especially I confuse cities with lots of little streets like Venice or Istanbul.
A: What in the world are you talking about?
B: Oh, I mean I _____ *(get confused by cities with lots of little streets)* _____.
A: I see. I do, too.

Figure 8.14 Repair task to develop form-meaning mappings

Assessing for output processing

Although learners may have developed an explicit knowledge of the form and meaning of a new grammatical point, this does not necessarily mean they can access this knowledge automatically in spontaneous communication. In order for learners to produce unplanned, meaningful output in real time (i.e., speaking), they need to be able to tap into grammatical knowledge that is already an unconscious part of their developing system of language knowledge (Lee and VanPatten, 2003). Thus, to assess the test-takers' implicit knowledge of grammar (i.e., their ability to process output), test-takers need to be presented with tasks that ask them to produce language in real time, where the focus is more on the content being communicated or on the completion of the task than on the application of explicit grammar rules.

One way of assessing test-takers' implicit knowledge of grammar (i.e., their ability to process output) is to present them with tasks that focus on meaning and that are cognitively engaging. While obviously this has clear implications for construct definition, cognitively engaging tasks are more likely to maintain a focus on information examination or information exchange than on applying grammar rules, and in this way they tap into a test-taker's implicit knowledge of grammar. This also invokes the test-takers' strategic competence in very complex ways.

Classroom assessments that are cognitively complex typically involve the processing of topical information from multiple sources in order to accomplish some task that requires complex or higher-order thinking skills (Burns, 1986). Based on an analysis of tasks in school subject classrooms (e.g., social studies), Marzano, Pickering and McTighe (1993) provide a list of commonly identified reasoning processes (which I have added to) that are used in cognitively complex tasks.

- Comparing
- Classifying
- Induction
- Deduction
- Investigation
- Error analysis
- Constructing support
- Analyzing perspectives
- Decision making
- Problem solving
- Experimental inquiry
- Invention
- Abstracting
- Diagnosis
- Summarizing

Some of these processes, I might add, are not uncommon in communicative language teaching or in language classroom assessment.

While cognitively complex performance tasks have much to recommend them in terms of providing authentic assessments and keeping a focus on information, they may measure more than a test-taker's implicit knowledge of grammar, and score-based inferences should reflect the broader construct.

In sum, the learning mandate in language classrooms requires that grammar assessments designed to promote learning draw on not only grammar-testing theory for the design and operationalization of grammar assessments, but also L2 learning theory. In this section, I have argued that in language classrooms teachers need to be aware of how learners process new grammar and they need to provide assessments targeting the stages in that process (i.e., intake, restructuring, output). In this way, learning-oriented assessment provides information that allows test-takers to notice their deficiencies, reanalyze their grammar hypotheses and further develop grammatical ability.

In the next section, I will illustrate how elements of learning-oriented assessment have been applied to an ESL classroom grammar achievement test.

Illustrative example of learning-oriented assessment

Let us now turn to an illustration of a learning-oriented achievement test of grammatical ability.

Background

The example is taken from Unit 7 of *On Target 1 Achievement Tests* (Purpura et al., 2001). This is a book of achievement tests designed to accompany *On Target 1* (Purpura and Pinkley, 1999), a theme-based, integrated-skills program designed for secondary school or adult learners of English as a second or foreign language at the lower–mid intermediate level of proficiency. *On Target* provides instruction in language (e.g., grammar, vocabulary, pronunciation), language use (e.g., listening, speaking, reading and writing) and thematic development (e.g., record-breaking, mysteries of science). The goal of the achievement tests is 'to measure the students' knowledge of grammar, vocabulary, pronunciation, reading and writing, as taught in each unit' (Purpura et al., 2001, p. iii). The test results are intended to indicate mastery of the learning points in the unit being tested and to determine if students are ready for the next unit or level of the program. They also aim 'to provide students with valuable feedback and teachers with empirical information on what students may need to review' (ibid.). In short, these books were designed as learning-oriented assessments with a focus on providing targeted feedback for further development.

Each *On Target* achievement test consists of five sections: grammar (containing at least two tasks), pronunciation, reading (not discussed here), and writing. Table 8.2 provides an overview of the test design (except for the reading section).

Each test is designed to be moderately speeded with an administration time of approximately 50–60 minutes.

The Unit 7 achievement test was structured in the following way. The unifying theme was 'Filling the bill' in the context of gaining employment or winning an award. Grammar task 1 was designed to measure the students' explicit knowledge of grammatical form (verb tenses) by presenting them

Table 8.2 *Overview of an 'On Target achievement test'*

Section	Areas of language knowledge	Possible task types	Scoring
1. Grammar	Grammatical knowledge (sentence level) • Grammatical form and/or meaning	• Selected-response • Limited-production	• Right/wrong (single or multiple criteria for correctness)
2. Grammar	Grammatical knowledge (discourse level) • Grammatical form and/or meaning	• Selected-response • Limited-production	• Right/wrong (single or multiple criteria for correctness) • Partial-credit
3. Pronunciation	Grammatical knowledge • Phonological form and/or meaning	• Selected-response • Limited-production	• Right/wrong

4. Writing	• Strategic competence
	  ▪ Brainstorming
	• Grammatical knowledge
	• Topical knowledge
	• Pragmatic knowledge
	  ▪ Organizational
		• Limited-production (brainstorming task)
		• Extended-production
			• Partial-credit (brainstorming task)
			• Analytic scoring

with a gapped and cued account of a person interviewing for a job. According to the test book, this task was designed to be scored dichotomously for grammatical form.

Grammar 1

Complete the passage with the correct form of the verb. Use the negative when appropriate.

This past June, Tim (1. graduate) _____ from college with a degree in business. He (2. work) _____ in his father's store since July. Now he (3. decide) _____ to find another job. He (4. be) _____interested in marketing for a long time. So far he (5. go) _____on a number of interviews, but he still (6. get) _____ an offer. Last week Tim (7. have) _____ his best interview of them all; he (8. interview) _____ at Nova Movie Studios. He thought he (9. have) _____ a good chance at getting this job. Yesterday morning the studio (10. give) _____ him a second interview. When he (11. call) _____the studio, the manager said to him, 'Congratulations! We (12. decided) _____to hire you! We don't have a marketing position right now, but we'd like you to jump out of an airplane in our next action movie!'

(Purpura et al., 2001, On Target 1. Unit 7)

The second grammar task, designed to measure knowledge of grammatical form and meaning (present perfect tense), presented test-takers with a résumé along with a gapped interview between an award judge and an award candidate. Test-takers have to read the interviewee's list of achievements and complete the conversation. They also have to include some questions with *how long* and *how many*. Each gap was designed to be scored using a three-point holistic rubric designed to measure grammatical form and meaning.

Grammar 2

You are interviewing Suki for the Student of the Year award. Read the list of her achievements in the box and complete the conversation. Include questions with *how long* or *how many*.

Suki Mikado

School record
Top student in the tenth-grade Chinese class
Top student in eleventh-grade math, English and science classes.

> **Clubs and societies**
> Student director of the Street Theater Club
> President of the Modern Dance Club
> Member of the National Hip-Hop Poetry Society
>
> **Prizes and awards**
> First-prize winner for the school dance contest
> Award for most popular student
>
> **Other activities**
> Photographer for school newspaper
> Volunteer at Senior Citizens' Homes for Retired Dancers

You: Suki, I see you are in the Street Theater Club and now serve as student director. (1.) _____?

Suki: For a few years now.

You: Good. And I also see that you're the president of the Modern Dance Club. (2.) _____?

Suki: Since October, 1999.

You: That's great! (3.) _____?

Suki: So far, only one. I got the first prize for the school dance contest.

You: Wow! First prize! What other activities have you been involved in recently?

Suki: _____
_____
_____

You: Thanks. That's all for now. It was a pleasure meeting you.

(Adapted from Purpura et al., 2001, *On Target 1.* Unit 7)

The pronunciation task was designed to measure the learners' understanding of phonological form. They are presented with a written job interview in which they have to underline the syllable of the word that carries sentence stress. This task was intended to be scored dichotomously for phonological form.

Pronunciation

In each thought group for Person B, underline the syllable of the word that carries the sentence stress. Look at the interviewer's questions to help you.

1. A: What was your last *job?*
   B: I was a waitress.

2. A: Where did you *work*?
  B: I worked in Andy's restaurant.
3. A: How long did you *work* there?
  B: For about a year now.
4. A: Do you have any *other* experience?
  B: Not until you hire me!

(Adapted from Purpura et al., 2001, On Target 1. Unit 7)

Finally, the writing section aimed to measure the test-takers' ability to write a recommendation paragraph using the present perfect tense. This task hoped to elicit the learners' implicit knowledge of grammatical form and meaning. Test-takers have to read a situation and brainstorm information. They then have to use this information to write a recommendation paragraph to the principal, justifying their choice for the award. They are reminded to check their work for organization and for the use of the present perfect tense.

Writing
Write a paragraph recommending someone for the award.

A. The principal at your school has asked you to recommend a student for this year's Student of the Year award. You have interviewed several students and chosen Keiko Suzuki. Make a list of the reasons why (supporting points and details) you chose Ms. Suzuki. Use the box below to organize your thoughts.

School record
Prizes and awards
Other activities

B. On a separate piece of paper, write a letter to your principal explaining why you think Ms. Suzuki should receive the award. When finished, check your work. Make sure you have a good topic sentence, supporting points, and details. Finally check your work for correct use of the present perfect tense.

Part A: 3 possible points (relevance/validity of information, task fulfillment): _____

Part B: 15 possible points (topical control, rhetorical control, grammatical control): _____

(Adapted from Purpura et al., 2001, On Target 1. Unit 7)

The brainstorming task was intended to be scored with a three-point holistic rubric defined in terms of topical control, task fulfillment and information relevance/validity. Scores for the letter should be derived from an analytic rubric consisting of three scales: content control, organizational control and grammatical control. The grammatical control scale was defined in terms of accuracy and range of structures and vocabulary. This scale could easily be adapted to include task-specific information.

In the next section, I will discuss how the Unit 7 achievement test draws on both grammar-testing theory and learning theory to fulfill the learning mandate.

Making assessment learning-oriented

The *On Target* achievement tests were designed with a clear learning mandate. The content of the tests had to be strictly aligned with the content of the curriculum. This obviously had several implications for the test design and its operationalization. From a testing perspective, the primary purpose of the Unit 7 achievement test was to measure the students' explicit as well as their implicit knowledge of grammatical form and meaning on both the sentence and discourse levels. More specifically, the test was intended to measure the degree to which test-takers had learned the present perfect tense with repeated actions (How many times have you been . . . ?) and with length of time actions (How long have you been . . . ?). Test inferences also included the learners' ability to use this knowledge to discuss life achievements. The test results were intended for use in deciding if students had adequately incorporated the grammatical form into their interlanguage system. If not, the test specifically aimed to identify what aspects of the target grammar needed further work. Claims about grammatical ability were to be based on the results of the grammar, pronunciation and writing sections of the test.

While the TLU domain was limited to the use of the present perfect tense to discuss life achievements, the constructs and tasks included in the test were both simple and complex. For example, the first gap-filling grammar task was intended only to assess the test-takers' explicit knowledge of morphosyntactic form and the pronunciation task focused only on their explicit knowledge of phonological form. The second grammar task was slightly more complex in that it aimed to measure the test-takers' ability to use these forms to communicate literal and intended meanings based on more extensive input. The writing task, however, was the most complex in that it was designed to measure strategic competence in the brainstorming task, and in the composing task, it measured topical knowledge, pragmatic knowledge (organizational control), and the test-takers' explicit and implicit knowledge of grammar. From a theoretical perspective, this test provides a relatively comprehensive assessment of grammatical knowledge with regard to the target grammar points.

In terms of scoring, the specification of participants was left to the teachers' discretion in case they wished to score the tasks themselves or involve students in self- or peer assessment activities. Each task contained a recommended number of points so that learners could receive a score for each task. To rate performance on the extended-production tasks, teachers were encouraged to use (and adapt) one of the scoring rubrics available in the front of the book. They were also able to decide how best to report the test results and to whom, how to provide learners with feedback, how to document progress and how to encourage student plans for improving.

From a learning perspective, the achievement test was based on the premise that students had had plenty of opportunities in class to demonstrate their understanding of the present perfect tense and to receive feedback. Thus, it was presumed that assessment was taking place at some point beyond intake. For this reason, no comprehension tasks were included in the test. It was also presumed that most students were well on their way toward incorporating the target grammar into their interlanguage and that it would make sense to have information on the degree to which students had learned the present perfect tense and the degree to which this knowledge was implicit. For this reason, both simple and complex tasks were used in the test.

The writing task was included in the test to assess the test-takers' implicit knowledge of grammar. In this task, test-takers had to maintain a focus on meaning as they wrote a grammatically accurate, meaningful and well-organized paragraph about past achievements.

In sum, the *On Target* achievement test attempted to take into consideration elements from both grammar-testing theory and L2 learning theory in achieving a learning-oriented assessment mandate.

Summary

In this chapter I argued that even though large-scale, standardized tests have an important role to play in school decisions, the primary mandate of learning-oriented classroom assessment is to provide formative information about learners that can be used to plan further learning and more focused instruction. In other words, the main role of classroom-based, grammar assessment is to help students understand how well they have learned the target grammar and what they need to work on in order to improve. Given this general assessment goal, I also argued that the development of classroom assessments needed to be rooted in a theory of grammar assessment and a theory of second language learning.

In describing learning-oriented assessment, I showed how the learning mandate has implications for how teachers make decisions about test design and operationalization. With regard to test design, I discussed how teachers could explicitly specify the test mandate by stating whom the assessment is for, why assessment information is needed and what kind of information is needed. This, of course, will influence the types of constructs that are assessed in classroom contexts and the types of tasks that could be used. In this regard, I demonstrated how the characteristics of test tasks could be varied to elicit grammar performance data as an integral part of instruction by using observation and reflection. I also discussed how the specification of the scoring method in classroom assessment contexts could vary to involve students. In this regard, I discussed in some detail teacher-, self- and peer-assessment procedures, and how this might promote further learning.

I then discussed learning-oriented grammatical assessment from a learning perspective, noting the critical moments in which assessments should take place and the goals that these assessments would serve. Drawing on research and theory in grammar processing, I discussed the importance of assessing for intake by providing assessments that measured students' understanding of the meaning of target grammatical features. I also discussed how assessment and the provision of feedback could serve to raise the learners' awareness of gaps between their interlanguage and target forms – a process which is designed to promote interlanguage development. Finally, this chapter discussed the importance of assessing for output so that inferences about the test-takers' implicit knowledge of grammar can be made. This could be done by designing grammar tasks that require test-takers to use the target feature while communicating meaning in real time. In sum, assessments that target the different phases of the learning process can give teachers some information on how to help learners improve.

CHAPTER NINE

Challenges and new directions in assessing grammatical ability

Introduction

Research and theory related to the teaching and learning of grammar have made significant advances over the years. In applied linguistics, our understanding of language has been vastly broadened with the work of corpus-based and communication-based approaches to language study, and this research has made pathways into recent pedagogical grammars. Also, our conceptualization of language proficiency has shifted from an emphasis on linguistic form to one on communicative language ability and communicative language use, which has, in turn, led to a de-emphasis on grammatical accuracy and a greater concern for communicative effectiveness. In language teaching, we moved from a predominant focus on structures and metalinguistic terminology to an emphasis on comprehensible input, interaction and no explicit grammar instruction. From there, we adopted a more balanced approach to language instruction, where meaning and communication are still emphasized, but where form and meaning-focused instruction have a clear role. Current research in grammar instruction involves investigations into the effect of teaching grammar explicitly or implicitly, reactively or proactively, and integrated in the curriculum at one point in time or sequentially (Doughty, 2002). Findings from SLA have also shown that the processing constraints underlying certain developmental orders (e.g., negation) cannot be contravened (Doughty, 2002) and that the optimal conditions for processing meaning, function and form in language learning are still to be discovered. All these developments have implications for how grammatical ability needs to be assessed and how assessments of grammatical ability might conceivably be used. However, theoretical discussions on the nature of grammatical ability, such as those initiated by Rea-Dickins (1991) and Larsen-Freeman (1991, 1997), have been few and far between, as have discussions of the construction of reliable and valid assessments. Equally absent from the literature have been discussions of the potential benefits (or caveats) of designing grammar assessments with reference to a theory of interlanguage development (e.g., Hudson, 1993; Ellis, 2001a, 2001b; Chang, 2004), to a theory of second or foreign language learning, (e.g., VanPatten and his colleagues), or to a theory of communicative language ability.

This book has endeavored to address this gap and further these discussions. In Chapters 1 and 2, I examined different notions of grammar and showed how these different conceptualizations could provide complementary information for use in the construction of grammar assessments. I then discussed how grammar is learned and taught, and the role that assessment plays in decisions about learning. In Chapters 3 and 4, I examined how grammatical knowledge has been conceptualized in models of communicative language ability and argued that grammatical knowledge should be defined in terms of a form and meaning component, and that this should be differentiated from pragmatic knowledge. I then proposed a model of grammatical knowledge that could be used in the construction and validation of grammar assessments. In Chapters 5 and 6, I discussed grammar test tasks and the process of grammar-test construction. In this discussion, I attempted to show how the qualities of test usefulness needed to be balanced and prioritized for each testing context. In Chapters 7 and 8, I described some large-scale grammar assessments in terms of their purpose and usefulness qualities. I then described classroom-based grammar assessments and the construction of learning-oriented grammar assessments.

In this final chapter, I will discuss how grammar assessment has evolved over the years and how it has begun to change. I will also highlight some of the persistent theoretical and practical issues and challenges language educators face in assessing grammatical ability.

The state of grammar assessment

In the last fifty years, language testers have dedicated a great deal of time to discussing the nature of language proficiency and the testing of the four skills, the qualities of test usefulness (i.e., reliability, authenticity), the relationships between test-taker or task characteristics and performance, and numerous statistical procedures for examining data and providing evidence of test validity. In all of these discussions, very little has been said about the assessment of grammatical ability, and unsurprisingly, until recently, not much has changed since the 1960s. In other words, for the past fifty years, grammatical ability has been defined in many instances as morphosyntactic form and tested in either a discrete-point, selected-response format – a practice initiated by several large language-testing firms and emulated by classroom teachers – or in a discrete-point, limited-production format, typically by means of the cloze or some other gap-filling task. These tests have typically been scored right/wrong with grammatical accuracy as the sole criterion for correctness. Tests of this kind are, as I have argued, appropriate for certain purposes, and make sense, for example, in situations where individual grammatical forms are emphasized, such as in form-focused instruction. However, we must recognize that separate tests (or subtests) of explicit grammatical knowledge such as these provide only a partial measure of grammatical ability, and that while scores from these tests might be related to those produced from more comprehensive measures of grammatical ability, they fall short in terms of an evidentiary basis for making such claims. We must also recognize that while discrete-point testing may be tolerated for certain assessment purposes by language teachers (Rea-Dickins, 2001), context-independent, discrete-point tasks, or those that lack authenticity of topic, are perceived by current and past students, teachers, administrators and content teachers as being 'old-fashioned' and 'out of touch' with their language learning goals (Purpura et al., 2003).

In recent years, the assessment of grammatical ability has taken an interesting turn in certain situations. Grammatical ability has been assessed in the context of language use under the rubric of testing speaking or writing. This has led, in some cases, to examinations in which grammatical knowledge is no longer included as a separate and explicit component of communicative language ability in the form of a separate subtest. In other words, only the students' implicit knowledge of grammar alongside other components of communicative language ability (e.g., topic, organization, register) is measured. The decision to eliminate the explicit testing of grammar in at least two cases was based on research showing that a separate subtest of grammatical knowledge could not be adequately differentiated from other sections of the test. Examples of this are the revised versions of the ESL Placement Exam (ESLPE) at the University of California, Los Angeles (see Cushing Weigle and Lynch, 1995), and the revised IELTS at the University of Cambridge (see Alderson, 1993). Also, the next generation TOEFL scheduled to be released in September 2005 by the Educational Testing Service in Princeton, New Jersey, has decided to eliminate its separate structure and writing section in favor of a more integrated test of the four language skills (http://www.toefl.org/nextgenerationcbt). The de-emphasis on explicit grammar assessment has also led, in some instances, to examinations with scoring rubrics in which notions of grammatical precision are closely linked to notions of communicative effectiveness or the degree to which grammatical forms promote or inhibit effective communication (e.g., the ESLPE). In these instances, grammatical ability is not scored separately by means of an analytic rubric; rather, it contributes holistically to a language performance score alongside other components of language knowledge. Tests of this kind are, as I have also argued, suitable for certain purposes and again make sense in situations, for example, where ideas and meaning are emphasized, such as in meaning-focused instruction or content-based language programs. This can also be appropriate in programs (e.g., English for Academic Purposes) where test-takers are assumed to have already acquired high levels of grammatical ability and where the goal of assessment is to determine how well test-takers can use grammatical resources to convey a wide range of meanings in completing some complex task. However, we must recognize, though, that writing and speaking tests (scored holistically) provide only a partial measure of grammatical ability, given the other constructs that might be tapped into and measured explicitly or implicitly in these complex tasks. In other words, when grammatical knowledge is fully integrated within a measure of speaking or writing ability and scored holistically for multiple areas of competence, we have no way of disentangling what in the ability to speak or write might be attributed to a knowledge of grammatical forms and meanings. If, however, we score these assessments analytically, such as with the current version of the IELTS, we can better estimate the relative contribution of grammatical knowledge to the assessment. We must also recognize that by eliminating the explicit assessment of grammar, we have no way of providing formative feedback to students who need to achieve superior or distinguished levels of proficiency in a second or foreign language.

In a few cases, grammatical ability has been tested in both ways – as 'a "body" of knowledge and "a means to an end" with attention to . . . conveying appropriate meanings in messages rather than an exclusive emphasis on accuracy of form and structure' (Rea-Dickins, 2001, p. 28). This has led to examinations in which grammatical ability is measured by one or more separate-and-explicit, selected-response or limited-production tasks of grammatical knowledge, as well as one or more extended-production tasks designed to measure, amongst other things, the test-takers' implicit knowledge of grammar while speaking or writing. Also, grammatical performance is rated by means of an analytic rubric in which at least one scale is explicitly designed to measure the test-takers' ability to use grammar to communicate their ideas and intended messages precisely and meaningfully in response to the task demands. Examples of this are the *Community English Program Placement Test* (the grammar, speaking and writing sections) at Teachers College, Columbia University, the *On Target Achievement Tests* (the grammar and writing sections) (Purpura et al., 2001) discussed in Chapter 7, and several tests in the University of Cambridge suite of exams, including the *FCE* (Cambridge ESOL, 2001a), the *Certificate in Advanced English* (Cambridge ESOL, 2001b), and the *Certificate of Proficiency in English* (Cambridge ESOL, 2002b). Tests of this kind are appropriate for certain purposes, and make sense, for instance, in situations where information on both the test-takers' explicit and implicit knowledge of grammar is relevant, such as in form-and-meaning-focused instruction. This method provides, as I have argued, a more comprehensive way of measuring grammatical ability, if, in fact, that is the goal of assessment. In the end, it is important for language educators to differentiate these different ways of testing grammar, not to prescribe how best to measure grammatical ability, but to allow language educators to select the type of assessments that best match their assessment goals.

Having discussed how grammar assessment has evolved over the years, I will discuss in the next section some ongoing issues and challenges associated with assessing grammar.

Challenge 1: Defining grammatical ability

One major challenge revolves around how grammatical ability has been defined both theoretically and operationally in language testing. As we saw in Chapters 3 and 4, in the 1960s and 1970s language teaching and language testing maintained a strong syntactocentric view of language rooted largely in linguistic structuralism. Moreover, models of language ability, such as those proposed by Lado (1961) and Carroll (1961), had a clear linguistic focus, and assessment concentrated on measuring language elements – defined in terms of morphosyntactic forms on the sentence level – while performing language skills. Grammatical knowledge was determined solely in terms of linguistic accuracy. This approach to testing led to examinations such at the *CELT* (Harris and Palmer, 1970a) and the *English Proficiency Test battery* (Davies, 1964).

Since the 1980s this depiction of language knowledge has been significantly broadened with a push towards communicative language teaching and with theoretical models of communicative competence, characterized by the work of Canale and Swain (1980), Bachman (1990b), and Bachman and Palmer (1982, 1996). These models supported a multicomponential view of language ability with grammar as an uncontested component. In most models, grammatical knowledge was defined in terms of phonology, morphology, lexis, syntax and sometimes semantics. Also, grammar at the discourse level was accounted for by the specification of cohesion, as well as rhetorical and conversational organization (Bachman and Palmer, 1996; Canale, 1983).

However, despite the overarching emphasis on meaning in communicative language teaching and learning, the role of meaning in models of language proficiency has been difficult to locate, since in none of these models has the role of meaning or its relationship to linguistic form been defined or specified. Nor has it been clear how literal meanings were related to or differentiated from pragmatic meanings. As I have argued in Chapters 3 and 4, the specification of grammatical meaning in a model of communicative language ability is critical if these models are to account for instances of language use in which the test-taker has effectively communicated the intended meaning of an utterance, but expresses it imprecisely (e.g., *I no understand*). Similarly, we must clearly specify (and score) grammatical meaning if we wish to account for instances of language use in which the test-taker has accurately expressed a grammatical utterance, but the utterance has not communicated the speaker's intended meaning. Examples of this are when a Spanish-speaking test-taker says *I borrowed her car* instead of *his* car (confusion of gender with reference to biological sex), or when a test-taker says *My boss is boring* instead of *My boss is bored* (confusion of stative and dynamic adjectives), or when he or she says *The cell phone dropped from me* instead of *I dropped my cell phone*. In communicative language testing, assessing both grammatical form and meaning, when relevant to the assessment purpose, provides teachers and learners with a more complete assessment of the test-takers' grammatical ability than just providing information on form or on meaning alone.

Therefore, responding to Bachman and Clark's (1987) appeal to 'refine the theoretical models of communicate language proficiency . . . with particular attention to defining the specific ability domains in operational terms' (p. 30), I have proposed in this book a model of grammatical knowledge that includes both grammatical form and meaning on the sentence and discourse levels (see Figure 4.2). I have articulated this model with the full understanding that at times it is impossible to observe the exact boundaries of form and meaning, and that for those who want clear and unambiguous distinctions, this depiction of grammatical knowledge might present a problem. However, I would argue that even though two dimensions of a single feature are encoded together and might not be observable separately at times, this does not refute the existence of two distinct dimensions. A case in point is the English modal auxiliary *must*, where form and meaning are entwined in the same word. In my experience of teaching English to speakers of other languages, learners have no problem learning the form of the modal auxiliary *must*, but acquiring its meanings present a challenge. Moreover, based on many years of experience teaching languages, I have found that with some grammatical structures learners find the form more challenging to learn than the meanings, whereas with other structures, they find the meaning(s) more difficult. Larsen-Freeman (1991) has written about these challenges, and Chang (2004) has investigated them with regard to the relative clauses.

With an expanded definition of grammatical knowledge, however, come several theoretical challenges. The first is for language educators to make clear distinctions between the form and meaning components of grammatical knowledge and, if relevant to the test purpose, to incorporate these distinctions in construct definition. Making finer distinctions between form and meaning will require adjustments in how we approach grammar assessment and may require innovation.

A clear example of an area in which much would be gained from making finer distinctions between form and meaning is in learner corpora research. In recent years, many corpus linguists and SLA researchers interested in the persistence of learner errors at different proficiency levels (e.g., Granger, 1999, 2003a, 2003b) have devoted a considerable amount of energy to compiling corpora of learner language and to tagging these corpora for a range of learner errors in speaking and writing – typically with regard to grammatical form at the sentence and discourse levels. The errors are then tallied by computers to better understand, for example, the types of errors students from different native languages make at different proficiency levels or the types of errors that persist after instruction. Granger (2002) recognizes that 'computer-aided error analysis often arouses negative reactions' (pp. 13–14) but argues convincingly that the examination of errors provides critical information for understanding interlanguage development and, I might add, for providing students with structured negative feedback designed to promote noticing.

While the current research on learner-oriented corpora has shown great promise, many more insights on learner errors and interlanguage development could be obtained if other components of grammatical form (e.g., information management forms and interactional forms) and if grammatical meaning were also tagged at both the sentence and the discourse levels. For example, in a talk on the use of corpora for defining learning problems of Korean ESL students at the University of Illinois, Choi (2003) identified the following errors as passive errors:

> 1: *The color of her face was changed from a pale white to a bright red.
> 2: *It is ridiculous the women in developing countries are suffered.

While it is true that the students may have overused the passive in these sentences, it is clear that they have a full understanding of passive form, but not of passive meaning, so that it can be used correctly. In sentence 1, the student has failed to learn that 'change' requires the active voice since it is an agentless 'change-of-state' or ergative verb, and in sentence 2, 'suffer' denotes a physical state and is intransitive, thereby making passivization unlikely. As a result, these sentences might be tagged for meaning and not form. This information could ultimately provide a more comprehensive understanding of learner errors than a depiction based solely on form. It would also root learner errors stemming from performance data to a broader model of language proficiency.

Challenge 2: Scoring grammatical ability

A second challenge relates to scoring, as the specification of both form and meaning is likely to influence the ways in which grammar assessments are scored. As we discussed in Chapter 6, responses with multiple criteria for correctness may necessitate different scoring procedures. For example, the use of dichotomous scoring, even with certain selected-response items, might need to give way to partial-credit scoring, since some wrong answers may reflect partial development either in form or meaning. As a result, language educators might need to adapt their scoring procedures to reflect the two dimensions of grammatical knowledge. This might, in turn, require the use of measurement models that can accommodate both dichotomous and partial-credit data in calculating and analyzing test scores. Then, in scoring extended-production tasks for both form and meaning, descriptors on scoring rubrics might need to be adapted to reflect graded performance in the two dimensions of grammatical knowledge more clearly. It should also be noted that more complex scoring procedures will impact the resources it takes to mark responses or to program machine-scoring devices. It will also require a closer examination (and hopefully ongoing research) of how a wrong answer may be a reflection of interlanguage development. However, successfully meeting these challenges could provide a more valid assessment of the test takers' underlying grammatical ability.

A clear example of the need to score for form and meaning can be seen in some of the latest research related to computer-assisted language learning (CALL). Several studies (e.g., Heift, 2003) have investigated, for example, the role or different types of corrective feedback (i.e., explicit correction, metalinguistic information, repetition by highlighting) on grammar development. Grammar performance errors in these studies were scored for form alone. In future studies, the scoring of both grammatical form and meaning, when applicable, might provide interesting insights into learner uptake in CALL.

Another challenge relates to the scoring of grammatical ability in complex performance tasks. In instances where the assessment goals call for the use of complex performance tasks, we need to be sure to use well-developed scoring rubrics and rating scales to guide raters to focus their judgments *only* on the constructs relevant to the assessment goal. McNamara (1996) stresses that the scales in such tasks represent, explicitly or implicitly, the theoretical basis upon which the performance is judged. Therefore, clearly defined constructs of grammatical ability and how they are operationalized in rating scales are critical. Questions related to whether topical knowledge or strategic competence are part of the construct or not need to be resolved, and the rating scales need to reflect these decisions. The advantage of using complex performance tasks that are highly authentic is the generalizability of the inferences these tasks allow us to make about grammatical ability. Their disadvantage, however, relates to the potential lack of accuracy with which we are able to infer what test-takers know about specific grammatical knowledge given the other constructs that may also be intentionally or unintentionally measured in such tasks by raters.

Challenge 3: Assessing meanings

The third challenge revolves around 'meaning' and how 'meaning' in a model of communicative language ability can be defined and assessed. The 'communicative' in communicative language teaching, communicative language testing, communicative language ability, or communicative competence refers to the conveyance of ideas, information, feelings, attitudes and other intangible meanings (e.g., social status) through language. Therefore, while the grammatical resources used to communicate these meanings precisely are important, the notion of meaning conveyance in the communicative curriculum is critical. Therefore, in order to test something as intangible as meaning in second or foreign language use, we need to define what it is we are testing.

Looking to linguists (and language philosophers) for help in defining meaning (e.g., Searle, 1969; Lyons, 1977; Leech, 1983; Levinson, 1983; Jaszczolt, 2002), we will soon realize that meaning is not only a characteristic of the language and its forms (i.e., semantics), but also a characteristic of language use (i.e., pragmatics). This, in turn, involves the links among explicitly stated meanings in an utterance, the language user's intentions, presuppositions and knowledge of the real world, and the specific context in which the utterance is made. We will also realize that boundary debates between semantics and pragmatics have been long and interesting, but have produced no simple answer with respect to the meaning of 'meaning' and the distinctions between semantics and pragmatics.

It then should come as no surprise that language testers have had varying opinions about the role of meaning in communicative language ability and communicative language use. Lado (1961) described 'linguistic meaning' as that seen in 'dictionaries and grammars'. He described language as a resource for conveying cultural meaning and individual meaning. Oller (1979) mentioned meaning at two levels: literal meaning and pragmatic meaning:

> In addition to the factive information coded in the words and phrases of the statement, a person who utters that statement may convey attitudes toward the asserted or implied states of affairs, and may further code information concerning the way the speaker thinks the listener should feel about those states of affairs.
>
> (p. 18)

Here, although Oller (1979) referred specifically to how language elements can encode a number of meanings, he provided no guidance for differentiating meanings from forms in language tests. Drawing on

Halliday's (1978) notion of language as a system of 'meaning potential', Canale and Swain (1980) listed semantics as a part of grammatical competence. This is described as word meaning and sentence meaning, or the emphasis on 'getting one's point across' (i.e., meaningful communication) (p. 15). Bachman and Palmer (1996), building on Bachman (1990b), referred to vocabulary, or word meaning, as a component of grammatical knowledge and to textual meanings derived from cohesion as well as from rhetorical or conversational organization. They also specified meaning related to communicative goals (i.e., language functions) under the broad rubric of pragmatic knowledge. What might be inferred from this discussion is that meaning in language use (lexical, cohesive, rhetorical and functional) occurs simultaneously at several levels and is produced as a result of the processes of language use. In other words, a test-taker uses language knowledge, topical knowledge, strategic competence, as well as information from the context, to construct meanings from utterances or from discourse (Bachman, personal communication). While this may be true for communicative language use, I also believe that if we wish to assess the product of language use in terms of communicative effectiveness, we need to specify precisely what that entails.

From the perspective of grammar assessment, we might consider the following questions with regard to meaning. How do we test the meaning of utterances when expressed in a situation where there is very little contextual information available, and where the meaning can be derived solely from the meaning of its component parts arranged in syntax (i.e., literal meaning)? For example, how do we assess the communicative effectiveness of a beginning learner unscrambling a sentence or writing sentences describing the relative size of people in a drawing? Also, how do we test a speaker's literal and intended meaning of utterances when expressed in context-reduced situations (i.e., grammatical meaning)? For example, how do we assess the communicative effectiveness of a beginning learner describing her family relations in a picture or of an intermediate student discussing her weekend activities? Finally, how do we test the meaning of utterances when expressed in context-rich situations – that is when the extensions of meaning are derived primarily from context and dependent upon an understanding of the shared norms, assumptions, expectations and presuppositions of the interlocutors in the communicative context (i.e., pragmatic meaning)? For example, how do we assess the communicative effectiveness of an advanced learner responding to a complaint from a customer in a polite manner or an intermediate learner expressing an indirect request of a work supervisor?

To address the qualitative differences among these various types of meaning, I have discussed in this book the assessment of meaning in terms of grammatical meaning and pragmatic meaning. As described in Chapters 3 and 4, grammatical meaning embodies the literal and intended meanings of an utterance derived both from the meaning of the words arranged in syntax and from the way in which the words are used to convey the speaker's intention. In other words, grammatical meaning refers to instances of language in which what is said is what is meant and intended. I have also argued that in grammar assessment the primary assessment goal is to determine whether learners are able to use forms to get their basic point across accurately *and meaningfully*. I have maintained that if meaning is construct-relevant, then communicative meaningfulness should be scored. Pragmatic meaning, also described in Chapters 3 and 4, embodies a host of implied meanings that derive from context relating to the interpersonal relationship of the interlocutors, their emotional or attitudinal stance, their presuppositions about what is known, the sociocultural setting of the interaction and participation of an interlocutor during talk-in-interaction. While the primary goal of this book is to focus on the assessment of grammatical forms and their meanings, I have extended the discussion to the assessment of pragmatic knowledge in an effort to highlight, to the extent possible, the boundaries I have drawn between grammatical and pragmatic meanings.

More specifically, in discussing the form–meaning mappings (see Table 3.2 in Chapter 3), I have characterized the relationship between grammatical meaning and pragmatic meaning in terms of directness and context. This relates to the degree to which the literal and intended meaning of an utterance could be derived *more* from the meaning of the forms arranged in syntactic structure than from the information in the context (relatively direct). It may equally relate to the degree to which the literal and intended meaning of an utterance depend *more* on the information in the context and *less* on the actual words expressed (relatively less direct). In this discussion, I have argued that much of what is taught and tested at the beginning, intermediate and sometimes at the advanced levels of language courses involves the grammatical resources needed to express grammatical meanings. In fact, much of what I have attempted to accomplish in this book involves the same – the use of grammatical resources to convey literal and intended meanings.

At the same time, we must recognize that the meaning of grammatical forms can be extended to convey a host of implied meanings that derive from context. As I stated in Chapters 3 and 4, these meaning extensions can involve contextual meanings, sociolinguistic meanings, sociocultural meanings, psychological meanings, rhetorical meanings and so forth. Furthermore, one or more of these meanings can be intended or understood at the same time. In terms of language assessment, an L2 learner would hardly be considered 'proficient' if he or she could not understand or express both grammatical and a wide range of pragmatic meanings. However, to what degree must he or she be able to understand and express certain sociocultural or sociolinguistic meanings in order to be considered fully functional in a second or foreign language – or in order to function in an English-medium environment? In my own personal experience in learning languages, it is my own inability to understand and communicate the subtle pragmatic meanings that categorize me as a near native speaker as opposed to a native speaker. In short, it resides not so much in the forms, but in the meanings and their extensions.

The existence of finer distinctions between the different types of 'meaning' poses several challenges for language educators interested in assessing both the precision with which utterances are expressed (i.e., accuracy) and the degree to which utterances are meaningful (i.e., meaningfulness – to be differentiated from task fulfillment). The first challenge, as I have mentioned earlier, is for language educators to understand the finer distinctions of meaning, so that they can assess the test-takers' ability to construct a range of meanings as part of language use, when relevant and appropriate. This has implications especially for construct definition, task selection, scoring and feedback. Information from these assessments could contribute to the research base in language testing. For example, I know of no empirical studies that have examined the relationship between form and meaning development with different grammatical features. I also know of no studies that have investigated the relationships among form–meaning directness, context and language ability. Finally, the distinction between the different types of pragmatic meanings, as described in Chapters 3 and 4, may serve as a basis for the development of future tests of pragmatic knowledge – ones that complement those that have examined intended meanings in speech acts (e.g., Cohen, 1994), sociolinguistic meanings (e.g., Hudson, Detmer and Brown, 1995; Yamashita, 1996) or sociocultural meanings (e.g., Cohen and Olshtain, 1981; Farhady, 1983). Results from this research could help us better understand the relationships between grammatical forms and the different types of meaning they convey.

Again I recognize that it is sometimes difficult to draw a clear and unambiguous boundary between grammatical and pragmatic meaning. However, distinctions between grammatical form and meaning become clear when L2 learners make mistakes – that is, when they appear to have mastered the meaning of a structure, but not the form, or vice versa. In the same way, distinctions between grammatical meaning and pragmatic meaning can be observed when L2 learners fail to understand how meanings might be extended or might be intentionally ambiguous – for example, in jokes or double entendres. It is also obvious when L2 learners unwittingly express certain pragmatic meanings inappropriately or in uncustomary ways. The challenges encountered by more specific and more complex definitions of meaning present numerous opportunities to re-examine our current assumptions and pave new directions in terms of measuring how learners are able to use the linguistic resources to create meanings in messages.

Practically speaking, language testers might need to test 'meaning' in ways that have perhaps not been done before. For example, we might wish to test our students' ability to resolve a problem for a client (grammatical meaning) and at the same time give the client a feeling of satisfaction with the resolution (pragmatic meaning – psychological inference). We would then need to devise procedures for scoring these performances, analyzing the data and interpreting the test takers' capacity to construct meaning from forms in language use.

Challenge 4: Reconsidering grammar-test tasks

The fourth challenge relates to the design of test tasks that are capable of both measuring grammatical ability and providing authentic and engaging measures of grammatical performance. Since the early 1960s, language educators have associated grammar tests with discrete-point, multiple-choice tests of grammatical form. These and other 'traditional' test tasks (e.g., grammaticality judgments) have been severely criticized for lacking in authenticity, for not engaging test-takers in language use, and for promoting behaviors that are not readily consistent with communicative language teaching. Discrete-point testing methods may have even led some teachers to have reservations about testing grammar or to have uncertainties about how to test it communicatively.

While there is a place for discrete-point tasks in grammar assessment, language educators have long used a wide range of simple and complex tasks in which to assess test-takers' explicit and implicit knowledge of grammar. In fact, in a small-scale study designed to discover teacher practices in testing grammar in primary, secondary and adult-school contexts, Rea-Dickins (2001) noted that 61 of the 70 teachers reported testing grammar explicitly, while 27 reported assessing it indirectly through the language skills. Furthermore, 67 out of the 70 teachers reported testing grammar, and only one actually stated that it should not be tested. In short, grammar testing in classrooms is alive and well.

In providing grammar assessments, the challenge for language educators is to design tasks that are authentic and engaging measures of performance. To do this, I have argued that we must first consider the assessment purpose and the construct we would like to measure. We also need to contemplate the kinds of grammatical performance that we would need to obtain in order to provide evidence in support of the inferences we want to be able to make about grammatical ability. Once we have specified the inferences, or claims, that we would like to make and the kinds of evidence we need to support these claims, we can then design test tasks to measure what grammar test-takers know or how they are able to use grammatical resources to accomplish a wide range of activities in the target language.

For example, if we wished to make claims about test-takers' ability to use grammar to argue for or against some public policy, a selected-response task would not be likely to provide the type of evidence needed to support this claim, since a selected-response task does not require students to understand and respond to an interlocutor's opinions, express a coherent set of opinions, provide support for opinions and work collaboratively to resolve policy implications. The challenge, then, is to specify the characteristics of a task that will, in fact, provide a consistent measurement of the construct we are trying to get at in this particular situation.

To provide guidance on specifying test tasks in this book, I have discussed Bachman and Palmer's (1996) framework of test-task characteristics (see Chapter 5), and I have shown how individual task characteristics can be varied to provide a wide range of test tasks for the purpose of measuring grammatical ability. In creating grammar-test tasks, language educators face the challenge of thinking beyond the traditional multiple-choice task or the gap-fill task. These tasks certainly serve their purpose in measuring test-takers' explicit knowledge of grammar; however, used alone, these tasks do not provide, as I have argued, a comprehensive depiction of grammatical ability, when that is the assessment goal. Therefore, language educators must reflect upon the constructs we wish to measure and consider carefully how tasks can be specified to elicit the samples of grammatical performance we are trying to tap into.

In a communicative language curriculum, our goal as educators is not only to create test tasks, but also to create assessments that are also authentic and engaging. In this respect, Bachman and Palmer (1996) have argued persuasively that in order to make inferences about language ability, that are generalizable beyond the language test, we need to design test tasks that engage test-takers in language use, or in the co-construction of meaning in communication. They have further argued that this engagement can be facilitated by presenting test-takers with test tasks that correspond to the types of tasks that one might encounter in a specific TLU situation, drawn from a broader TLU domain. The relative correspondence between the TLU tasks and the test tasks constitutes 'authenticity'. Therefore, when it comes to designing highly authentic measures of performance from which we can make claims about grammatical ability, language educators are faced with further related challenges.

We need first to consider the degree to which authenticity should be given priority for a given test purpose. In other words, we need to determine the degree to which we are willing to accept moderate or low levels of authenticity in a task for a given assessment goal, so that we will have an idea of the effect that this might have on our ability to generalize interpretations from performance on the test task to performance beyond the test. We need to consider, for example, the degree to which we can tolerate the lack of correspondence between the language or topic of the input of a test task and the language or topic of a similar task in the TLU domain. We also need to consider what effect this lack of correspondence will have on the generalizability of score interpretations.

In reflecting upon the design of authentic tasks, we must acknowledge that not all grammar assessments in large-scale or classroom contexts need to have 'communication' as their primary assessment goal. There are, in fact, times when we simply wish to know if students have understood the meaning of a form or if they have acquired explicit knowledge of a particular grammatical structure without the complexities of rich context or on-line, spontaneous performance. For example, I can think of many instances as a French teacher when I just wanted to know if my students knew how to form the passé composé (a past tense) with the correct auxiliary verb and past participle, or if they could recognize when to use the passé composé as opposed to the imperfect (another past tense) in certain contexts. In this situation, students were able to attend selectively to the aspects of grammar they had learned to complete the task, and in this case a selected-response or limited-production task was capable of providing the evidence I needed to make inferences about their explicit knowledge of these forms. Again, however, in deciding to assess in this fashion, I had to acknowledge that performance on these tasks alone did not provide sufficient evidence for me to infer that my students could use these forms on some other task beyond the test. The score-based interpretations I was justified in making were, therefore, limited to inferences about my students' explicit knowledge of these forms – my actual assessment goal. While selected-response and limited-production tasks provide limited generalizability, they can serve an important purpose in language-instructional domains. In this respect, we can argue that the characteristics of the TLU tasks and those of the test tasks match, thereby providing evidence of authenticity with respect to the instructional TLU domain. The obvious challenge for communicative language educators who wish to maintain a perception of authenticity despite the selected or limited-production nature of the response is to create test tasks that display a high degree of authenticity of topic and language. This can be accomplished by presenting students with tasks that are clearly aligned with the unit theme, that are content-rich and that use natural-sounding language for the situation.

In many other instances of communicative language teaching, our goal is to present students with highly authentic assessment tasks to measure the degree to which they can actually use a defined set of grammatical resources to accomplish something in the target language. In these cases, the primary focus of assessment is the degree to which grammatical forms can be used to understand and convey a range of meanings in a given context. Imagine, for example, that we wished to measure our students' implicit knowledge of the past and past continuous tenses, or the degree to which they had internalized these new grammar points so that they could use them in spontaneous interaction. Here, the construct relates to claims about the test-takers' ability to use the past and past continuous tenses to have a discussion. Before thinking about the tasks we might use to assess this knowledge, we need to imagine some real-life language-use situation in which these forms would not only emerge naturally, but the use of these forms would also be 'essential' or obligatory. One discursive practice that naturally elicits the past and past continuous tenses is the 'eyewitness report' between an eyewitness to some sudden event or close call and a reporter. For example:

Reporter: 'What **were you doing** when the electricity **went out**?'
Interviewee: 'I **was having** a heaping plate of pasta.'

As seen in the example, this task appears likely to elicit samples of the past and past continuous that could serve as an evidentiary basis for inferring the test-takers' ability to use these tenses to communicate. With this information, we could then design an eyewitness report task in which test-takers first hear a brief news summary about the electricity going out due to a massive grid failure. They would then be asked to play the roles of a reporter and an eyewitness to the event. Other characteristics of the test task could also be specified, such as the channel (aural), vehicle (taped or 'live') and procedures for the task, the length, channel and vehicle of the news summary, and length, channel and vehicle of the response. The scoring method would also need to be specified. In this task, we are likely to find a high degree of correspondence between the TLU task and the test task. Moreover, this task displays authenticity of topic (sudden event), authenticity of task (interviewing) and authenticity of language response. Finally, as the goal of this task was to measure the test-takers' implicit knowledge of the past and past continuous tenses, this task needed to elicit spontaneous discourse in which test-takers had to understand and use the target structures to communicate their ideas about the sudden events. Therefore, we can assume that no irrelevant variance in the scores would be attributed to the test-takers' topical knowledge (e.g., prior experience with sudden events and eyewitness news interviews), their strategic competence (e.g., their ability to assume a role, plan, clarify, link with prior knowledge) and their affective schemata (e.g., coping strategies) in performing the task. In other words, the test-takers would be fully familiar with the topic to be discussed and the demands of the task such that neither the topic nor the task would detract from the test-takers' use of grammar. If we had found that in fact the task had unexpectedly engaged these other areas of communicative language ability, as seen, for example, in fluctuations in the scores due primarily to the topic, we would likely not have achieved our assessment goal. In other words, if our intention was to tap into grammatical ability but instead our task tapped into other constructs not defined by the test, then this particular task would produce score variance irrelevant to the construct of grammatical ability. In this way it would blur the very construct we hoped to measure.

When language teachers and testers begin with a grammar assessment goal such as the one just described, the challenge then is to identify tasks within the TLU domain that elicit only those aspects of the grammatical ability that we wish to measure. In task-based assessments, for example, where we begin with a communicative task such as an eyewitness report interview, the challenge again is to ensure that the task elicits aspects of grammatical knowledge that conform with our assessment goals. As seen in the previous example, construct and task considerations need to work in concert to provide performances from which score-based inferences can be drawn. If, at the same time, the tasks are highly authentic, this justifies the generalization of the score-based interpretations beyond the test itself.

In selecting test tasks to measure grammatical ability in communication, there are many occasions in which assessment might call for highly authentic, interactive, extended-production tasks to elicit samples of grammatical performance. The questions in complex assessments such as these are: What exactly is being measured? and Should we give test-takers time to prepare their answers? Ellis (1997, 2001a) argued that administering the task with no preparation time provides a good measure of the test-takers' implicit knowledge of grammar due to the on-line, spontaneous nature of the task, whereas if planning time were allowed, the task would provide a measure of the test-takers' explicit as well as their implicit knowledge of grammar. In designing complex tasks with preparation time, however, language testers have often questioned what effect planning might have on performance. In other words, if test-takers were allowed to use planning time to prepare their ideas, this could free up on-line processing resources while completing the task, and grammatical performance might be more fluent, more complex and more accurate (Skehan, 1998). Furthermore, score variability might be explained in terms of the test-takers' explicit as well as their implicit grammatical knowledge (Ellis, 1997, 2001a).

In examining the effects of a planning-time task characteristic on complex test performance, Wigglesworth (1997) found that test-takers improved their performance in terms of fluency (i.e., number of self-repairs), accuracy (i.e., suppliance of plural -*s*, verbal morphology, and indefinite articles) and complexity (amount of subordination). Skehan (1998) also found that planning time seemed to have a significant positive effect on performance in terms of increased fluency, accuracy, and complexity of language used. However, Iwashita, McNamara and Elder (2001), in a replication of Skehan's study, failed to confirm these results, suggesting that we still have much more to learn about the relationship between planning time and grammatical performance. Given the complex nature of the tasks used to measure grammatical ability and the constructs that they could be tapping into other than knowledge of grammatical form, it comes as no surprise that these studies produced mixed results. In terms of the assessment of grammatical ability, these studies looked at the relationship between planning time as a task characteristic and grammatical ability defined in terms of fluency, accuracy and complexity of grammatical forms. It would be interesting to see how planning time might also impact the range of grammatical forms used. More compelling yet, we are left to wonder, in fact, how planning time might influence the degree to which test-takers provided 'meaningful' responses in completing the tasks (different from task fulfillment). Until we learn more about the effects of planning time on performance, language testers are left with their own understanding of the research findings regarding the use of planning time in complex tasks of grammatical ability.

Challenge 5: Assessing the development of grammatical ability

The fifth challenge revolves around the argument, made by some researchers, that grammatical assessments should be constructed, scored and interpreted with developmental proficiency levels in mind. This notion stems from the work of several SLA researchers (e.g. Clahsen, 1985; Pienemann and Johnson, 1987; Ellis, 2001b) who maintain that the principal finding from years of SLA research is that structures appear to be acquired in a fixed order and a fixed developmental sequence. Furthermore, instruction on forms in non-contiguous stages appears to be ineffective. As a result, the acquisitional development of learners, they argue, should be a major consideration in the L2 grammar testing.

In terms of test construction, Clahsen (1985) claimed that grammar tests should be based on samples of spontaneous L2 speech with a focus on syntax and morphology, and that the structures to be measured should be selected and graded in terms of order of acquisition in natural L2 development. Furthermore, Ellis (2001b) argued that grammar scores should be calculated to provide a measure of both grammatical accuracy and the underlying acquisitional development of L2 learners. In the former, the target-like accuracy of a grammatical form can be derived from a total correct score or percentage. In the latter, the developmental proficiency can be derived from scores linked to different stages of the interlanguage continuum. In this view, it was argued, students and teachers can be provided with information that reflects both target-like and developmental criteria with regard to knowledge of specific grammatical forms. If these claims are accepted, the ensuing challenge to language testers and SLA researchers is to adapt current test design and scoring procedures to incorporate findings from this research.

As intuitively appealing as the recommendation for developmental scores might appear, the research based on developmental orders and sequences is vastly incomplete and at too early a stage for use as a basis for assessment (Lightbown, 1985; Hudson, 1993; Bachman, 1998). Furthermore, as I have argued in Chapters 3 and 4, grammatical knowledge involves more than knowledge of morphosyntactic or lexical forms; meaning is a critical component. In other words, test-takers can be communicatively effective and at the same time inaccurate, they can be highly accurate but communicatively ineffective and they can be both communicatively effective and highly accurate. Without more complete information on the patterns of acquisition relating to other grammatical forms as well as to grammatical meaning, language testers would not have a solid empirical basis upon which to construct, score and interpret the results from grammar assessments based solely on developmental scores. At this point, I would recommend that grammar assessments based on developmental sequences be used only in research, and not for decision-making. With those few acquisitional sequences that have shown a clear fixed order of acquisition (i.e., relative clauses), the incorporation of a meaning (grammatical or pragmatic) dimension could provide interesting information for teaching, learning and assessment.

Despite the incompleteness of the developmental sequence research, the suggestion that grammar-test tasks be designed to 'give credit to learners who demonstrate knowledge of advanced interlanguage forms' (Ellis, 2001a, p. 260) is well taken. As I have shown in Chapters 5 and 6, this can be addressed by means of more elaborated scoring procedures. In other words, with selected-response or limited-production grammar tasks, we can use right/wrong or partial-credit scoring with multiple criteria for correctness to provide credit for partial achievement. For example, in selected-response tasks in a multiple-choice format, the key would obviously get full credit, some response options which represent varying levels of interlanguage development would get partial credit, and others would get none. Also, with limited-production and extended-production tasks, we can devise analytic rating scales that allow us to judge performance at different levels of grammatical ability. In other words, relevant information that relates to development could be incorporated into the rating-scale descriptors. Finally, we might consider using developmental criteria as a basis for weighting tasks in a test. In other words, tasks that elicit the use of grammatical features shown to be somewhat resistant to instruction and acquired late by students of certain language backgrounds (e.g., ergative passives in English for Korean speakers, the past subjunctive in

Spanish for English speakers) could be given more credit or weighted more heavily. In this respect, research from learner corpora has much to offer language assessment. This criterion-referenced approach to incorporating developmental information into assessment would be particularly implementable and justifiable for certain assessment contexts.

With regard to selected-response or limited-production tasks, the challenge to language educators interested in incorporating developmental information in grammar assessment is to identify an empirical basis, or at least a logical rationale, for attributing partial credit to a response option that is not the key. In order to do this, language educators might consult the research in SLA that examines learner errors (e.g., contrastive analysis, error analysis, interlanguage analysis, learner corpora research, CALL). This research has attempted to identify, categorize and explain errors in grammatical performance. Then, in terms of scoring, most language teachers know from experience that some grammar errors reflect partial development (e.g., incomplete application of a rule or overgeneralization of a rule), whereas others reflect no development (e.g., total ignorance of a rule or misinformation of a rule). In these cases, the allotment of full, partial or no credit is somewhat straightforward. However, the causes of errors in actual responses or in response options are often difficult to establish consistently across test-takers, especially when they come from different native language backgrounds and different learning contexts. In these cases, the errors in actual responses or in response options would be difficult to score. For example, how should we score a teacher- or textbook-induced error or a task-related error? Is a transfer-related error evidence of more development than an error involving ignorance of rule restrictions? Clearly, more research is needed before the scoring can become highly differentiated. In the meantime, as discussed in Chapters 5 and 6, right/wrong or partial-credit scoring with multiple criteria for correctness provides a more precise measure of accuracy or meaningfulness.

With regard to limited- or extended-production tasks, we can give learners credit for what they know and feedback on what they do not know by judging performance on these tasks by means of analytic rating scales. I have argued that in grammar assessment, these scales need to be created by means of construct- and task-based methods so that the different levels of grammatical ability can be fully described. The descriptors in these scoring rubrics then need to articulate clearly the kinds and amount of evidence learners must demonstrate in order to support claims of grammatical ability at each level of performance.

In sum, the challenge for language testers is to design, score and interpret grammar assessments with a consideration for developmental proficiency. While this idea makes sense, what basis can we use to infer progressive levels of development? Results from acquisitional development research have been proposed as a basis for such interpretations by some researchers. At this stage of our knowledge, other more viable ways of accounting for what learners know might be better obtained from the way grammatical performance is scored. Instead of reporting one and only one composite, accuracy-based score, we can report a profile of scores – one for each construct we are measuring. Furthermore, in the determination of these scores, we can go beyond dichotomous scoring to give more precise credit for attainment of grammatical ability. Finally, scores that are derived from partial credit reflect different levels of development and can be interpreted accordingly. In other words, acquisitional developmental levels need not be the only basis upon which to make inferences about grammatical development.

Final remarks

Despite loud claims in the 1970s and 1980s by a few influential SLA researchers that instruction, and in particular explicit grammar instruction, had no effect on language learning, most language teachers around the world never really gave up grammar teaching. Furthermore, these claims have instigated an explosion of empirical research in SLA, the results of which have made a compelling case for the effectiveness of certain types of both explicit and implicit grammar instruction. This research has also highlighted the important role that meaning plays in learning grammatical forms.

In the same way, most language teachers and SLA researchers around the world have never really given up grammar testing. Admittedly, some have been perplexed as to how grammar assessment could be compatible with a communicative language teaching agenda, and many have relied on assessment methods that do not necessarily meet the current standards of test construction and validation. With the exception of Rea-Dickins and a few others, language testers have been of little help. In fact, a number of influential language proficiency exams have abandoned the explicit measurement of grammatical knowledge and/or have blurred the boundaries between communicative effectiveness and communicative precision (i.e., accuracy).

My aim in this book, therefore, has been to provide language teachers, language testers and SLA researchers with a practical framework, firmly based in research and theory, for the design, development and use of grammar assessments. I have tried to show how grammar plays a critical role in teaching, learning and assessment. I have also presented a model of grammatical knowledge, including both form and meaning, that could be used for test construction and validation. I then showed how L2 grammar tests can be constructed, scored and used to make decisions about test-takers in both large-scale and classroom contexts. Finally, in this last chapter, I have discussed some of the challenges we still face in constructing useful grammar assessments. My hope is that this volume will not only help language teachers, testers and SLA researchers develop better grammar assessments for their respective purposes, but instigate research and continued discussion on the assessment of grammatical ability and its role in language learning.

References

Alanen, R. (1995). Input enhancement and rule presentation in second language acquisition. In R. Schmidt (ed.), *Attention and Awareness in Foreign Language Learning and Teaching* (pp. 259–302). Honolulu: University of Hawai'i Press.

Alderson, J. C. (1993). The relationship between grammar and reading in an English for Academic Purposes test battery. In D. Douglas and C. Chapelle (eds.), *A New Decade of Language Testing Research* (pp. 203–19). Alexandria, VA: TESOL.

Alderson, J. C., Clapham, C. and Wall, D. (1995). *Language Test Construction and Evaluation*. Cambridge: Cambridge University Press.

Allen, P., Swain, M., Harley, B. and Cummins, J. (1990). Aspects of classroom treatment: toward a more comprehensive view of second language education. In B. Harley, P. Allen, J. Cummins and M. Swain (eds.), *The Development of Second Language Proficiency* (pp. 57–81). Cambridge: Cambridge University Press.

Austin, J. L. (1962). *How to Do Things with Words*. Oxford: Clarendon Press.

Azar, B. S. (1998). *Understanding and Using English Grammar*. White Plains, NY: Pearson Education.

Bachman, L. F. (1988). Language testing – SLA interfaces. In L. F. Bachman and A. D. Cohen (eds.), *Interfaces Between Second Language Acquisition and Language Testing Research* (pp. 177–95). Cambridge: Cambridge University Press.

Bachman, L. F. (1990a). Constructing measures and measuring constructs. In B. Harley, P. Allen, J. Cummins and M. Swain (eds.), *The Development of Second Language Proficiency* (pp. 26–38). Cambridge: Cambridge University Press.

Bachman, L. F. (1990b). *Fundamental Considerations in Language Testing*. Oxford: Oxford University Press.

Bachman, L. F. (1998). Appendix: Language testing – SLA research interfaces. In L. F. Bachman and A. D. Cohen (eds.), *Interfaces Between Second Language Acquisition and Language Testing Research* (pp. 177–95). Cambridge: Cambridge University Press.

Bachman, L. F. (March, 2000). Some reflections on task-based language performance assessment. Paper presented at Language Testing Research Colloquium, Vancouver.

Bachman, L. F. (2002). Alternative interpretations of alternative assessments: some validity issues in educational performance assessments. *Educational Measurement: Issues and Practice, 21* (3), 5–19.

Bachman, L. F. (2004). *Statistical Analyses for Language Assessment.* Cambridge: Cambridge University Press.

Bachman, L. F. and Clark, J. L. (1987). The measurement of foreign/second language proficiency. *Annals of the American Academy of Political and Social Science, 490,* 20–33.

Bachman, L. F. and Cohen, A. D. (1998). *Interfaces Between Second Language Acquisition and Language Testing Research.* Cambridge: Cambridge University Press.

Bachman, L. F. and Palmer, A. S. (1982). The construct validation of some components of communicative proficiency. *TESOL Quarterly, 16,* 449–65.

Bachman, L. F. and Palmer, A. S. (1996). *Language Testing in Practice.* Oxford: Oxford University Press.

Bailey, N., Madden, C. and Krashen, S. (1974). Is there a 'natural sequence' in adult second language learning? *Language Learning, 21,* 235–43.

Bangert-Downs, R. L., Kulik, C-L. C., Kulik, J. A., and Morgan, M. T. (1991). The instructional effect of feedback in test-like events. *Review of Educational Research, 61* (2), 213–38.

Beebe, L. and Cummins, M. (1996). Natural speech act data vs. written questionnaire data: how data collection method affects speech act performance. In J. Neu and S. Gass (eds.), *Speech Acts Across Cultures.* Berlin: Mouton de Gruyter.

Beebe, L. and Takahashi, T. (1989). Do you have a bag? Social status and patterned variation in second language acquisition. In S. Gass, D. Madden and L. Selinker (eds.), *Variation in Second Language Acquisition,* vol. I: *Sociolinguistic Issues.* Clevedon, Avon: Multilingual Matters.

Beretta, A. and Davies, A. (1985). Evaluation of the Bangalore Project. *ELT Journal, 29,* 121–7.

Berwick, R. (1993). Towards an educational framework for teacher-led tasks. In. G. Crookes and S. M. Gass (eds.), *Tasks in a Pedagogical Context: Integrating Theory and Practice* (pp. 97–124). Clevedon, Avon: Multilingual Matters.

Biber, D., Conrad, S. M. and Reppen, R. (1998). *Corpus Linguistics: Investigating Language Structure and Use.* Cambridge: Cambridge University Press.

Biber, D., Conrad, S. M., Reppen, R., Byrd, P., Helt, M., Clark, V., Cortes, V., Csomay, E. and Urzua, A. (2004). *Representing Language Use in the University: Analysis of the TOEFL 2000 Spoken and Written Academic Language Corpus* (TOEFL Monograph No. 25). Princeton, NJ: Educational Testing Service.

Blau, E. K. (1990). The effects of syntax, speed and pauses on listening comprehension. *TESOL Quarterly, 25*, 746–53.

Bloomfield, L. (1933). *Language*. New York: Holt, Rinehart and Winston.

Brinton, D. M., Snow, M. A. and Wesche, M. B. (1989). *Content-Based Second Language Instruction*. New York: Newbury House.

Brown, J. D. (1996). *Testing in Language Programs*. Upper Saddle River, NJ: Prentice Hall Regents.

Brown, J. D. (ed.) (1998). *New Ways of Classroom Assessment*. Alexandria, VA: TESOL.

Bull, W. (1960). *Time, Tense and the Verb: A Study in Theoretical and Applied Linguistics, with Particular Application to Spanish*. Berkeley and Los Angeles: University of California Press.

Burns, M. (1986). Teaching 'what to do' in arithmetic vs. teaching 'what to do and why.' *Educational Leadership, 43* (7), 34–8.

Butler, R. (1987). Task-involving and ego-involving properties of evaluation: effects of different feedback conditions on motivational perceptions, interest and performance. *Journal of Educational Psychology, 79* (4), 474–82.

Butler, R. (1988). Enhancing and undermining intrinsic motivation: the effects of task-involving and ego-involving evaluation on interest and performance. *British Journal of Educational Psychology, 58*, 1–14.

Cambridge ESOL (1995). *FCE – First Certificate in English: Specifications and Sample Papers for the Revised FCE Examination*. Cambridge: University of Cambridge Local Examinations Syndicate.

Cambridge ESOL (1996). *FCE – First Certificate in English: Handbook*. Cambridge: University of Cambridge Local Examinations Syndicate.

Cambridge ESOL (2001a). *FCE – First Certificate in English: Handbook*. Cambridge: University of Cambridge Local Examinations Syndicate.

Cambridge ESOL (2001b). *CAE – Certificate in Advanced English: Handbook*. Cambridge: University of Cambridge Local Examinations Syndicate.

Cambridge ESOL (2002a). *First Certificate of English Anchor Test*. Cambridge: University of Cambridge Local Examinations Syndicate.

Cambridge ESOL (2002b). *CAE – Certificate of Proficiency in English: Handbook*. Cambridge: University of Cambridge Local Examinations Syndicate.

Cambridge ESOL (2003). *Research Notes, 13*. Cambridge: University of Cambridge Local Examinations Syndicate.

Canale, M. (1983). On some dimensions of language proficiency. In J. Oller (ed.), *Issues in Language Testing Research* (pp. 333–42). Rowley, MA: Newbury House.

Canale, M. and Swain, M. (1980). Theoretical bases of communicative approaches to second language teaching and testing. *Applied Linguistics, 1*, 1–47.

Carroll, J. B. (1961). Fundamental considerations in testing for English language proficiency of foreign students. In H. B. Allen and R. N. Campbell (eds.), *Testing the English Proficiency of Foreign Students* (pp. 30–40). Washington, DC: Center of Applied Linguistics.

Carroll, J. B. (1968). The psychology of language testing. In A. Davies (ed.), *Language Testing Symposium: A Psycholinguistic Approach* (pp. 46–69). London: Oxford University Press.

Celce-Murcia, M. (1991). Grammar pedagogy. In M. Celce-Murcia (ed.), *Teaching English as a Second and Foreign Language*. Rowley, MA: Newbury House.

Celce-Murcia, M. and Larsen-Freeman, D. (1999). *The Grammar Book: An ESL/EFL Teacher's Course*. Boston: Heinle and Heinle Publishers.

Center for Applied Linguistics (2002). *Basic Skills of English Test Plus*. Washington, DC: Center for Applied Linguistics.

Chang, J. (2002). Construct validation of models of grammatical knowledge: an exploratory study. Unpublished paper for A&HL6500. Teachers College, Columbia University.

Chang, J. (2004). Examining models of second language knowledge with specific reference to relative clauses: a model-comparison approach. Doctoral dissertation, Teachers College, Columbia University, New York City.

Chapelle, C. (1998). Construct definition and validity inquiry in SLA research. In L. F. Bachman and A. D. Cohen (eds.), *Interfaces Between Second Language Acquisition and Language Testing Research* (pp. 32–70). Cambridge: Cambridge University Press.

Chastain, K. (1976). *Developing Second-Language Skills: Theory to Practice*. Chicago: Rand McNally College Publishing Company.

Chaudron, C. (1983). Research on metalinguistic judgments: a review of theory, methods, and results. *Language Learning, 33* (3), 343–77.

Chihara, T., Oller, J. Jr., Weaver, K. A. and Chavez, M. A. (1977). Are cloze items sensitive to constraints across sentence? *Language Learning, 27*, 63–73.

Choi, H. E. (2003). The use of corpora for defining learning problems of Korean ESL learners. Paper presented at The Conference on Technology for Second Language Learning at Iowa State University.

Chomsky, N. (1965). *Aspects of the Theory of Syntax*. Cambridge, MA: MIT Press.

Chomsky, N. (1981). *Lectures on Government and Binding*. Dordrecht: Foris.

Chomsky, N. (1995). *The Minimalist Program*. Cambridge, MA: MIT Press.

Clahsen, H. (1985). Profiling second language development: a procedure for assessing L2 proficiency. In K. Hyltenstam and M. Pienemann (eds.), *Modelling and Assessing Second Language Acquisition* (pp. 283–331). Clevedon, Avon: Multilingual Matters.

Clapham, C. (1996). *The Development of IELTS: A Study of the Effect of Background Knowledge on Reading Comprehension*. Cambridge: Cambridge University Press.

Cohen, A. (1984). On taking language tests: What the students report. *Language Testing, 1*, 70–81.

Cohen, A. (1993). The role of instructions in testing summarizing ability. In D. Douglas and C. Chapelle (eds.), *A New Decade of Language Testing Research* (pp. 132–60). Alexandria, VA: TESOL.

Cohen, A. (1994). *Assessing Language Ability in the Classroom.* Boston: Heinle & Heinle Publishers.

Cohen, A. (1998). *Strategies in Learning and Using a Second Language.* New York: Longman.

Cohen, A. and Olshtain, E. (1981). Developing a measure of sociocultural competence: The case of apology. *Language Learning, 31* (1), 113–34.

Community English Program. (2002). *Community English Program Placement Exam.* New York: Teachers College, Columbia University.

Corder, P. (1967). The significance of learners' errors. *IRAL, 5,* 161–9.

Cummins, J. (1980). The cross-lingual dimensions of language proficiency: implications for bilingual education and the optimal age question. *TESOL Quarterly, 14,* 175–87.

Cummins, J. (1983). Language proficiency and academic achievement. In J. Oller (ed.), *Issues in Language Testing Research* (pp. 108–30). Rowley, MA: Newbury House.

Cushing Weigle, S. and Lynch, B. (1995). Hypothesis testing in construct validation. In A. Cumming and R. Berwick (eds.), *Validation in Language Testing* (pp. 58–71). Clevedon, Avon: Multilingual Matters.

Darling-Hammond, L., Ancess, J. and Falk, B. (1995). *Authentic Assessment in Action: Studies of Schools and Students at Work.* New York: Teachers College Press.

Davidson, F. and Lynch, B. (2002). *Testcraft: A Teachers' Guide to Writing and Using Language Test Specifications.* New Haven, CT: Yale University Press.

Davies, A. (1964). *The English Proficiency Test, Version A.* London: The British Council.

Davies, A. (1991). Language testing in the 1990s. In J. C. Alderson and B. North (eds.), *Language Testing in the 1990s: The Communicative Legacy* (pp. 136–49). London: Modern English Publications, Macmillan.

DeKeyser, R. (1995). Learning second language grammar rules: an experiment with a miniature linguistic system. *Studies in Second Language Acquisition, 17* (3), 379–410.

DeKeyser, R. (1998). Beyond focus on form: cognitive perspectives on learning and practicing second language grammar. In C. Doughty and J. Williams (eds.), *Focus on Form in Classroom Second Language Acquisition* (pp. 42–64. Cambridge: Cambridge University Press.

Doughty, C. (1991). Second language acquisition does make a difference: evidence from an empirical study of SL relativization. *Studies in Second Language Acquisition, 13* (3), 431–69.

Doughty, C. (2002). Focus on form: the latest word for teachers. Third Annual Apple Lecture, Teachers College, Columbia University, New York City.

Doughty, C. and J. Williams (eds.) (1998). *Focus on Form in Classroom Second Language Acquisition.* Cambridge: Cambridge University Press.

Douglas, D. (1997). *Testing Speaking Ability in Academic Contexts: Theoretical Considerations* (TOEFL Monograph Series, No. MS-8). Princeton, NJ: Educational Testing Service.

Douglas, D. (2000). *Assessing Language for Specific Purposes.* Cambridge: Cambridge University Press.

Douglas, D. and Selinker, L. (1985). Principles for language tests within the 'discourse domains' theory of interlanguage. *Language Testing, 2,* 205–26.

Douglas, D. and Selinker, L. (1993). Performance on a general versus a field-specific test of speaking proficiency by international teaching assistants, In D. Douglas and C. Chapelle (eds.), *A New Decade of Language Testing Research* (pp. 235–54). Alexandria, VA: TESOL.

Douglas, D. and Smith, J. (1997). *Theoretical Underpinnings of the Test of Spoken English Revision Project* (TOEFL Monograph Series, No. MS-0). Princeton, NJ: Educational Testing Service.

Dulay, H. and Burt, M. (1973). Should we teach children syntax? *Language Learning, 23,* 245–58.

Eckman, F. (1977). Markedness and the contrastive analysis hypothesis. *Language Learning, 27,* 315–30.

Eckman, F., Bell, L. and Nelson, D. (1988). On the generalization of relative clause instruction in the acquisition of English as a second language. *Applied Linguistics, 9,* 1–11.

Ekbatani, G. and Pierson, H. (eds.) (2000). *Learner-Directed Assessment in ESL.* Mahwah, NJ: Lawrence Erlbaum Associates.

Ellis, R. (1990). *Instructed Second Language Acquisition: Learning in the Classroom.* Cambridge: Basil Blackwell.

Ellis, R. (1993). Second language acquisition and the structural syllabus. *TESOL Quarterly, 27* (1), 91–113.

Ellis, R. (1994). *The Study of Second Language Acquisition.* Oxford: Oxford University Press.

Ellis, R. (1997). *SLA Research and Language Teaching.* Oxford: Oxford University Press.

Ellis, R. (2001a). Investigating form-focused instruction. In R. Ellis (ed.), *Form-Focused Instruction and Second Language Learning* (pp. 1–46). *Language Learning, 51, Supplement 1.*

Ellis, R. (2001b). Some thoughts on testing grammar: an SLA perspective. In C. Elder, A. Brown, E. Grove, K. Hill, N. Iwashita, T. Lumley, T. McNamara, K. O'Loughlin (eds.), *Experimenting with Uncertainty: Essays in Honour of Alan Davies* (pp. 251–63). Cambridge: Cambridge University Press.

Farhady, H. (1983). New directions for ESL proficiency testing. In J. Oller (ed.), *Issues in Language Testing* (pp. 253–69). Rowley, MA: Newbury House.

Feldt, L. S. and Brennen, R. L. (1989). Reliability. In Linn (ed.), *Educational Measurement* (3rd edition). American Council on Education, Macmillan.

Fillmore, C. (1968). The case for case. In E. Bach and R. Harms (eds.), *Universals in Linguistic Theory.* New York: Holt, Rinehart and Winston.

Francis, W. N. and Kučera, H. (1964). *Manual of Information to Accompany 'A Standard Sample of Present-Day Edited American English for Use with Digital Computers.'* Providence, RI: Department of Linguistics, Brown University.

Fries, C. (1940). *American English Grammar.* New York: Appleton Century Company.

Gardner, R. C. (1985). *Social Psychology and Language Learning: The Role of Attitudes and Motivation.* London, Ontario: Edward Arnold.

Gardner, R. C., Lalonde, R. N., Moorcroft, R. and Evans, F. T. (1987). Second language attrition: the role of motivation and use. *Journal of Language and Social Psychology, 6,* 29–47.

Garrett, N. (1986). The problem of grammar: what kind can the language learner use? *The Modern Language Journal, 70,* 133–48.

Gass, S. (1994). The reliability of grammaticality judgments. In E. Tarone, S. Gass and A. Cohen (eds.), *Research Methodology in Second Language Acquisition* (pp. 303–22). Hillsdale, NJ: Lawrence Erlbaum Associates.

Gass, S. and Selinker, L. (1994). *Second Language Acquisition: An Introductory Course.* Hillsdale, NJ: Lawrence Erlbaum Associates.

Genesee, F. (1987). *Learning Through Two Languages.* New York: Newbury House.

Gipps, V. V. (1994). *Beyond Testing: Towards a Theory of Educational Assessment.* London, England: Falmer Press.

Grabowski, E. and Mindt, D. (1995). A corpus-based learning list of irregular verbs in English. *ICAME Journal, 19,* 5–22.

Granger, S. (1999). Use of tenses by advanced EFL learners: evidence from a learner-tagged computer corpus. In H. Hasselgard and S. Oksefjell (eds.), *Out of Corpora – Studies in Honour of Stig Johansson* (pp. 191–202). Amsterdam: Rodopi.

Granger, S. (2002). A bird's-eye view of learner corpus research. In S. Granger, J. Hung and S. Petch-Tyson (eds.), *Computer Learner Corpora, Second Language Acquisition and Foreign Language Teaching* (pp. 3–33). Amsterdam/Philadelphia: John Benjamin.

Granger, S. (2003a). Error-tagged learner corpora and CALL: a promising synergy. *CALICO, 20* (3), 465–80.

Granger, S. (2003b). The international corpus of learner English: a new resource for foreign language learning and teaching and second language acquisition. *TESOL Quarterly, 37* (3), 538–46.

Grice, H. P. (1957). Meaning. *Philosophical Review, 67.* (Reprinted in D. Steinberg and L. Jakobovits (1971). *Semiotics: An Interdisciplinary Reader in Philosophy Linguistics and Psychology,* (pp. 53–59). Cambridge: Cambridge University Press.

Halliday, M. A. K. (1978). *Language as Social Semiotic.* London: Edward Arnold.

Halliday, M. A. K. (1994). *An Introduction to Functional Grammar* (2nd edition). London: Edward Arnold.

Halliday, M. A. K. and Hasan, R. (1976). *Cohesion in English.* London: Longman.

Halliday, M. A. K. and Hasan, R. (1989). *Language, Context, and Text: Aspects of Language in a Socio-semiotic Perspective.* Oxford: Oxford University Press.

Hammond, R. (1988). Accuracy versus communicative competence: the acquisition of grammar in the second language classroom. *Hispania, 74,* 408–17.

Harley, B. and Swain, M. (1984). The interlanguage of immersion students and its implication for second language teaching. In A. Davies, C. Criper and A.

Howatt (eds.), *Interlanguage* (pp. 291–311). Edinburgh: Edinburgh University Press.

Harley, B., Allen, P., Cummins, J. and Swain, M. (1990). *The Development of Second Language Proficiency*. Cambridge: Cambridge University Press.

Harris, D. (1969). *Testing English as a Second Language*. New York: McGraw-Hill.

Harris, D. P. and Palmer, L. A. (1970a). *CELT Listening Form L-A, Structure Form S-A, Vocabulary Form V-A*. New York: McGraw-Hill.

Harris, D. P. and Palmer, L. A. (1970b). *CELT Technical Manual for Listening Form L-A, Structure Form S-A, Vocabulary Form V-A*. New York: McGraw-Hill.

Harris, D. P. and Palmer, L. A. (1986). *CELT Listening Form L-A, Structure Form S-A, Vocabulary Form V-A* (2nd edition). New York: McGraw-Hill.

Hatch, E. (1992). *Discourse and Language Education*. Cambridge: Cambridge University Press.

Hatch, E. and Lazaraton, A. (1991). *The Research Manual: Design and Statistics for Applied Linguistics*. New York: Newbury House.

Heaton, J. B. (1975). *Writing English Language Tests*. London: Longman.

Heift, T. (2003). Corrective feedback and learner uptake in CALL. Paper presented at The Conference on Technology for Second Language Learning at Iowa State University.

Herman, J. L., Aschbacher, P. R. and Winters, L. (1992). *A Practical Guide to Alternative Assessment*. Alexandria, VA: Association for Supervision and Curriculum Development.

Hillocks, G. and Smith, M. W. (1991). Grammar and usage. In J. Flood, J. M. Jensen, D. Lapp, and J. R. Squire (eds.), *Handbook of Research on Teaching the English Language Arts* (pp. 591–603). New York: Macmillan.

Hinkel, E. (2002). Why English passive is difficult to teach (and learn). In E. Hinkel and S. Fotos (eds.), *New Perspectives on Grammar Teaching in Second Language Classrooms* (pp. 233–59). Mahwah, NJ: Lawrence Erlbaum Associates.

Hinkel, E. and Fotos, S. (eds.), (2002). *New Perspectives on Grammar Teaching in Second Language Classrooms*. Mahwah, NJ: Lawrence Erlbaum Associates.

Homburg, T. J. (1984). Holistic evaluation of ESL compositions: can it be validated objectively? *TESOL Quarterly, 18* (1), 87–107.

Hudson, T. (1993). Nothing does equal zero. *Studies in Second Language Acquisition, 15*, 461–93.

Hudson, T., Detmer, E. and Brown, J. D. (1995). *A Framework for Testing Cross-Cultural Pragmatics*. Honolulu, HI: University of Hawai'i Press.

Hughes, A. (2003). *Testing for Language Teachers* (2nd edition). Cambridge: Cambridge University Press.

Hulstijn, J. (1989). Implicit and incidental language learning: experiments in the processing of natural and partly artificial input. In H. Dechert and M. Raupach (eds.), *Interlingual Processing* (pp. 49–73). Tübingen: Gunter Narr.

Hymes, D. (1967). Models of the interaction of language and social setting. *Journal of Social Issues, 23*, 8–28.

Hymes, D. (1971). Competence and performance. In J. B. Pride and J. Holmes (eds.), *Language Acquisition: Models and Methods* (pp. 3–34). London: Academic Press.

Hymes, D. (1972). On communicative competence. In J. Gumperz and D. Hymes (eds.), *Directions in Sociolinguistics* (pp. 35–71). New York: Holt, Reinhart and Winston.

Iwashita, N., McNamara, T. and Elder, C. (2001). Can we predict task difficulty in an oral proficiency test? Exploring the potential of an information-processing approach to task design. *Language Learning, 51* (3), 401–36.

Jacobs, H. L., Zingram, D. R., Wormuth, D. R., Hartfiel, V. F. and Hughey, J. B. (1981). *Testing ESL Composition: A Practical Approach*. Rowley, MA: Newbury House.

Jaszczolt, M. (2002). *Semantics and Pragmatics: Meaning in Language and Discourse*. London: Longman.

Johansson, S., Leech, G. and Goodluck, H. (1978). *Manual of Information to Accompany the Lancaster-Oslo-Bergen Corpus of British English, for Use with Digital Computers*. Oslo: Department of English, Oslo University.

Jones, R. (1979). Performance testing of second language proficiency. In E. J. Brière and F. B. Hinofotis (eds.), *Concepts in Language Testing: Some Recent Studies* (pp. 50–7). Washington, DC: TESOL.

Katz, J. J. and Fodor, J. A. (1963). The structure of a semantic theory. *Language, 39*, 170–210.

Kennedy, G. (1998). *An Introduction to Corpus Linguistics*. London: Longman.

Korsko, P. (2003). The narrative shape of two-party complaints in Portuguese: a discourse analytic study. Doctoral dissertation, Teachers College, Columbia University, New York City.

Krashen, S. (1977). Some issues relating to the Monitor Model. In H. Brown, C. Yorio and R. Crymes (eds.), *On TESOL '77: Teaching and Learning English as a Second Language Trends in Research and Practice* (pp. 144–78). Washington, DC: TESOL.

Krashen, S. (1981). *Second Language Acquisition and Second Language Learning*. Oxford: Pergamon.

Krashen, S. (1982). *Principles and Practice in Second Language Acquisition*. Oxford: Pergamon.

Krashen, S. D. and Terrell, T. D. (1983). *The Natural Approach: Language Acquisition in the Classroom*. San Francisco: Alemany Press.

Kunnan, A. (1990). DIF in native language and gender groups in an ESL placement test. *TESOL Quarterly, 20* (4), 740–6.

Lado, R. (1961). *Language Testing*. New York: McGraw-Hill.

Lakoff, G. and Johnson, M. (1980). *Metaphors We Live By*. Chicago: University of Chicago Press.

Larsen-Freeman, D. (1991). Teaching grammar. In M. Celce-Murcia (ed.), *Teaching*

English as a Second or Foreign Language (pp. 279–96). Boston, MA: Heinle and Heinle Publishers.

Larsen-Freeman, D. (1997). Chaos/complexity science and second language acquisition. *Applied Linguistics, 48,* 141–65.

Larsen-Freeman, D. (2002). The grammar of choice. In E. Hinkel and S. Fotos (eds.), *New Perspectives on Grammar Teaching in Second Language Classrooms* (pp. 103–18). Mahwah, NJ: Lawrence Erlbaum Associates.

Lazaraton, A. and Wagner, S. (1996). *A Revised Test of Spoken English (TSE): Discourse Analysis of Native Speaker and Nonnative Speaker Data.* Princeton, NJ: Educational Testing Service.

Lee, J. F. and VanPatten, B. (2003). *Making Communicative Language Teaching Happen* (2nd edition). Boston: McGraw-Hill.

Leech, G. (1983). *Principles of Pragmatics.* London: Longman.

Levinson, S. C. (1983). *Pragmatics.* Cambridge: Cambridge University Press.

Liao, Y. (2002). *CEP Placement Test Results for Grammar.* Community English Program Test Committee Meeting handout, Teachers College, Columbia University, New York City.

Lightbown, P. M. (1985). Can language acquisition be altered by instruction? In K. Hyltenstam and M. Pienemann (eds.), *Modelling and Assessing Second Language Acquisition* (pp. 101–12). Clevedon, Avon: Multilingual Matters.

Lightbown, P. M. (1992). Getting quality input in the second and foreign language classroom. In C. Kramsch and S. McConnell-Ginet (eds.), *Test and Contexts: Cross-Disciplinary and Cross-Cultural Perspectives on Language Study* (pp. 187–97). Lexington, MA: Heath.

Lightbown, P. M. (1998). The importance of timing in focus on form. In C. Doughty and J. Williams (eds.), *Focus on Form in Classroom Second Language Acquisition* (pp. 177–96). Cambridge: Cambridge University Press.

Lightbown, P. M., Spada, N. and White, L. (1993). The role of instruction in SLA: introduction. *Studies in Second Language Acquisition, 15* (2), 143–6.

Long, M. (1991). Focus on form: a design feature in language teaching methodology. In K. de Bot, R. Ginsberg and C. Kramsch (eds.), *Foreign Language Research in Cross-Cultural Perspective* (pp. 39–52). Amsterdam: John Benjamins.

Long, M. and Robinson, P. (1998). Focus on form: theory, research, and practice. In C. Doughty and J. Williams (eds.), *Focus on Form* (pp. 15–41). Cambridge: Cambridge University Press.

Loschky, L. and Bley-Vroman, R. (1993). Grammar and task-based methodology. In G. Crookes and S. Gass (eds.), *Tasks and Language Learning: Integrating Theory and Practice* (pp. 123–67). Clevedon, Avon: Multilingual Matters.

Lyons, J. (1977). *Semantics.* 2 vols. Cambridge: Cambridge University Press.

Madden, H. (1982). Determining the debilitative impact of test anxiety. *Language Learning, 32,* 133–43.

Marzano, R. J., Pickering, D. and McTighe, J. (1993). *Assessing Student Outcomes:*

Performance Assessment Using the Dimensions of a Learning Model. Alexandria, VA: Association for Supervision and Curriculum Development.

McLaughlin, B. (1987). *Theories of Second Language Acquisition.* London: Edward Arnold.

McNamara, T. (1990). Item response theory and the validation of an ESP test for health professionals. *Language Testing, 7* (1), 52–75.

McNamara, T. (1996). *Measuring Second Language Performance.* New York: Longman.

McTighe, J. and Ferrara, S. (1998). *Assessing Learning in the Classroom.* Washington, DC: National Education Association.

Messick, S. (1993). Validity. In R. L. Linn (ed.), *Educational Measurement* (3rd edition) (pp. 13–103). New York: Oryx Press.

Mislevy, R. J. (1995). Test theory and language-learning assessment. *Language Testing 12* (3), 341–69.

Mislevy, R. J., Steinberg, L. S. and Almond, R. G. (2002). Design and analysis in task-based language assessment. *Language Testing, 19* (4), 477–96.

National Research Council. (2001a). *Knowing What Students Know: The Science and Design of Educational Assessment.* The Committee on the Foundations of Assessment. James W. Pellegrino, Naomi Chudowsky and Robert Glaser (eds.), Bureau of Testing and Assessment. Washington, DC: National Academy Press.

National Research Council (2001b). *Classroom Assessment and the National Science Education Standards Committee.* The Committee on Classroom Assessment and the National Science Education Standards. J. Myron Atkin, P. Black and J. Coffey (eds.), Center for Education, Division of Behavioural and Social Sciences and Education (p. 63). Washington, DC: National Academy Press.

Newmark, L. (1966). How not to interfere in language learning. *International Journal of American Linguistics, 32,* 77–87.

Norris, J. (2001). Identifying rating criteria for task-based EAP assessment. In T. Hudson and J. D. Brown (eds.), *A Focus on Language Test Development: Expanding the Language Proficiency Construct Across a Variety of Tests* (pp. 163–204). Honolulu, HI: University of Hawai'i Press.

Norris, J. M, Brown, J. D., Hudson, T. and Yoshioka, J. (1998). *Designing Second Language Performance Assessments.* Honolulu, HI: University of Hawai'i Press.

Norris, J. and Ortega, L. (2000). Effectiveness of L2 instruction: a research synthesis and quantitative meta-analysis. *Language Learning, 50* (3), 417–528.

North, B. (2000). Defining a flexible common measurement scale: descriptors for self and teacher assessment. In G. Ekbatani and H. Pierson (eds.), *Learner-Directed Assessment in ESL* (pp. 12–47). Mahwah, NJ: Lawrence Erlbaum Associates.

Nunan, D. (1989). *Designing Tasks for the Communicative Classroom.* Cambridge: Cambridge University Press.

Nunan, D. (1993). Task-based syllabus design: selecting, grading and sequencing tasks. In G. Crookes and S. M. Gass (eds.), *Tasks in a Pedagogical Context: Integrating Theory and Practice* (pp. 55–68). Clevedon, Avon: Multilingual Matters.

O'Malley, M. J. and Chamot, A. U. (1990). *Learning Strategies in Second Language Acquisition.* Cambridge: Cambridge University Press.

O'Malley, M. J. and Valdez-Pierce, L. (1996). *Authentic Assessment for English Language Learners: Practical Approaches for Teachers.* White Plains, NY: Addison-Wesley.

Oller, J. W., Jr. (1979). *Language Tests at School.* London: Longman.

Oller, J. W., Jr. and Jonz, J. (eds.) (1994). *Cloze and Coherence.* Cranbury, NJ: Associated University Presses.

Ong, W. (1982). *Orality and Literacy.* London: Methuen.

Oskarasson, M. (1978). *Approaches to Self-Assessment in Foreign Language Learning.* London: Pergamon.

Park, T. (2004). An investigation of an ESL placement test of writing using many-facet Rasch Measurement. Teachers College, Columbia University. *Working Papers in TESOL and Applied Linguistics* 4(1). Retrieved May 1, 2004, from http://www.tc.columbia.edu/tesolalwebjournal/Taljoon2004.pdf.

Pellegrinio, J., Baxter, G. and Glaser, R. (1999). Addressing the two disciplines problem: Linking theories of cognition and learning with assessment and instructional practice. In A. Iran-Nejad and P. D. Pearson (eds.), *Review of Research in Education* (pp. 309–55). Washington, DC: AERA.

Pica, T. (1983). Adult acquisition of English as a second language under different conditions of exposure. *Language Learning, 33,* 465–97.

Pica, T. (1994). Research on negotiation: what does it reveal about second language learning, conditions, processes, outcomes? *Language Learning, 44,* 493–527.

Pienemann, M. (1989). Is language teachable? Psycholinguistic experiments and hypotheses. *Applied Linguistics, 10,* 52–79.

Pienemann, M. and Johnston, M. (1986). An acquisition-based procedure for second language assessment. *Australian Review of Applied Linguistics, 9,* 92–122.

Pienemann, M. and Johnston, M. (1987). Factors influencing the development of language proficiency. In D. Nunan (ed.), *Applying Second Language Acquisition Research* (pp. 45–141). Adelaide: National Curriculum Resource Centre.

Pienemann, M., Johnston, M. and Brindley, G. (1988). Constructing an acquisition-based procedure for second language assessment. *Studies in Second Language Acquisition Research, 10,* 217–24.

Prabhu, N. S. (1987). *Second Language Pedagogy.* Oxford: Oxford University Press.

Pressley, M. (1995). *Advanced Educational Psychology for Educators, Researchers and Policy Makers.* New York: HarperCollins.

Purpura, J. E. (1999). *Learner Strategy Use and Performance on Language Tests: A Structural Equation Modeling Approach.* Cambridge; Cambridge University Press.

Purpura, J., Bino, A., Gallagher, J., Ingram, M., Kim, H-J., Kim, H-J., Kim, J-W. and Tsai, C. (2001). *On Target 1 Achievement Tests.* White Plains, NY: Pearson Publishers.

Purpura, J., Graziano-King, J., Chang, J., Cook, K., Kim, J., Krohn, N. and Wiseman, C. (2003). *An Analysis of the Foreign Language Needs of SIPA Students at Columbia University: The SIPA Needs Assessment Project.* Investigation monograph pursuant to a grant from the Mellon Foundation to the Arts and Sciences at Columbia University.

Purpura, J. and Pinkley, D. (1999). *On Target 1* (2nd edition). White Plains, NY: Addison Wesley Longman.

Purpura, J. and Pinkley, D. (2000). *On Target 2* (2nd edition). White Plains, NY: Addison Wesley Longman.

Radford, A. (1988). *Transformational Grammar: A First Course.* Cambridge: Cambridge University Press.

Radford, A. (1997). *Syntax: A Minimalist Introduction.* Cambridge: Cambridge University Press.

Rea-Dickins, P. (1991). What makes a grammar test communicative? In J. C. Alderson and B. North (eds.), *Language Testing in the 1990s: The Communicative Legacy* (pp. 112–35). New York: HarperCollins.

Rea-Dickins, P. (2001). Fossilization or evolution: the case of grammar testing. In C. Elder, A. Brown, E. Grove, K. Hill, N. Iwashita, T. Lumley, T. McNamara and K. O'Loughlin (eds.), *Experimenting with Uncertainty: Essays in Honour of Alan Davies* (pp. 251–63). Cambridge: Cambridge University Press.

Rea-Dickins, P. and Gardner, S. (2000). Snares and silver bullets: disentangling the construct of formative assessment. *Language Testing, 17* (2), 215–43.

Ricento, T. K. (1987). Aspects of coherence in English and Japanese expository prose. Doctoral dissertation in applied linguistics, UCLA.

Rief, L. (1990). Finding value in evaluation: self-assessment in a middle school classroom. *Educational Leadership, 47* (6), 24–9.

Robinson, P. and Ross, S. (1996). The development of task-based assessment in English for academic purposes programs. *Applied Linguistics, 17,* 455–76.

Rutherford, W. (1987). *Second Language Grammar: Learning and Teaching.* New York: Longman.

Rutherford, W. (1988). Grammatical consciousness raising in brief historical perspective. In W. Rutherford and M. Sharwood Smith (eds.), *Grammar and Second Language Teaching* (pp. 15–18). Boston, MA: Heinle and Heinle Publishers.

Savignon, S. J. (1983). *Communicative Competence: Theory and Classroom Practice.* Reading, MA: Addison-Wesley.

Savignon, S. J. (1985). Evaluation of communicative competence: the ACTFL Provisional Proficiency Guidelines. *The Modern Language Journal, 69* (2), 129–34.

Saville, N. (2003). The process of test development and revision within UCLES EFL. In C. Weir and M. Milanovic (eds.), *Continuity and Innovation: Revising the Cambridge Proficiency in English Examination 1913–2002* (pp. 57–120). Cambridge: Cambridge University Press.

Schachter, J., Tyson, A. and Diffley, F. (1976). Learner intuitions of grammaticality. *Language Learning, 26,* 67–76.

Scherer, A. and Wertheimer, A. (1964). *A Psycholinguistic Experiment in Foreign Language Teaching.* New York: McGraw-Hill.

Schmidt, R. (1983). Interaction, acculturation, and the acquisition of communicative competence: a case study of an adult. In N. Wolfson and E. Judd (eds.), *Sociolinguistics and Language Acquisition* (pp. 137–74). Rowley, MA: Newbury House.

Schmidt, R. (1990). The role of consciousness in second language learning. *Applied Linguistics, 11,* 129–58.

Schmidt, R. (1993). Awareness and second language acquisition. *Applied Linguistics, 13,* 206–26.

Searle, J. R. (1969). *Speech Acts: An Essay in the Philosophy of Language.* Cambridge: Cambridge University Press.

Searle, J. R. (1975). Indirect speech acts. In. P. Cole and J. L. Morgan (eds.), *Syntax and Semantics, vol. III: Speech Acts* (pp. 59–82). New York: Academic Press.

Seliger, H. (1979). On the nature and function of language rules in language teaching. *TESOL Quarterly, 13,* 359–69.

Selinker, L. (1972). Interlanguage. *International Review of Applied Linguistics, 10,* 209–31.

Sharwood Smith, M. (1981). Consciousness-raising and second language acquisition theory. *Applied Linguistics, 2,* 159–68.

Sharwood Smith, M. (1988). Consciousness-raising and the second language learner. In W. Rutherford and M. Sharwood Smith (eds.), *Grammar and Second Language Teaching* (pp. 51–60). Boston, MA: Heinle and Heinle Publishers.

Sharwood Smith, M. (1993). Input enhancement in instructed SLA: theoretical bases. *Studies in Second Language Acquisition, 15,* 165–79.

Shepard, L. A. (2000). The role of assessment in a learning culture. Presidential address presented at the annual meeting of the American Educational Research Association, New Orleans, April 26.

Shohamy, E. (1983). The stability of oral proficiency assessment on the oral interview testing procedure. *Language Learning, 33,* 527–40.

Shohamy, E. (1995). Performance assessment in language testing. *Annual Review of Applied Linguistics, 15*, 188–211.

Short, D. J. (1993). Assessing integrated language and content instruction. *TESOL Quarterly, 27* (4), 627–56.

Sinclair, J. and Renouf, A. (1988). A lexical syllabus for language learning. In R. Carter and M. McCarthy (eds.), *Vocabulary and Language Teaching* (pp. 140–60). London: Longman.

Skehan, P. (1998). *A Cognitive Approach to Language Learning.* Cambridge: Cambridge University Press.

Smith, P. (1970). *A Comparison of the Audiolingual and Cognitive Approaches to Foreign Language Instruction: The Pennsylvania Foreign Language Project.* Philadelphia: Center for Curriculum Development.

Spada, N. and Lightbown, P. M. (1993). Instruction and the development of questions in L2 classrooms. *Studies in Second Language Acquisition, 15*, 205–24.

Sperling, D. (1993). What's worth an 'A'? Setting standards together. *Educational Leadership, 50* (5), 73–5.

Stiggins, R. (1987). Design and development of performance assessments. *Educational Measurement: Issues and Practice, 6*, 33–42.

Sunderland, J. (1995). Gender and language testing. *Language Testing Update, 17*, 24–35.

Swain, M. (1985). Communicative competence: some roles of comprehensible input and comprehensible output in its development. In S. Gass and C. Madden (eds.), *Input and Second Language Acquisition* (pp. 235–53). Rowley, MA: Newbury House.

Swain, M. (1991). French immersion and its offshoots: getting two for one. In B. Freed (ed.), *Foreign Language Acquisition: Research and the Classroom* (pp. 91–103). Lexington, MA: Heath.

Swain, M. (1995). Three functions of output in second language learning. In G. Cook and B. Seidlhofer (eds.), *Principles and Practices in Applied Linguistics: Studies in Honour of H. G. Widdowson.* Oxford: Oxford University Press.

Swan, M. (1995). *Practical English Usage.* Oxford: Oxford University Press.

Tarone, E. (1998). Research on interlanguage variation: implications for language testing. In L. Bachman and A. Cohen (eds.), *Interfaces Between Second Language Acquisition and Language Testing* (pp. 71–89). Cambridge: Cambridge University Press.

Terrell, T., Gomez, E. and Mariscal, J. (1980). Can acquisition take place in the classroom? In R. Scarcella and S. Krashen (eds.), *Research in Second Language Acquisition.* Norwood, NJ: Ablex. *TESOL Quarterly, 25* (3), 92–113.

Trussell-Cullen, A. (1998). *Assessment in the Learner-Centered Classroom.* Carlsbad, CA: Dominie Press.

TSE Program Office. (1995). *TSE Score User's Manual.* Princeton, NJ: Educational Testing Service.

TSE Program Office. (2003). *Test of Spoken English*. Princeton, NY: Educational Testing Service.

Tuz, E. (1993). From controlled practice to communicative activity: does training transfer? *Temple University Japan Research Studies in TESOL, 1*, 97–108.

van Ek, J. A. (1975). *The Threshold Level in a European Unit: Credit System for Modern Language Teaching*. Strasbourg: Council of Europe.

VanPatten, B. (1996). *Input Processing and Grammar Instruction in Second Language Acquisition*. Boston: McGraw-Hill.

VanPatten, B. (2003). *From Input to Output: A Teacher's Guide to Second Language Acquisition*. Boston: McGraw-Hill.

VanPatten, B. and Cadierno, T. (1993a). *Explicit Instruction and Input Processing. Second Language Acquisition, 15*, 225–41.

VanPatten, B. and Cadierno, T. (1993b). SLA as input processing: a role for instruction. *Modern Language Journal, 77*, 45–57.

VanValin, R. D. and LaPolla, R. J. (1997). *Syntax: Structure, Meaning and Function*. Cambridge: Cambridge University Press.

Weigle, S. C. (2002). *Assessing Writing*. Cambridge: Cambridge University Press.

White, E. (1984). Holisticism. *College Composition and Communication, 35*, 400–9.

White, L. (1989). *Universal Grammar and Second Language Acquisition*. Amsterdam: John Benjamins.

White, B. and Frederiksen, J. (2000). Metacognitive facilitation: an approach to making scientific inquiry accessible to all students. *Cognition and Instruction, 16* (1), 3–118.

Wigglesworth, J. (1997). An investigation of planning time and proficiency level on oral test discourse. *Language Testing, 14*, 85–106.

Wilkins, D. A. (1976). *Notional Syllabuses*. Oxford: Oxford University Press.

Wolfson, N. (1989). *Perspectives: Sociolinguistics and TESOL*. Rowley, MA: Newbury House.

Wolfson, N., Marmor, T. and Jones, S. (1989). Problems in the comparison of speech acts across cultures. In S. Blum-Kulka, J. House and G. Kasper (eds.), *Cross-Cultural Pragmatics: Requests and Apologies*. Norwood, NJ: Ablex.

Yamashita, S. O. (1996). *Six Measures of JSL Pragmatics*. Honolulu, HI: University of Hawai'i Press.

Zeidner, M. (1986). Are English language aptitude tests biased toward culturally different minorities? Some Israeli findings. *Language Testing, 3*, 80–9.

Zeidner, M. (1987). A comparison of ethnic, sex, and age bias in the predictive validity of English aptitude tests: some Israeli data. *Language Testing, 4*, 55–71.

Index

A
affective strategies 160
Alanen, R. 38
Alderson, J.C. ix–x, 120, 155, 179, 254
Allen, P. 29, 54
alternative assessment 215
analytic rating scales
  CEP Placement Test 255
  extended-production tasks 175–76
  FCE Use of English paper 190, 191
  versus holistic rating scales 226,
    230–31, 254–55
  learning-oriented assessments 226,
    230–31
  test task design 120–21
Ancess, J. 235
anecdotal records 231, 232
applied linguistics research 137–38,
  251
appropriateness 18–19, 58, 59, 76, 77,
  86, 106–7
  see also pragmatic meaning
archiving, of test tasks 179
Aschbacher, P.R. 214
assessment practices, calls for reform
  of 214–15
audio-lingual methods 27–28

Austin, J.L. 16–18
authentic assessment 215
authenticity
  discrete-point measurement
    151–52
  levels of 265–66
  test 103, 104
  test usefulness 151–52
  TLU tasks 192, 200–201, 202, 208,
    209–10
Azar, B.S. 22

B
Bachman, L.F. ix–x, 26, 29, 53, 54–56,
  59, 86, 101, 102, 103, 111,
  112–26, 145, 148–55, 156, 159,
  160, 161, 167, 168, 174, 176, 179,
  181, 215, 256, 257, 261, 265, 266,
  271
Bailey, N. 31
Bangert-Downs, R.L. 234
basic interpersonal communication
  skills (BICS) 158
Baxter, G. 213
Beebe, L. 138
Bell, L. 43
Beretta, A. 32–33